SVENSKA FORTITUDE

Memoirs of John Ostlund, A Swedish Immigrant Pioneer in Minnesota.

Jenny Ostlund - Evens

I have been blessed to have access to my grandfathers original journals and photo collections and have created this book of memoirs by reading, sorting, and matching parts, combining them into a chronological journey through his lifetime of adventures.

All of the photos and images included in this book are from John Ostlund's collection. Many of them are from his camera.

All inquiries, including distributor information, should be addressed to: Jevensartist@gmail.com

ISBN13: 9780578376004

Library of Congress Control Number: 2022913520

Dedication

I compiled this book of memoirs and photographs with love, to honor my grandfather, John Ostlund, who blessed us with his writings and had the forethought to translate them to English for future generations.

In addition, it is dedicated to my grandmother, Olga (Flank) Ostlund, who was also a Swedish Immigrant pioneer. She lived with us for most of my childhood and was a loving influence, teaching me bits of the Swedish language, culture and customs.

And, to my parents, Kenneth and Barbara Ostlund, who raised us to embrace and celebrate our Swedish heritage and kept it alive in our everyday life through the foods we ate, the customs we celebrated, the way our house was decorated, and the stories we were told.

I would also like to sincerely thank Edna Siniff for taking me under her wing and helping me make my dream of publishing my grandfather's memoirs come true! Her incredible generosity, knowledge, patience, and encouragement made publishing this book enjoyable.

Table of Contents

Table of Contents

Table of Contents

Introduction
by Jenny Ostlund - Evens

My grandfather, John Ostlund, was a Swedish Immigrant to Minnesota in 1902. From boyhood on, he recorded his life adventures as short stories in his diary. They were originally written in Swedish, but his hope was that future generations would find his experiences interesting, so he re-typed them in English once he was fluent. He died one month after I was born, so I didn't have the opportunity to get to know him as a grandfather. However, I still grew to know and love him through his stories and have always felt a strong connection to him. Thus, as a teenager, I vowed to someday honor his memory and my heritage by publishing his memoirs, not just for family, but for other Swedish Americans or anyone who has a relative that immigrated to America or is curious about what that experience and time was like.

My grandfather's stories cover his life as a child in Sweden, growing and working there, deciding to emigrate to America and the journey, his adventures establishing himself here, homesteading, working as a lumberjack, a locomotive engineer, a farmer, a public servant, etc. They include his adventures as a pioneer in northern Minnesota and other wilderness and life experiences, becoming a husband and father, visiting his homeland of Sweden and bringing family back to America, as well as coping with the hardships of the Great Depression and World War II.

Both of my paternal grandparents were Swedish Immigrants to the United States and established themselves in the state of Minnesota, where I have lived my entire life. My parents raised us to embrace and celebrate our Swedish heritage. There has always been strong Swedish influence in our daily lives through the foods we ate and the decor of our home. Holidays always had a Scandinavian theme as well. I have carried on the same traditions with my family.

Although I was born in Minneapolis, Minnesota, we moved to the area of the first Swedish settlement in the state when I was young. Our church celebrated the traditional customs like St. Lucia, lutefisk dinners and Midsommar. My parents both volunteered at the Gammelgården Museum in Scandia, Minnesota, which is the only open-air museum devoted to preserving, presenting and promoting Swedish immigrant heritage in the United States. My dad gave tours in the Swedish language (and in English) and my mom worked in the gift shop and also sewed traditional Swedish costumes for the Kirsten American Girl dolls to sell there. The buildings there have been carefully preserved and restored so visitors can get a glimpse of the daily lives and artifacts of immigrants. When my daughters were young, they participated in the summer camps there called "Comin'

To America" where they had the chance to explore what it may have been like to grow up in an immigrant family in the mid 1800's. They were given Swedish names and homeland identities as they prepared to make their passage to America. They put together passports, acted out making their way through Ellis Island and created a lifestyle with make-shift homes and families. They performed chores and activities typical of this era. There was craft time where they chose a traditional craft to try and ate a typical meal from that era. They experienced what a typical school day would've been like. It was a great learning experience for them. In 2013, my oldest daughter was married there at the Gammelkyrkan (which, after restoration, was rededicated in 1982 by Prince Bertil of Sweden). She also completed a semester of Study Abroad in Orebro, Sweden while in college.

I always dreamed that someday I would go to Sweden, but didn't think it would ever be financially possible for me. In fact, I even applied to be a contestant on the Swedish reality television show Allt för Sverige (The Great Swedish Adventure) hoping for a chance to go to Sweden. I was actually interviewed, and was in the running, but didn't make the final cut. Then, in 2019 an opportunity presented itself. My youngest daughter was on Study Abroad in London and had decided that she was going to visit Sweden on her own. My mother encouraged me to join her there and so did my husband. In a flurry, things all fell into place. Flights were booked for us to meet in Oslo, Norway where we rented a car and drove into Sweden. We were on a mission to see the places we'd read about in my grandfather's stories, to touch the soil where my ancestor's broke ground and generations were born and raised, and to connect with relatives that I had met when they visited America. It was a very short trip. I only had three full days in Sweden, but Victoria and I made the most of it and had such an exciting time! We were hosted for most of the trip by my second cousin Monica and her husband Tomas. They were simply amazing, and words could not express how much we appreciated their hospitality. While there, purely by luck and circumstance, I met three new relatives in my family tree, and discovered that both my grandfather's and grandmother's ancestral homes are still in the family. One has been in the family since my 4-times great grandfather broke ground there over 250 years ago in the year 1770. It's kind of a cool story. Here it is in a nutshell:

At the age of nineteen, my 4-times great grandfather, Anders Johansson, was engaged to his sweetheart Annika. It was decided that after their marriage, Anders would take over the farm of his father-in-law, as Annika was an only child. Everyone predicted they would be very happy together. However, predictions don't always come true. On a dark winter evening, while returning home from a visit with a friend across the frozen Lake Fryken, Annika was tragically lost when she broke through the ice and drowned. No one had heard her calls for help and they did not find her body until the ice melted in the spring. Anders was so heartbroken that he put a bag of barley flour and an old griddle in his pack sack, grabbed a sheepskin quilt and an axe, and headed north through the dense timber wilderness to live in solitude far away from Lake Fryken, where nothing would remind him of his lost happiness. When he found a place on a hill far from civilization and suitable to build a cabin, he set to work. A Finlander who was born out there in the wilderness happened by one day and said he and his family lived a few miles away. He offered to help Anders build his cabin. They made a deal to trade work with each other. Through his new friend, he became acquainted with a small Finnish colony near the Swedish/Norwegian border. They had been driven out of Finland. Since he was the only Swede they knew, they called him Svensk-Anders, and named his homestead on the hill "Svensk-Andersberg". After a time, he got lonely. When a church was built in nearby Östmark, he attended and met his bride. They had one daughter before Anders was killed by a bear at age 36. His wife and daughter stayed and worked on the farm they had built. The daughter, Catharina, eventually married a man who they hired to help with the farm...and so started the generations at Svensk-Andersberg.

More than 250 years later, Svensk-Andersberg is still there and remains in the family, and Victoria and I were able to locate it! I stood on the same soil and enjoyed the same view that Anders had all those years ago! I get teary every time I think about how incredible that moment was for me. I also met the man who currently lives there and we found him in the family tree that I brought with me. He was my second cousin and we were around the same age. I was so thankful that he could speak some English.

During our stay with Monica and Tomas in Älvdalen, they took us to the home where my grandmother and Monica's grandfather were born in Sörsjön, which, for the most part remains as it was originally. To actually sit on the porch of the house my grandmother was born in, in Sweden, and imagine her playing in the yard as a child, sailing little stick boats on the river that ran through the property, was incredible. I could so strongly feel her presence and that of my father (who has also passed) that day. While there, we noticed a couple of neighbors were out tending their yards, so we decided to pay them each a visit. It turned out that both of the neighbors we spoke with were also second cousins and had lived in the family home at some point. They did not speak English, but when Monica told them that I came to visit from America and I was the granddaughter of Olga Flank and John Ostlund, they both got very excited. They each told the same story of remembering being young boys in 1956 when my grandparents visited Sweden, and that when they met my grandfather, he pulled a shiny American dollar coin from his pocket and gave it to them. That visit to Sweden will be a memory I'll cherish forever.

Another of my grandfather's hobbies was to gather information about his ancestors and their families. He chronicled stories, dates, and facts from elderly relatives to help trace and build his family tree. In those writings he reveals that the early ancestors on his father's side settled and farmed in the valley of Lake Fryken in the province of Värmland, Sweden. They raised their own flax and spun their own linen to make their clothing. They tanned their own hides to make their shoes, gloves and caps. All of their furniture was made at home in the evenings by the light of their wood torches. When help was needed from outside, neighbors helped each other out. The following is an excerpt from his diary:

"I am proud to be a descendant of those hardy and independent people. Though I am living far away from the ancestral homeland, I feel like an invisible tie is connecting me with those ancestors. As far as I know, all of my relatives who have descended from those hardy forefathers are gentle, honest and peace-loving people. No gangsters or criminals are found in our family record, and I hope that invisible tie will remain with my descendants in years to come."

I definitely feel that invisible tie, and it is what planted the seed in my heart to want to publish his memoirs. May these stories be the string that connects future generations to their ancestors. I believe our ancestors had a hand in shaping who WE are and learning about our ancestors and where we come from teaches us important things about life, our families, history and even helps us understand ourselves a bit better.

Preface
by John Ostlund

"Vid skrivmaskinen, mitt nöje på lediga stunder.
Olga står bakom och tjuvläser." John.
"At the typewriter, is my pleasure in my free time.
Olga stands behind and reads." John

Since my early youth, I have kept a diary and thus all more noteworthy incidents through my life have been recorded and preserved. All my first diaries were of course written in the Swedish language, but in order to gather it all in one volume, I have tried to translate it into English. In doing so, it is my hope that future generations will find these stories interesting.

We all realize, however, that any story will lose some of its originality in being translated from one language into another, especially when its translator is as inexperienced and unschooled as I am. Many times, I have been quite unable to find the words I would need to express the true meaning in my Swedish manuscript. Furthermore, it has all been done in spare moments, and may this be my excuse for the incompleteness and faults in my stories.

As a reference in finding certain events, I will try to summarize it as follows:

PART 1 - My memoirs from first recollections to the time when I emigrated to America are included here. My diaries from that time were rather incomplete, and only more outstanding events in my life were recorded. At that time, when the first part was concluded, I was eighteen years of age.

PART 2 - Constitutes my story of the journey from Järpen, Sweden to Worthington, Minnesota in America in 1902.

PART 3 - The first three years in America, commonly called the "Dog Years" are included here. I had many adventures and often quite narrow escapes during my eighteenth to my twenty-first year.

PART 4 - Here is my story when I was "getting acclimatized" in my adopted country. During that time, I become a citizen of the United States. It includes my age from twenty-one to twenty five years.

PART 5 - The story of my trip back to the land of my birth in 1908-09 is told here. At that time, I was in the prime of my manhood, and I enjoyed the visit in Sweden immensely.

PART 6 - This includes the time from 1909 to 1915. During that time, I purchased my land in Gheen, where I prepared for my future home. I was also married during that time, and Alvin was born. It was the most carefree part of my life. I had a good job, always plenty of cash in my pocket and life seemed like a beautiful dream ahead of me.

PART 7 - When we left the Mesabi Range and moved to our future home at Gheen, and the first nine years there make up this part. This includes the years from 1915 to 1924.

PART 8 - From 1923 to 1933. Life on the farm is about our struggles to wrest a living out of the new soil. During this period, the worldwide depression set in and for several years we could not sell our products to any advantage. But we lived through it, and we never went without a square meal.

PART 9 - When I turned 50, I thought the best part of my life was behind me and what happened after would not matter much, so would not be worth relating and that my autobiography was closed. However, now, 15 years later I am resuming it. Many interesting events have happened since, which I will summarize to the best of my ability. Also included is a brief inventory of the public offices I have had over the last 40 years. During my life I have tried to do my part as a citizen and to serve my community to the best of my little ability.

Perhaps someday in the future these stories may make interesting reading for someone.

John's typwriter

PART 1
"My Youthful Years"

Thinking back to the time I was growing up, memories flit by like incidents in a dream. They are like old paintings, some clear and bright, others dim, dull and less distinct.

Per and Christine Ostlund with 8-month-old son, John. 1884
John Ostlund photo collection

1
The Most Carefree Days of My Life

The "Rista" waterfall in Sweden, near John's childhood home.

In the province of Jämtland, in the northern part of the country of Sweden, where the Indalsälven river empties into Lake Storsjön, is located a little thrifty village by the name of Trångsviken. Here I first saw the light of day on October 9th, 1883. My father was a log-scaler at the local sawmill and my mother was a farmer's daughter. Our home at that time was a little, red-painted frame house with two rooms owned by the sawmill company my dad was working for. The company had built several apartment houses which were rented out to their employees. Almost every apartment consisted of two large rooms, as that was considered sufficient for any size family at that time. I remember families, up to ten or more, living in two room apartment houses.

My first memories were from the time I was about 2 ½ years old. My grandmother died, and my mother took me and my little sister Mae and took the train to grandfather's home where she remained for several months. I distinctly remember how I followed my grandfather around the place, and how he made a little sled for me which I hauled a few sticks of wood on, from the woodshed to the house. I also remember when we rode the train back home and Dad met us. Those memories however are like dreams.

In the fall of 1888, my sister Ester was born. I was then nearly five years old and my memories from that time are more distinct and clear. On the day she was born a fair was held in the community and father took me and Mae for a walk through the fairground. This was the first and only fair that ever was held in Järpen as long as I was there and as far as I can remember. At any rate, it was the first fair that I attended. When we towards evening returned home, little sister had arrived. I still remember my wonder over the fact that mother had to stay in bed when the rest of us were up.

My parents were bringing us children up very strictly and we were not allowed to play with other children in the street. They evidently thought that we might be spoiled and that we might pick up cuss words and learn bad habits. However, I remember that I sometimes sneaked out when mother was busy with her housework and Dad was at work, and I must confess that I looked forward to these occasions when I could play with other boys of my age.

I commenced school in the fall of 1889. I was not yet six years old but was big for my age. The teacher, whose name was Kristina Anderson, occupied two rooms next to ours in the same apartment house, and she was my mother's intimate friend. I was "teacher's pet" long before I started school and that fact remained as long as I went through the primary grades. There was no regular schoolhouse in the village at that time but the I.O.G.T. (International Order of Good Templars) hall was rented for school. Miss Anderson was the only teacher, and she taught the higher grades in the forenoon and the primary grade in the afternoon. Mother made me a canvas schoolbag with my initials J.O. on it and dad bought a slate and an A-B-C book. The schoolhouse was located only a quarter of a mile from home, on top of a large hill. I did not know very many of my classmates when I commenced school. The result was that I felt almost a stranger with them the first weeks. I was backward and shy and consequently was the target of their teasing remarks. However, the teacher always took my defense when she was around, a fact that perhaps done more harm than good. I had a good memory and a natural talent for learning. Study was a play, and I enjoyed every minute of classwork. I never missed a day if I could help it and I felt proud over that I always was one of the highest in the class.

In the year of 1890 my father bought five acres of land in the center of the village and built a house of his own. It was not very large, only two rooms downstairs and two small attic rooms upstairs. He also built a barn and bought two cows and a dozen chickens. A small creek ran through the lot and past the barn, coming from a large spring in the hillside not far from our home. Here my dad built a little dam and below the dam he built a small waterwheel and connected to the wheel axle was a hammer that pounded on a small anvil, giving a ringing sound that could be heard a block away. Here I had a lot of fun and it attracted other boys living nearby and we could play together that we worked at a sawmill. If they were caught there when Dad came home from work, he chased them away. Consequently, Dad was not much liked by the neighbors, particularly the younger generation. However, there were a couple families living nearby who belonged to the same church denomination, and their children were tolerated in and around our home.

My best friend was a neighbor boy by the name of Fredrik. The other boys called him "the Lapp" because his mother was a Laplanders daughter. He was always timid and shy towards the other boys in our class but never with me. We got along well together. Out of school we also managed to spend some time together. We were both forbidden to go near the river, but we sneaked down there, and we had a lot of fun tossing "sandwiches" over the water. This game consisted in finding small flat stones and tossing them low over the water, making them bounce a number of times. The one whose stone made the most leaps before it sank, was the champion sandwich tosser. Often, we remained too long at the river and someone would come and look for us. Then we knew that we had earned a spanking.

It was very seldom that we could get money from our parents for sweets, but for a while Fred and I had plenty of cash to buy candy and Licorice. We roamed the dumping grounds and garbage piles in the backyards and picked bones which we could sell at the local stores. These bones were ground up into bone meal and used in fertilizing the gardens. A gunny sack of bones was worth 50 ore and this was a lot of money to us. I never told my mother about these bone hunting expeditions because I knew that she would not approve of it. I did not dare to carry the money in my pants pockets either fearing that she might find it, so I hid it under a piece of slab in the woodshed. That went along for several weeks until one day I came to look for my money and it was gone. Fred and I had gathered and sold two sacks full of bones and had received a shining silver krona. Some other boys had been in the store and saw us get the money. They wanted us to buy licorice and treat them, but we refused. Evidently, they must have followed us home and saw me go into the woodshed before going into the house. My total loss in the robbery was 90 ore, which was a fortune for me at that time. Crying, I went to Mother and confessed everything. I knew who the boys were that had robbed me, and I told her to see their parents and try to get the money back. However, she told me that it just served me right as I had no business sneaking around the backyards picking up dirty, stinking bones. If she found out that I had done it again, she would tell Dad and then I knew what my penalty would be. That ended the bone business as far as I was concerned. Now that my mother knew about it, she would watch me closer, and I had too much respect for the willow switch to break the rules again. In regard to spanking, I believe that I had my full share of it. It did not take much of an offence by me before Dad applied the switch on my bare rump. The willow switch was part of the furniture in our bedroom, stuck in behind the bed so as to be handy. However, what I dreaded most was that he made me kneel after the spanking and tell God that I was sorry and that I would not do the terrible sin any more. And perhaps I had just told a little white lie, of no importance whatsoever, as most children usually do. But I suppose that those spankings and forced prayers, in Dad's opinion, would help to make me a better man, and he felt that he had done his duty in that respect.

Not far from our home was a ruin of an old fort built during the war with Norway about 1808. Fred and I often played "cop and robber" in and around the old stone breastworks, still standing after almost 100 years. From the inside of the fort a shaft or tunnel led deep underground a distance of about 800 feet or more and ended near the riverbank. At several places the tunnel was almost caved in, and we knew it was dangerous to play in it. One afternoon however we decided to explore the entire length of it. Nobody knew that we were at the old fort, and I have thought many times that if we had been trapped there, nobody would have found us.

We had a few matches with us but before we were half ways the matches were used up and we were in complete darkness. In some places we could walk erect but most of the way we crawled on hands and knees just feeling our way through the passage. Several times we were on the verge of returning but we didn't. Finally, we noticed a shaft of light peeping through between two large boulders which blocked the entire passage. We had to dig with our hands an opening around one of the boulders and we finally squeezed through and came out into the sunshine. We never went exploring that tunnel again.

In our village about the year 1890, lived a man who generally was considered odd and peculiar in many ways. His name was Ekvall, but everybody called him "the Socialist", and people seemed to avoid him. The women warned their children not to speak to him, because he was a dangerous character. He advocated dividing the properties of the rich people, or in other words, robbing them of what they had accumulated or inherited.

One afternoon when Fred and I sat on the riverbank fishing for minnows, the "socialist" came up behind us. We pulled up our lines and grabbed our minnow bucket, prepared to run for it when he spoke to us. He sat down on a rock and told us that he too used to catch minnows when he was a boy. He told us he was born near the water, and he enjoyed fishing. When he saw that we only had common pins as fishhooks, he said he had some fishhooks in his trunk, and he would give some to us next time he saw us. He did not sound so dangerous after all. When I came home, I told Mother who we had met and what he had told us. She seemed scared and when I asked her what the word socialist meant, she said she did not know but it was the opposite to Baptist, she thought. She had heard that Ekvall did not believe in God and the king, but she thought that he was pretty ignorant.

Fred and I did not expect Edvall to live up to his promise, but he did. He was back the next day and in a little bag he had the finest fish hooks we had seen. And he also brought us new fishlines. We had only sewing thread before. He helped us tie the hooks on and thread the worms on the hooks. Then he pulled a bag of candy out of his pocket and treated us, and from that day we were not scared of the socialist anymore.

Farther up the river from our home was the pulp factory, the main industry of our village. It burned down in the summer of 1890 when I was about seven years old. When I came out of the house and saw the immense dark smoke clouds rolling down over the community, I stood fascinated by the gate. Father was called out with the rest of the men to fight the fire, but before he left he told me to stay close to the house and under no circumstances could I come out there. But how could a red-blooded boy, seven years old stay away from such an important and interesting event? Mother was busy and I sneaked out to the road. On the road people were hurrying to the fire, men, women, and children, many of them younger than I was. Before I realized it I was out on the road running for all I was worth towards that fascinating spectacle. When there, I was pushed into a line of women and children who had formed a bucket brigade, passing empty pails and buckets from hand to hand down to the river where the pails were filled with water and passed back along a long line of men to the firefighters. I felt quite important at first, feeling that I was able to help in fighting the fire, but soon I was tired, and the buckets dropped from my hands and I began to cry. A kind woman took me out to the road and told me to run home. When I arrived home wet and dirty, I had to tell Mother about where I had been. She scolded me and when Dad came home and heard of it, I received a session with the willow switch. But the adventure was well worth a spanking.

The sawmill where my dad worked was across the river from the main part of the village where our home was and a long wooden bridge led across the river which here was almost a quarter of a mile across. As soon as mother thought that I was old enough to carry the lunch basket to Dad, this was my daily chore. Dad worked as logscaler out on the scaling bridge and a long boardwalk led out there. The boardwalk was only between two and three feet wide and built on floating logs and at first it was with difficulty that I could balance myself with that heavy lunch basket. One day it was quite windy and several times I almost slipped off the walk before I reached the scaling bridge. When I finally made it, I felt pretty good and, when the men working with Dad bragged about me and told me what a frisky riverman I was, I grabbed a boathook and commenced pushing logs down the channel. But I was only seven years old at the time and before I realized it a strong gust of wind picked me up and tossed me headfirst in the water. The men were close by, and they soon fished me out. I did not feel so proud when Dad took me on his back and carried me to shore and into the warm boiler room where he undressed me and dried my clothes. It was the first time I took a similar dunking, but it was not the last time, as during the next eleven years I worked on the river and visited under water many times.

About that time my grandfather came to visit us. He was past 70 and his hair and his long beard were grey. Grandpa and I became great pals, and I followed him around the community wherever he went. When we sat down for a rest, he told me stories from his long life which I still remember. He had been a sailor in his youth and had seen many foreign lands and cities. He told me of the black negroes of Africa and about the Chinese and Japanese people and their customs and religions, something I never heard before. One day when we sat resting on the long bridge across the river, where they had built in benches just at the center of the bridge, grandpa told me about the time the freighter he was captain on, foundered in the Baltic Sea. With one member of the crew, grandpa laid in the icy water for three days and nights before he was rescued by a passing vessel. He said that was the time his hair turned grey. He also told me a lot about the sun, the moon, the planets and the fixed stars, things that I had never known before. He told me that they were bodies which like our earth were whirling about in the universe. I had been told that the stars were peepholes into heaven.

As soon as I was strong enough to pull the bucksaw, I had to saw and split all the wood for the house. Every night after school I had to work a couple hours in the woodshed. Oh, how I hated that saw and the sawbuck. Other boys could run about and play after school, but not me. I had to work, and I remember how my arms often ached at night after pulling that heavy saw.

I was only nine and a half years old when I had to help earn my own living. It was in the spring of 1893 when father got me a job at the sawmill. I was put to work hooking logs unto the endless chain that brought them into the mill. For this work I received one krona (27 cents) for 10 hours. My leisure days were over. I had to get up before six in the morning and accompany Dad to the mill where work commenced at seven o'clock. Every other week I had to work the night shift, from seven in the evening until six in the morning. When school started, I was relieved at the mill and took my seat in school. In the spring when school was out for the summer, I resumed my work at the mill. From then on, my carefree days were ended, and it was work, work and responsibility all through life.

2
Losing Mother

My mother left us February 13th, 1894. I was then only 10 years old. I believe that I was the only one of us children who fully realized our great loss. She had been ailing for a long time. Tuberculosis is a slow killer, and while all the grownups must have known that she was going to die, it was unknown to us youngsters. During her sickness and afterwards, we had housekeepers, but I missed mother and many times I used to go out in the woodshed and cry my heart out for her. Brother Peter was only two years old when mother died. He was rather sickly and constantly coughing and everybody thought that he would soon follow his mother, but he rallied and has been well and strong ever since.

After mother was gone, my father sold the place. He made a contract with the Mill company, whereby he was to get about ten acres of land near the sawmill. This was all wild land with a lot of large pine stumps and overgrown with brush. This land was to be cleared, stumped, and plowed at the expiration of the contract, which was for a period of seven years. The company would furnish lumber for buildings needed, but father had to pay the carpenter and furnish doors, windows, brick, and nails, etc. In this enterprise went all the money father received for the old place and when we finally moved in with our furniture, our two cows and our chickens, father was broke. In order that we would get enough land cleared in a hurry so we could raise hay and feed for our stock, he hired two men to clear and grub stumps. These men had to be paid out of our earnings that first summer. I have often wondered if dad could have been sober when he signed that contract.

From that time on, we never managed to get out of debt. We generally had a steady income the year around and we lived as cheap as possible, but whenever payday come, there were bills to pay. The usual fare on our table was potatoes and herring, with barley porridge always for supper. Only occasionally on Sundays did we have some meat or liver instead of herring. We children always drank oatmeal water at breakfast every morning.

Our furniture consisted of a kitchen table, a few chairs, a cupboard, a sofa and a cookstove in the kitchen. In the bedroom we had two wooden beds, a bureau, a bookcase, a washstand, a dresser, and another kitchen table. Nothing elaborate or expensive about our furniture. When finally sold, it did not bring enough to pay two months board for father.

For a period of four years after mother's death we hired housekeepers. It was hard to keep anybody for any length of time. Sister Ester found a home with a couple of father's friends, Anders Olsson's in Ytterån, about 30 miles from Järpen. An old maid by the name of Anna-Lisa kept house for us during my mother's sickness and until after the burial. Then my dad's sister Kristina Liljequist, who had lost her husband about the same time, came home and worked for us for a while. However, father was hard to please and they were often quarreling. While she was there, Grandmother Gertrud Bengtson came up from Värmland. Then for a while we had a young housekeeper who had a baby. She was from another parish a few miles from Järpen. However, she soon got married and left. Finally, through an advertisement, father hired another woman from the province of Jelsingland, who had two children. Her name was Mrs. Aslund, and she worked for us for about a year. When she left, sister Mae was eleven years old, and she had to take over the household duties. Besides keeping house, she milked our two cows and still kept up her studies in school, so I guess she had her hands full, but she managed good.

John's mother, Kristina Fredrika Ostlund.

John Ostlund collection

3
A Life Saved

This episode happened in the summer of 1894. I was 10 years old and was working at the Husa Sawmill in my hometown, Järpen in Sweden. My duties were to lead the saw logs in to the endless chain which brought them up into the mill. With me was another boy, by the name of Anders Person, a year older than I. A deep channel had been dug through the otherwise shallow water near the shore below the mill, and through this channel we brought the logs. The channel was approximately ten feet wide and reached out into deeper water about 150 feet from shore.

While I was working at the shore end of the channel, hooking the logs on the chain, Anders worked at the other end, where he had to turn many of the logs as all logs had to be sent into the mill top end first. The logs were too long to turn after they had entered the channel, and if we sent them up with the butt end first, we were due for some cussing and scolding by the sawyers. Anders and I had a good reputation and it was very seldom we broke the rule in this respect.

One day when I was busy at the chain, I happened to look over to where Anders was, and I did not see him. Leaving my work, I ran as fast as I could down the boardwalk to where he had been working. When I arrived on the turning bridge I looked down in the water and I saw my buddy sitting on the bottom of the channel. I screamed at the top of my voice and was heard by the logscalers, working about 150 feet farther out on the river. Meanwhile I stuck my pike-pole, which fortunately I had brought with me, down in the water and hooked it in the back of the jacket Anders wore. I pulled him up to the surface but was unable to drag him up on the boardwalk. But now two of the scalers arrived and helped me. Anders was unconscious but we rolled him on the boardwalk and succeeded in getting the water out of his throat and stomach and after a while he came to life. He was pretty groggy, but the men brought him to shore and took him to his home. The next day he was back at work again as usual.

If I had not happened to miss him when I did, or if I had not reached him as soon as I did, he would have been dead. For several days I was lauded and praised as a hero by my fellow workers at the mill, and if it had happened during later years, I would have received a medal from the government for saving a life.

Anders and I emigrated to America together eight years later and we saw each other here during the first two years as he came to Worthington, where I was working, and worked on a neighboring farm. But we lost track of each other, and I never heard from him again.

4
The Trolls

In my youth, many of the people believed in mysterious beings called "trolls, nymphs, dwarfs and giants" who were supposed to live underground, in caves or in the mountains, in creeks or small lakes and other out-of-the-way places. And ignorant people believed that "spooks" or souls of dead people could take human form and walk about visiting their former homes and often appear in visible form during these visits. It was superstition, inherited from generation to generation, things that if they were told now, would only be considered as jokes.

I never really believed in spooky tales as I had never seen anything that could not be explained naturally. But, seeing is believing and this is how it happened.

I had been up the river fishing one evening and just about midnight, when according to witnesses, spooks are visible, I returned home along an old trail winding along the riverbank. It was in the later part of the summer, and it was getting dusk around midnight in northern Sweden. Nobody lived near this old trail, and it was seldom used, except by an occasional fisherman like myself. Suddenly I stopped in my tracks, surprised, when I saw a light which appeared to be about fifty feet ahead. It appeared to be a fire burning and around this fire I saw several dwarfs jumping around making passes at each other. Tales that I had heard came to my mind. There really existed mischievous dwarfs and trolls after all. Here I saw them with my own eyes.

Fully five minutes I must have stood there looking at the scene and debating with myself whether I should proceed and pass them, or if I should go back about a mile and cross the river on a small bridge and go home that way. But this would lengthen my way home considerably. I was now convinced of one thing. These supernatural beings really existed after all.

Finally I decided to continue my way past the dwarfs and pretend that I never saw them. Perhaps they would make themselves invisible when I came nearer. With my heart literally in my throat I proceeded. I soon discovered that the fire was farther away from me than I had imagined and that it had first appeared to be. When I finally reached it, I saw a crew of rivermen camping around the fire and cooking coffee while they rested and waited for daylight. The distance and my imagination had played a nasty trick on me. If I had turned back and taken another road home, I would have been convinced for the rest of my life that I had seen supernatural beings with my own eyes. However, this incident has convinced me more than anything else, that it is easy to be fooled through imagination and superstition.

5
Visiting The Laplanders

The Laplander of Sweden can well be compared with the Indian of North America. They belong to the mongolian race and very rarely mix with the native Swedes, who are Caucasians. There are three kinds of Laplanders. The mountain Lapps support themselves by raising reindeer herds and move constantly from place to place in the mountain regions, following their herds from one grazing place to another. Then there are the fishing Lapps, who have only a few reindeer and generally live close to some lake where they sustain themselves by fishing, trapping, and hunting. The third kind is the beggar Lapps, who do not own any animals and generally live close to inhabited villages or hamlets, where they often go begging for food or clothing and are considered outcasts.

Many of the mountain Lapps are quite well to do. They own herds of thousands of reindeer, and they send their children to good schools built by the government, where they receive free education.

I was about twelve years old when I first visited a Laplanders camp. It was not very often the Lapps came so close to the village where I grew up. That winter they had camped by a large tarn, about three miles from the village. It was two brothers, Jon, and Pal Palson, with their families and two hired men, all Laplanders, and they had a herd of about 1,200 reindeer. When the rumor spread around, many of the villagers decided to visit the Lapp camp one Sunday, and I was permitted to follow a couple neighbor boys who knew their way out to "Long tarn", as the little lake was called. When we walked out there, we had a lot of company. At the camp several hundred people were gathered that afternoon. On the ice were the herd of reindeer held together by several small but rugged dogs and the two hired men. Some of the animals were laying down while others were walking about restlessly. The horns or antlers of the bucks were sticking up like craggy bushes over the dark mass of animals. It was a very impressive sight that never is forgotten.

Close to their wigwams (kator,) a large log fire was built where the visitors could warm themselves. The Lapp women served coffee to those who wished for it and were willing to pay. One of my companions ordered a cup, but when he tasted it, he handed it to me. I took a swallow but that was enough. It was black as ink and salted and no sugar or cream was served with it.

One of the visitors wanted a ride after a reindeer. A Lapp took a piece of rope and walked out towards the herd on the ice. Near the herd he tossed the rope and lassoed a large buck. Soon he had him harnessed and hitched before a boat-like sled (Atcha,) The harness consisted only of a heavy leather strap around the animal's neck and a tog running between the deer's legs to the sleigh. The customer took his place in the bottom of the sleigh and the Laplander sat on the prow with one leg on each side in order to steer or brake, if need be. Off they went in a shower of snow around the lake and whirled around on the verge of turning over. But they returned safe to the camp. I heard the rider say to a friend that it was the greatest thrill he ever had, that ride behind a reindeer.

6
The Fight on Main Street

My old hometown, Järpen, in Sweden was somewhat divided into two different localities. The older part of the community was built near the long bridge spanning the river. There were several stores and business establishments, there were the assembly halls of the Order of Good Templars, the Baptist and Methodist chapels, the Salvation Army barracks and a large community dance hall.

Farther to the west was a later built community around the large paper factory. There were several large barracks built by the paper manufacturing company, housing the families of the factory workers, several boarding houses and a couple grocery stores and a large schoolhouse, the Racklov School, attended by all the children who were above third grade.

Between the workers in the older part of town and the factory workers a certain rivalry existed which often broke out in fistfights, particularly if both parties had imbibed too much intoxicating liquor, which often happened. The young workers at the factory seemed to think that they were a step higher in education and culture than the sawmill workers who lived in the old part of town, who mostly derived their income from the sawmill. Thus, two factions were formed within the same community.

Once when I was about 12 years old, I happened to witness a rather bloody melee between the two factions. It began at the Salvation Army Hall when about twenty young men assembled on the main street cussing at each other. Soon it became a fistfight. Down the street a couple blocks lived a man by the name of Knut Hamrin and his son, Karl. Both were intoxicated that evening and they were the ones who started the fight by teasing a group of factory boys. When the crowd came near Hamrin's home, he ran in and returned with a hammer and a large wood chisel. Karl gave the hammer to his dad and they both jumped on the factory boys wielding their weapons. Shouts, cuss words and screams filled the air when several men were wounded and bled from cuts by the sharp chisel. People from nearby houses came out and were helping the Hamrin's as this was in their neighborhood. Bricks, rocks, and board pieces were used as weapons in the general melee.

We were about half a dozen young boys who followed at a discreet distance, but we were so interested that several times we almost were hit by flying missiles. This only increased our interest in the outcome. Suddenly we heard somebody shout, "The sheriff is coming." The fight stopped instantly, and the crowd scattered. But several men were unable to get away. The younger Hamrin had received a wound from a knife that ripped up his right arm above the elbow and had to be taken to the community nurse to have it sewn up. The older Hamrin was not hurt much and stayed to help his son. He was arrested by the sheriff. Several of the factory boys were also arrested and confined in the county jail.

We boys who had seen the whole thing, were envied by our schoolmates and we had to repeat the whole story many times.

7
The Village Cobbler

I will never forget the first time I saw the little old cobbler, from a nearby community, come to our home. He carried a gunny sack on his back in which he had several pair of homemade shoes of various sizes which he was peddling. One pair fitted me, so Dad bought them. It was getting late in the day and Dad invited Sven Bengtsson, as his name was, to stay overnight. After that he often called on us when he made his regular trips peddling shoes, boots, or slippers that he had made.

When I, at the age of thirteen, graduated from school, Dad induced Bengtsson to teach me in his trade. While I at that time had not yet made up my mind what work I wanted to take up, I knew that I did not want to become a shoemaker, but I had no choice in the matter. Dad was the one who decided, and I obeyed his decision. So, a few days after my graduation I followed the little old man to his home.

With his wife and four-year-old daughter, Maria, he lived in a little cabin about ten miles from my hometown. The cabin contained only two rooms of which the inner room was the barn. There they had two milk cows and a large steer who was broken in as a draft ox. When the cattle were let out for water, they had to walk through the kitchen, dining room and bedroom, all in one, and they often had a bad habit to leave droppings on the kitchen floor. Consequently, we had to get used to the barn smell. The shoemaker shop was in the barn room just behind the tails of the cattle. There was no door between the two rooms, but nobody seemed to care, even though the food had a taste of the barn odor.

Here I was installed and learned the mysteries of cobbling. The principal part of my work was to patch old shoes and resole shoes and boots. When I made mistakes, as I often did, I was loudly bawled out. If Bengtsson was satisfied with my work he did not show it but commenced singing. Then I knew my work was O.K. It was monotonous work and I often felt like crying, but I then thought that I was making my own living at any rate and let that thought be my consolation. We both worked long days, from six in the morning until eight and sometimes nine in the evening, that is except Saturday evening. Then, according to Bengtsson's religion, the "sabbath" commenced and promptly at six o clock all work was laid aside. After supper he brought out his prayer book and for one hour we had to sit and listen to his singsong reading from the book. I often fell asleep during those services but if the woman noticed it, she kicked me and woke me up. Sundays I was free and roamed around in the woods or near the rapids in the river that ran by the little farm.

Bengtsson had harvested some barley the previous summer and that was stored in a little shed a stone's throw from the house. This was to be threshed and that had to be done in our spare time. So for about two weeks in March the alarm clock was set and woke us up at three o' clock in the morning and we tramped through the snow in the dark night out to the shed. The sheaves were placed in a row on the floor and with homemade flayes we threshed out the grain. After the first sessions with those flayes, I was quite exhausted but after a few days I did not mind the hard work. It was good exercise and I needed it after sitting still all day by the shoemaker desk.

It was in the middle of April and the spring sun melted the ice and snow on the manure pile outside our shop window. I resented the monotonous cobbler work and was unable to concentrate on what I was doing. The master noticed it and one day he asked me to haul home some firewood that he had cut in the woods about a quarter of a mile from the farm. I sure appreciated this change in my daily routine, the draft ox was led out and harnessed and hitched to a long sleigh. Bengtsson helped me get the ox ready and when he turned over the reins I rode away on the sleigh proud and happy. The ox had been standing in his stall for several days and seemed just as happy as I was. He danced away along the broken winter road like a colt. Soon we reached the wood piles and after some difficulty I was able to turn the sled around. However, to make the ox stand still while I loaded the wood was another problem. He did not have a bit in his mouth, only a halter in which the reins were fastened, and I was quite unable to hold him. For a while he dragged me in the snow behind the sleigh, while I held the reins, but when I saw that I could not stop him, I crawled up on the empty sleigh and let him go for full speed towards home.

There the old cobbler and his wife stood grinning at me. When I tossed him the reins of the ox he laughed outright and said. "I knew that Petter would give you a ride before you left here. He is strong and he is stubborn. But perhaps it was a good lesson for you."

I did not answer him back. Disgusted and humiliated I went in and sat down by the shoe desk and picked up the work I had been working on. And I resolved then and there that it would be the last time I tried driving oxen. My self-respect had received a setback that it took a long time to recover from. If they had not laughed and made fun of me, I would have forgiven them, but they probably could not help it.

It was not long afterwards that I resigned and went home. When I said goodbye Bengtsson handed me fifty ore, enabling me to take the train to my home village. Otherwise, I would have had to walk home. This cash payment and a pair of secondhand boots, was my remuneration for three months work.

Eleven years later I again visited Sven Bengtsson and his family. I had then spent six years in the United States and was back for a visit in Sweden. One day I happened to be in the vicinity of the old cobbler's home farm, so I called on them. They had now built a living house and had a fairly nice home. Maria had grown up to a young lady and while she still remembered me, she was shy and bashful and would hardly speak to me. The old man was so happy when I honored them with a visit, that tears were running down his nose. We visited the old granary and saw his grain, he showed me his four cows and a flock of chickens, and in overwhelming generosity he offered to give me everything, including his daughter Maria, if I would stay in Sweden and accept his offer. But the memory of the three months I served as his slave was too fresh and I declined.

8
Climbing Mount Åreskutan

About 20 miles from my hometown, Järpen, was the majestic mountain, "Åreskutan". It was well visible from home as it towered in the southwest. Most of the year the top was white with snow.

I was about fifteen years old when I first had the opportunity to visit and climb this mountain. It was the summer of 1899. Three of the young men on the assorting bridge where I worked were going and invited me to accompany them. We took the night flyer train Saturday night and after a 40-minute train ride we arrived in the village of Åre just at midnight. In the waiting room at the depot, we were allowed to wait for morning, and we slept a couple hours on the benches. It was about 4 o' clock in the morning when we left the depot and walked up the hillside towards the mountain. We were all hungry, but no restaurants were open that early. We reached a cafe above the village after a while and found it open. So we went in and ordered coffee and sandwiches for four, and were told that it would be served as soon as the cook had it made. She had just gotten up when we came.

Outside the dining room was a porch with a table and chairs and we went there and waited. We waited an hour and no service. Other tourists came and were waited on, but she had forgotten us four who were first. I was the youngest in our company and was sent in to remind the lady that we still waited for our order. When I respectfully inquired how soon we would be waited on, she answered sharply, "If you don't want to wait until you are served, you can leave." I came back and told the others, and we decided to not accept our order when it came, but were going to leave, just to show her that she could not treat us like a bunch of children. Finally the lady came with our order. One of us told her that now we had waited so long that we were not hungry anymore, and we left her with her long face.

We continued up the steep trail, hungry but happy, feeling that we showed the haughty woman that we were independent. We reached a plateau in the mountainside where a tourist cabin was erected, and there we found two good looking ladies serving lunch to tourists and other mountain climbers. Here we also were served good sandwiches and coffee, and we rested a while. The weather was clear and sunny when we left the village of Åre, but before we reached the top about 10 o'clock we had walked through a thick cloud formation, and we were afraid that we might get a shower. However, at the top it was clear and sunny, and the clouds were below us shielding the view of the landscape. To the west we saw the tops of other mountains in Norway and towards the south we saw the mighty "Sylarne" mountains like islands in a sea of clouds. Where we stood at the peak of the highest mountain, it looked like we were on a high island in an ocean and a bleak and lonely island at that. We did not see any forests or lakes or rivers. Nothing but clouds all around us. A cold wind swept the mountaintop and we shivered from the cold though we were well dressed. We were glad to descend the marked trail towards the clouds. Before we reached the above-mentioned tourist cabin, we ran into rain and became almost soaked. In the heated and warm cabin, we rested and enjoyed coffee and sandwiches again. About 5 o'clock in the evening the rain ceased, and the sun reappeared over the beautiful landscape around the village of Åre. We returned there and took the night train home.

9
The Wonder Field

I have always enjoyed listening to older people telling tales of the past, and I usually jotted down in my diary what I thought most interesting. This is one of them translated from Swedish.

I was only about 15 years old when Gullik Sefastsson, an old peddler who bought up hides and wool, stayed overnight in our home. He owned a farm about four miles from my hometown, Järpen, which he had inherited from his parents. He was born and raised on that farm and had made his living on it but now that he was up in age, he had turned the farm over to his son in law. However, old Gullik was quite ambitious yet and picked up good money buying hides and wool from the farmers which he sold in the city of Östersund. He was quite a talker and enjoyed these trips when he could meet many people. Here are his own words as I remember them.

"I took over the farm after my parents in the year 1860, when I returned home after finishing my 90 days of military training. The first summer I cleared off a tract of timberland close to where the river forms a waterfall, which we now call "Prästforsen". On that field I received good crops as the constant mist from the falls spread over the field and watered it.

The year 1867 was a year of famine over a large part of northern Sweden. People and animals starved to death, and thousands barely lived through it subsisting on bark and moss. After an unusually cold and stormy winter the frost stayed in the ground until July, and there was hardly any pasture for the cattle. In August it commenced snowing again and we had full winter in September. I seeded barley on the field by the falls in June. It was the only field that could be worked. In spite of frost and snow flurries the barley sprouted and grew and headed out when all other fields were black and nothing grew on them. I remember it was snowing when my wife and I cut the barley that fall. It was of course way below average in yield but then it was the only crop of grain harvested in our province, as far as I know. Every straw and every kernel was saved and I had enough barley for our own use and was even able to share some of our barley flour with our neighbors when they were on the verge of starving the following winter."

The story of Gullik's barley field spread around and people came from many nearby communities to see the "wonder field" that had produced grain that summer. A few years later, 1873, the parish was organized, and they called it "Undersåker" (wonder field). Later in 1886 the railroad was built through the province and Gullik's wonder field was split up by the railroad. A new church was also built on Sefastsson's farm, and a cemetery was laid out and dedicated. A large living-house was erected for the priest and there was not much left of the original farm

I have visited the place many times during my walks up the river fishing for salmon and harr. Just below the falls the large trouts were lurking, and I had to cross the wonder field to get there. Perhaps that was the reason why I jotted down Gullik's story in my diary as I well knew the field that gave our parish its name.

10
Mutt and Jeff

The once so popular comic strip "Mutt and Jeff" reminds me of farmer Hedman's two hired men, Halvar Nilsson and Lars Isaksson in my home community of Järpen. When Hedman was in a jolly mood, he bragged that he had the world's tallest and the world's shortest men working for him on his farm. This was of course an exaggeration, but the fact was that "Lang-Halvar", as he usually was called, was almost seven feet tall, while his companion "Lil-Lasse" was about two feet shorter, hardly five feet in length. The men were, when I remember them, well in their middle age, between 35 and 40, and they were both good workers, which evidently was the main reason why Hedman rehired them from year to year. Despite their difference in stature, they seemed to get along well with each other, and when you saw one of them, the other one was not far away.

When we boys met Lill-Lasse, someone always asked him when he was going to come to school. Lars always took it as a joke and laughingly replied, "When you become schoolmaster" or else "When I get too old to work, as I cannot afford to commence school now." But it was different with Halvar. He was short tempered and when some joking lad asked him, "How are the angels getting along up there?" then the boy had to be ready to run because if Halvar caught up with him he received a good licking.

I remember once when Lars had an accident that almost ended his life. He had been to the sawmill after a load of planks and was driving home sitting on top of the load. In the steep hill leading up to Hedman's farmyard, one front wheel fell off the wagon and Lars fell down on the road with part of the heavy load falling over him. When he was pulled out everyone thought that he was dead, but the doctor patched him up and he lived. However, he was carried to his room unconscious. Word reached Halvar who was ditching some distance away. He left his work and ran home and when he saw his partner bloody and unconscious, he cried like a child. He refused to leave the room even for meals, until he was assured that Lars was recuperating and would eventually get well again.

One cold winter day when Halvar was hauling water from the nearby lake, he slipped and fell in the open waterhole. He was able to crawl up on the ice alone but before he reached home his clothes were frozen stiff and he caught a cold that ended with pneumonia. Now it was Lars that nursed him back to health. Nobody else was allowed to enter the room. Lars gave him his medicine at regular intervals and nursed him day and night for nine days until finally the fever had broken and Halvar began to recuperate. Then Lars climbed the ladder to the attic and slept for nearly two days and nights after his long vigil.

Many years later I heard that Lars and Halvar had retired from regular work and had bought a little two room house outside the village. They lived together until they became unable to care for themselves and the parish council gave them a home until they died. None of them were ever married.

11
As a Factory Worker

In the fall of 1900, I applied for work at the pulp factory in my home town, Järpen. I had just celebrated my 17th birthday. Dad warned me that the work would be too hard, but I decided to make a try at it. I was strong for my age and considered myself good for any kind of hard work.

At the factory I was placed at the peeling machines and my job was to pile the heavy 20-inch-long blocks to the men who were peeling. It sure was heavy work and particularly if the logs had just been pulled out of the water when they were wet and slimy. The wages were 3.50 kronor per ten-hour day, and that was considered very good wages at that time.

The process of developing paper from timber logs is worth describing. The logs were brought up from the river on a long endless chain with hooks to hold the log. They were then rolled into the large circular saw which cut the logs up in 20-inch lengths. The log blocks were then taken to the peeling machines and all bark was removed. Then to the knotter where the knots were bored out. When the block was free from bark and knots it went to other machines and was cut up into slivers. On an endless belt the slivers, or "flis" as it was now called, were poured into the large boilers where it was mixed with strong acid and boiled for several days. When ready it consisted of a soup like, ill smelling substance and was poured into large cisterns or bins to cool off. Then it ran through the drying machine and from this to other machines where it was pressed into large sheets which were cut into sizes about 4 x 4 feet, and now it was baled, and the bales sown with burlap for transportation to other factories in England or Norway where the pulp bales were made into printing paper.

The factory was running night and day the year around and we changed shifts every other week. One week on days and the next on nights. At Christmas the machines were closed down for two days, but then repairs were made, and the smoke vents should be cleaned. I was ordered out the second day to help with cleaning the vents and I think it was the toughest and dirtiest day that I ever put in. When I walked home that night, I was blacker than a Cong Negro and my clothes were torn to pieces all over. We received double pay for that day, but we earned it.

On Jan. 1st, 1901, a law went into effect excluding boys under 18 years of age to work more than 8 hours a day. Our foreman had to place an older person on my job. He told me that he was well satisfied with my work and offered me to stay on by doing some lighter work 8 hours a day, but my wages would be only 2 kronor. I told him that before I worked for kids' wages, I would quit, and so I did. I had worked at the factory for about three months and had saved a little money, so I felt independent.

12
My First Experience as a Lumberjack

During part of the winter 1900-01, I worked as a lumberjack near the little hamlet of Fröån in northern Sweden. It was the first time I had been away from home, and I was 17 years old and considered myself a full grown man. My companion was an elderly man, Magnus Dahlin, a hard and experienced woodsman.

We rented a little room from a peasant farmer, Anders Hoglund, and boarded ourselves. We had about three miles to walk morning and evening to where we were working cutting pine and spruce logs. The first week I was unable to keep pace with my companion but after I became used to my axe, I soon caught up with him. The logs had to be peeled and the ends trimmed as they had a long way to be transported before they reached the sawmill. We were paid from 8 to 20 ore for each log, according to size and we managed to earn an average of three crowns a day, which was considered fair wages at that time.

It was a monotonous existence out there and no opportunities for recreation, but we were informed that plans were made for a big celebration at Easter, and we were looking forward to it. Several days before the holidays a man was sent to the city to buy whiskey, as no celebration could be without intoxicants. Strong beer was brewed by two of the women, to be consumed at the Easter festivities. Two violinists were hired from a nearby hamlet, to play for a dance on Saturday night and everybody was looking forward for a great time.

I had joined a Good Templar lodge in my hometown, and I refused to expend any money in the kitty for the purchase of liquor, but my companion liked his liquor and joined with the other men. The celebration commenced on Good Friday. A large room in a nearby house was to be the headquarters for the festivities and there gathered men and women, lumberjacks and peasants, for what they considered a good time. On Saturday afternoon the fiddlers arrived, and dancing commenced. I was alone in our little room and across the yard I could hear the music and the noise from the dancehall. Hoglund's hired maid came with a bowl of milk for us and she asked me why I wasn't at the dance. So after a while I accompanied her over there.

The dance was in full swing with men and women dancing in pairs or alone. The whiskey keg stood on the table and in a corner, I saw a barrel filled with homemade beer. It smelled terrible and I almost backed out when I opened the door. I tried to dance with the hired girl but I was not much of a dancer, and we were jolted and pushed by the other dancers so it was no fun. As soon as the dance ended, I ran out and went home to bed.

The next morning, I went there again to look for Magnus, who had not come home during the night. The place sure was a mess. In the bunks drunken men and even some women were sleeping and snoring. The whiskey keg was laying on the floor empty and the beer barrel was overturned. I did not find Magnus there but later I found him sleeping in the little backhouse by the barn. I had to get the hired maid to help me get him in the house and to bed.

Witnessing this carousal perhaps helped a great deal to make me an abstainer from alcohol for life.

13
On a Log Drive

It was in the spring of the year 1900. I had been working as a lumberjack near a little hamlet by the name of Fröån during the winter. The logs had been hauled out on a little lake or tarn, and from there they were to be floated down a small river into a larger lake and ultimately to the sawmills in my hometown of Järpen.

When the cutting ended, I was selected as one of a crew of four to be stationed two miles down the river and patrol the river to see that the logs did not jam up in their transportation down to the lake.

We were to live in a small hut near the river which had been un-inhabited for years. In this hut, we were told, a traveling peddler had been killed by a laplander and superstitious people believed that the peddlers ghost was still haunting the premises and warned us to not tease or disturb him.

The first thing we had to do when we reached the hut was to repair the hearth or fireplace so it could be used. Then the bunks were almost rotted down and had to be repaired. With birchbark we patched the roof of the cabin and built mattresses in our bunks from fragrant spruce boughs. We now had a cozy little home in the wilderness but had any of us believed in spooks or ghosts, we could well imagine that we heard them when the wind whistled through the walls of the cabin. However, we all slept undisturbed.

The next morning the first logs came tumbling down the river. We worked together two and two, but sometimes when a log jammed up against some large boulders in the river, we had to get together all four of us to jerk it loose and prevent a logjam. It was wet and often dangerous work. A log would get wedged in between some rocks and in a few minutes other logs would be caught until there was a pack of several hundred logs which often would dam up the water. Then a man had to go out on the logjam and cut off the log holding it. When the jam broke loose that man would be in a dangerous position. He had to jump from log to log trying to get to shore. Often, he was caught between rolling logs and injured and it happened quite often that men were drowned in the breaking up of log-jams. We were fortunate however in not having any serious accidents but almost every night we came home wet, sometimes up to our neck, and during the two weeks we remained in the hut, wet ill-smelling clothes hung before the fireplace every night. "That", said my bunkmate Magnus Dahlin, "was enough to keep all spooks and ghosts away from our cabin."

Finally came the day when the little river was clear from logs, and we followed "the tail" down to the lake "Hälgesjön". The river drive was over but now we were going to join three larger crews in transporting the logs across three lakes, "Hälgesjön", "Sås-sjön" and "Brattlands sjön". At the mouth of the river, twenty men were waiting and had the logs partitioned off into three different log-rafts or "skutor" as they were called. The logging company we worked for had built a bunkhouse nearby, a shed about 16 x 16 feet. It was built for a crew of eight and now we were 24 men to occupy it overnight. Every man was his own cook and preparing something to eat on the open fireplace that evening was a memorable event in itself. Cuss words fell like hailstones on a tin pan and for several minutes it looked like there would be a fistfight around that hearth.

There were no beds or bunks in this camp to sleep on, but two wide shelves along one wall, one above the other, originally built to accommodate four men on each shelf. That night we had to sleep 12 men on each shelf and consequently we were packed like sardines in a can. It was impossible to turn over during the night, but we were all tired and I for one, slept soundly all night.

It took us the most of the first day to get our rafts in order. The first raft left about three in the afternoon and a couple hours later the second raft pulled out. I was with the last crew to get ready, and it was after six in the evening before we rowed out our anchor and pulled away from the shore. We had about 4,000 logs ringed in and confined within our boom behind our windlass platform. We had two anchors or drags fastened to 1-inch manilla rope about 500 feet long. Two men rowed out the anchor and dropped it to the bottom of the lake. When they gave the sign that anchor was dropped four men commenced winding the rope around the windlass, thereby pulling the entire raft ahead. We were eight men on the windlass crew and while thus six men were working, the other two men rested or prepared the food, consisting principally of coffee, bread and salt pork. When one anchor was pulled in, the second anchor was rowed out the full distance and dropped. The rope was exchanged on the windlass and the procedure was continued. If the weather was favorable, we kept going day and night, 24 hours a day, until we reached our destination, and changed about so two men slept while six worked.

The second day out on the lake the wind suddenly turned against us, and the drags slid. We were unable to make any headway and had to pull in behind a small islet where we were in the lee and the wind could not reach our raft. There we remained for two full days while a strong east wind lashed the lake and threatened to break up the raft. The time was spent in exploring the little island and playing cards. On the south shore, about a mile from where we were marooned was a little farmstead. The second day some of our crew rowed over in the skiff and bought fresh eggs and milk which made a welcome change in our diet.

There were, as mentioned before, three lakes we had to cross. These lakes were connected with narrow straits, just barely wide enough to let a raft pass through in calm weather. When we reached the straits, a man was posted on each side to watch and signal if the raft grounded. Passing the first strait, I was sent to the post on one side. It was raining and was pitch dark. I had a lantern to signal with and every time I swung that lantern, it went out and I had to relight it. The raft kept going meanwhile and I heard the groaning of the boom when it scraped against the rocks on the shore. If the boom would break, I would get the blame for not giving signals to stop. However, it held and it was with a deep breath of relief I saw the raft leave the shore into open water again. A little while later the skiff came and picked me up.

Everything went fine after that, and we reached the eastern end of the last lake one Saturday afternoon. We had been on the lake just a week. It was an experience I would long remember.

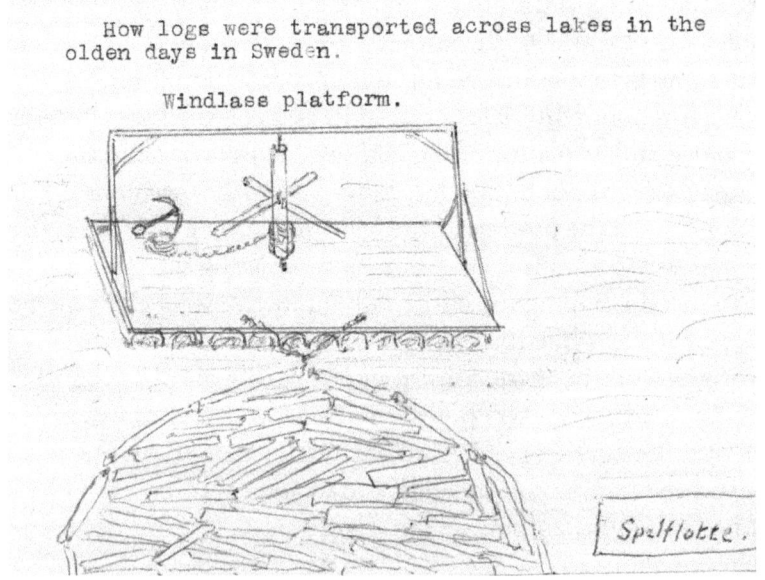

How logs were transported across lakes in the olden days in Sweden.

Windlass platform.

Spelflotte.

Logging sketch by John Ostlund.

14
My First Vacation

It was Midsommar in the year 1901, and I was almost 18 years old, and had never been to the city. Neither had I ever carried any money that I could say really belonged to me. My Dad had collected my earnings and spent them, giving me occasionally a 25 or 50 ore as my allowance at each payday.

An international youth meeting was to be held in the city of Östersund and special trains were chartered to bring young people from the city of Trondheim in Norway and from Copenhagen in Denmark. Also from the nation's capital, Stockholm, a special train was bringing people to our province. Several of the younger men in the crew where I was working, were going and they induced me to come along. I doubted very much that Dad would allow this extra expenditure but one night, when I thought that he was in good humor, I asked him if I could have some money and go to the city with the other boys. He hesitated at first, but when I reminded him that I earned more money than he did being enumerator at the assorting boom where we both worked, he did not feel that he could refuse my request.

Nobody could have been happier than I was when at the next payday he handed me 15 kronor for the trip. I never before had that much money that I could call my own. At the depot I joined three other youngsters of the assorting crew, and we boarded the train for Östersund. It was packed on the train, and we did not find a seat, but we did not care. After a two-hour train ride, we were in the city. All hotels were filled but we were fortunate to find a member of the reception committee who directed us to a place where cots had been placed in a large hall, and, where we registered for the night.

However, we had not come to the city to just sleep, so after we had registered, we left and went down to the lake harbor where several steamboats were loading to take people out to various places along the Lake Storsjön, where midsummer wakes and dances were arranged. We four boys purchased tickets on "Karl XV" a nice steamboat destined to take us out to a place called "Önöudden" where a dance was held. When we arrived there, the pavilion floor was so packed that they did not allow us to enter. We went back to the boat and when it left for another dance pavillion, called "Sandviken" we went along. I was not much of a dancer at that time but here I was a stranger, and I was bold enough to invite a girl and mix with the dancers on the floor. I had fun and if I made missteps, I blamed it on the crowd.

It was quite early Midsummer day morning when we returned to the city and found our cots. We did not sleep long, however. Soon we were out on the streets again. The great Good Templar Hall was the place of the Youth meeting, but we did not go there. Instead, we returned to the harbor and took a steamboat to "Kungsgården", the military training post. There we watched the soldiers doing their maneuvers, which was very interesting. Later, we watched an open-air dramatic play called "Arnjlot Gällinot" where the actors were dressed like the old vikings who lived there about the year 1000. It was a wonderful performance.

Back in the city we met a couple boys from our hometown who were serving in the artillery, and we were invited to accompany them there. A dance was arranged in the mess hall and again we mixed with the dancers and had a good time. It was after midnight when we took the night train back to our home.

15
The Great Forest Fire

The summer of 1901 was one of the warmest and driest summers in northern Sweden. Forest fires were reported from many communities and rangers were kept busy. One smoky afternoon, the foreman on the sorting bridge where I was working received orders to send six men out to a small forest fire about six miles from our village and try to check it before it spread any further. We were to take food with us for a couple of days after which we would be relieved by another crew.

Before daybreak the next morning, I joined the foreman and four other men, and we were on our way. We followed a trail through the tall timber for a couple miles. When the trail ended at a little tarn we continued through the wild woods. We saw a little cloud of smoke ahead of us which became darker and denser the closer we came. But it was farther away than we thought, and we walked all day before we reached it. Then the wind died down, the smoke raising horizontally, and we could get to work. We cleared off the edge of the burned area all around and it was after 3 o'clock in the morning before our foreman called for a rest. He had made coffee and it sure tasted good after almost 24 hours of hard tramping through the woods and strenuous work all night. After eating we stretched out on the ground and fell asleep. It was about 8 o'clock a.m. when I was awakened. In a nearby creek, we filled our pails with water and went along the fireline extinguishing sparks and glowing tinders wherever we saw any. It was still smoking from old windfalls and rotten stumps but there was no wind and it seemed that we had everything under control.

We had a good breakfast and then our foreman decided that we just as well could return home. There he made a grave mistake, a mistake that cost him his job later on. We were supposed to remain at the fire until we were relieved. After we had left the wind increased and must have thrown sparks across the line we had cleared off. When we neared home and looked back, dark smoke again was visible behind us. We met a crew sent out to relieve us. We came home ragged and tired late at night.

One day we rested but then were ordered out to fight the fire again. Meanwhile it had spread out and every available man in the community had been sent there. Emergency calls were sent to military posts in the province and even from other provinces special trains brought firefighters. When we reached the fireline we were placed under military control too and ordered to clear a 20 ft. wide strip between two little tarns or lakes. The fire had not reached there yet but when it did, we had strict orders to stop it. We worked like mad clearing and backfiring as we went. When we had the fireline ready we were handed pails which we filled and placed at intervals along the open strip. When the main conflagration hit us, we were almost blinded by the smoke and the sparks set fire to our clothes. Almost ready to drop from exhaustion we were relieved by a new troop of soldiers who took over our pails and told us to get out. I stumbled down to the little lake, undressed and took a refreshing bath in the cool water. In a nearby saeter cabin the military cooks served mess and I had a good meal after which I fell asleep on the floor among a dozen other exhausted firefighters. 84 eng. square miles of valuable timber was destroyed in this fire.

16
At a Cottage Dance in Norway

During the winter of 1901 - 1902, I worked a few weeks at the little border village of Storlien, about sixty miles from my hometown in Sweden. We were employed by the railroad company and sent up there to remove the snow from the tracks in and around the railroad depot. Never in man's history had so much snow accumulated there before. It drifted in from the surrounding mountains and covered the tracks in places more than twenty feet deep and packed so hard that a person could walk on top of it like walking on a road and the large snowplows were quite unable to penetrate the snow masses. Many of the buildings in the village were quite covered over and buried, and tunnels had to be dug up to the surface. At several of the larger houses, entrances were made by some window on the second story. In order to keep the Railroad yard open for the trains, the snow had to be cut in squares by man labor and loaded onto flatcars which were hauled out to a deep ravine called "Great Hell" where it was dumped or unloaded. Often the thermometer dropped to 40 below zero, but there was no rest. From daylight to dark, Sunday or weekday, we were driven out to battle the snowdrifts.

A few kilometers west from Storlien, on the Norwegian side is the little hamlet of Taeverdalen. One Saturday evening when we returned to the hotel where we were staying, we were informed that a dance was to be held out there. Working for weeks without any change or recreation of any kind becomes quite monotonous and particularly so for young people. We were eager to get out there. After supper three of us youngsters borrowed each a pair of skis and set out on a well broken ski trail across the mountainside with the intention to attend the dance. It was not only the dance itself that tempted us to go there, but none of us had ever been across the border before and the idea of attending a dance in a foreign country was the main motive of the trip. We looked ahead for that dance both as a pleasure and as an adventure.

When we arrived to Taeverdalen the full moon was bright over the landscape, but not a house could we see. The snow had covered every house and only a few trees emerged through the white blanket. Smoke was seen here and there, bringing evidence that we had reached the place of habitation. We met a couple men who were going to the dance and followed them. Reaching the opening of a tunnel, the men left their ski's outside and stepped down a stairway hewn out in the snowbank. We done the same and entered a semi-dark room where a small kerosene lamp on a shelf left the room in a pleasant twilight. We three foreigners found a seat on an old trunk in a corner and sat down listening to the chatter of the other occupants in the room. We did not understand much of the language spoken by the natives here. Nobody seemed to notice us and we did not try to speak to anybody. After a while a man arrived with an accordion and the dance commenced. We watched it with interest for a while. There were only two young girls and the rest of the feminine part of the dancers were older, married women. I was the youngest of us three and I was waiting for the others to join the dance and partake of the fun. However, none of my companions made any attempt to dance and when I no longer could resist the temptation to dance, I boldly stepped over to one of the girls and bowed. She looked surprised and shook her head. Dejected I returned to the corner, where my companions seemed to enjoy my embarrassment. When I suggested that we should return to Storlien, they only laughed telling me to wait and they would show me how to handle the Norwegian lassies. Now one of the other boys tried and was refused and I felt better. Soon we left and scrambled out through the tunnel and found our ski's.

One of the men who had shown us the place when we came, now came out and we told him how disgusted we were when none of the girls wanted to dance with us. He comforted us by saying. "Consider yourself lucky boys, that the girls refused you. If you had danced with any of them, their steady fellows would have given you a licking. They will not tolerate any foreigner playing with their lassies."

We returned to Storlien and resolved that our luck with the Norwegian girls was nothing to brag about. But it was an experience and an adventure to be remembered.

PART 2 -
"My Journey to America"

I believe that I was too happy to sleep the first nights after receiving the ticket to America. I was looking forward to a great adventure. I was going to cross foreign countries, Norway, and England, I would see and meet people of other lands and speaking other languages and the future looked bright and rosy ahead.

The Cunard Line Steamer SS Ultonia. The ocean liner that John Ostlund took from Liverpool, England to Boston, United States of America in 1902.
Wikipedia public domain

17
Crossing the Atlantic Ocean

The greatest event in my young life was when I emigrated to America in the spring of 1902. Disgusted with conditions in Sweden and particularly the prospect of serving three years in the army, made me resolve to emigrate to a land where there was no military service required from its young citizens. How to get there was now my greatest problem. I had no money with which to buy a ticket and no rich friends or relatives whom I could ask for assistance. My only hope was that I could induce my old boss, Mr. Paulsson, to lend me the amount necessary to get across. However, I knew that unless I could get my father's consent, it would be no use to talk to Paulsson. When I came home from Storlien, I brought the subject up but dad was solidly against it at first. He was getting up in age and he depended on my support. If I emigrated, he would never have any hopes of ever seeing me again. However, when I insisted, he gave in but suggested another plan. He had met a farmer from Minnesota at a Baptist conference in Östersund the previous summer and now he suggested that I should write to him. If he needed any help on his farm, he might advance my ticket and I could work it out. This plan would have the advantage that I was assured of a job when I arrived in the new country.

I wrote to Charles Wickstrom in Worthington, Minnesota, explaining my problem and practically begged him to help me out by sending me a ticket for the fare and I would pay him by working on his farm when I arrived there. I did not depend much on this letter, as I did not know Mr. Wickstrom, nor did he know me. However, a few weeks later I received a message from my father that the ticket to America had arrived with a long letter informing me of what I needed and how to conduct myself with the customs and other problems meeting me during the trip. I am unable to express my feelings when this news reached me. After all, I was going to emigrate to the wonderful land across the ocean that I had heard so much about. My dreams had come true, my longings were to be fulfilled. My chest filled and my heart felt like it was coming up in my throat. I had to work the day out, loading logs in Gevsjön, but it was one of the longest days of my life. It did not take me long to get my few belongings together and the first train carried me home to Järpen.

I believe that I was too happy to sleep the first nights after receiving the ticket to America. I was looking forward to a great adventure. I was going to cross foreign countries, Norway and England, I would see and meet people of other lands and speaking other languages and the future looked bright and rosy ahead. What little money I had saved was spent for a good suit of clothes, new shoes and underwear and when I was through shopping I was nearly dead broke. A friend of mine offered me a loan of 40 kronor and I was glad to accept it. I accompanied my father to the Lutheran priest to get his references for my passport. The old fellow was in an ugly mood when we arrived. As I had not been confirmed and had not been in touch with him or that church, how could I come to him for any references. Before he could do anything, he would have to inquire and secure information in regard to my previous life and character, and he told me to come back in two weeks or thereabout. I informed him that I was leaving within that time, whether I had his permit or not, and if he wanted to give me a respectable sendoff, he should have my reference ready within one week. A week later I visited the priest again and my paper was ready for me. No further examination was requested.

Saying goodbye to friends and schoolmates was not as hard as I had imagined. At that age everything comes so naturally. No thought about possible disaster or probability of never seeing each other again. Someday I would surely return loaded with riches and experiences. I believe that I promised everybody to write to them, but I am sorry to state that these promises were forgotten and never fulfilled.

In the letter I received from Mr. Wickstrom, he advised me to not bother with a trunk. Consequently, I packed my few clothes in a satchel, some food in another and I was all ready for the long journey. All the money in my possession was about fifty crowns or about fourteen dollars. However, I did not worry at all.

Two weeks after I had received my ticket, I was ready and boarded the train for Trondheim, Norway. I was fortunate to get a traveling companion from my hometown, Andrew Pearson, who was going on the same boat across the North Sea and also across the Atlantic. Other emigrants were also leaving Järpen on the same train, but they were from nearby communities, and we did not know them before. We were all decorated with flowers and on the station platform our friends and relatives had gathered to bid us farewell and wish us good luck. It is impossible to describe a person's feelings at a time like this. When one after another of my friends, schoolmates and fellow workers came up to shake my hand, and I saw tears glistening in their eyes, a peculiar lump lodged in my throat and my own tears were not far away. A last goodbye, a last handshake with father and we were on our way. The whole platform was like a rolling sea with waving handkerchiefs. When we rode through the village, we saw white waving objects all over, waving us a last goodbye, goodbye. Our journey had begun.

When our hometown was out of sight and we no longer saw any white waving handkerchiefs, we sat there looking foolishly at one another. I am sure everybody had the same feelings that I had, a feeling that cannot be put in words, only experienced. It was not a word said in the coach, only the monotonous click, click, when the wheels passed over the joints in the rails. But while we were thus meditating, we had reached the next station, Hålland, and here, more friends were on hand to bid us farewell. We were already decorated with flowers on both sides of our coats, but here more flowers were pinned on our breasts.

Soon we were on our way again and the sadness gradually gave way. The comment was made that never had we realized before how many friends we had left behind. So we passed the well-known villages, Undersåker, Björnänge, Åre and Duved. When we passed the little farm, Kläppen, where I, four years earlier, had attempted to learn the shoemaker trade, I went out on the rear platform to see if anybody was in sight. The little cottage was there, just as forlorn as it had been when I lived in it, and beside it I saw little Maria. She had grown since I left but I recognized her and waved to her. I wonder if she recognized me.

After about an hour's ride, we reached Gevsjön, and I had only been there two months. So, when I thought of the gathering at the depot, and realized that they had all come down just to say goodbye to me, a lump lodged in my throat again.

In Storlien, on the border between Sweden and Norway, we had to change trains. After a light lunch in the Railroad restaurant, we were soon comfortably installed on the Norwegian train, which would carry us to Tronheim. In our coach we met two jolly farmer girls from the province of Ångermanland, also emigrating to America, and soon we were gaily chatting like old friends. We were all enthused and sometimes awed at the scenery and the landscape we were passing through. The mountain on one side was several hundred feet high and towering almost over us. On the other side, hundreds of feet below us a silvery river was winding its way to the ocean. Small farms ere scattered here and there along the riverbank and a little white church could be seen occasionally.

Before we reached the first station on the Norwegian side which was Meraker, the custom officers entered our coach. We were ordered to open all handbags and grips for inspection. At Meraker those who had trunks had to open them for custom inspection. As soon as we got rid of the custom officials, the emigration agents appeared. These agents represented the different steamship lines traversing the Atlantic Ocean, and they were all eager to find customers. Those of us who had tickets however were left alone. In pleasant company the time flies fast and soon we saw the blue-grey water of the Bay of Tronheim. At ten o'clock our train rolled in on the depot of Tronheim, the old "Nidaros" as it was named by the vikings.

The noise and the traffic of this busy little city almost stunned us, but soon we were taken care of by the General Agent of the Cunard Steamship Line, Mr. Olaf Solem, who personally took us to a hotel and assisted us in getting a room. The hotel was filled but a small room was vacated by some of the hotel employees and Andrew and I moved in. The entire city was decorated with bunting and flags, and we were wondering if the celebration was on our account. We were soon taken out of illusions when we were informed that King Oscar II had just left the city.

In the morning we were awakened by a pretty waitress, with a tray of coffee and cookies. This was a pleasant surprise for us and we gratefully told her so. She informed us that this was the custom in Norway, and she also told us that we had been sleeping in her room and bed. We laughingly told her that if we had known that we would gladly have shared the room with her.

After breakfast we went out to see the sights of the city. On the street we suddenly met an old acquaintance from Järpen, who now lived here. He at once offered to show us around. First we saw the harbor and he pointed out the steamer on which we were going to cross the North Sea. It's name was "Tasso", belonging to the Wilson Steamship Line, and was the largest steamboat we had ever seen up to that time. Walking along the pier, we saw many fishing schooners. Many of them had just arrived loaded with freshly caught fish. At several places, boys and even full-grown men were fishing from the pier. They used snails for bait and were fishing for a kind of fish called "Sej".

Later our guide took us to the Cathedral, a building well known and famed all through the Scandinavian Peninsula. This was first built during the regime of Olaf Tryggvason, about the year of 1050. It had been razed several times during the various wars and rebuilt again. History relates that during one war, it was used as a stable by the invading cavalry troops. The entire structure is a work of art.

The Ihlewold Park was visited next. We did not linger long as our guide's time was limited, and he wanted us to see as much as possible of the sights of Tronheim. Soon we came to a ship-building yard and dry dock, and we came just in time to see a steamer being launched. this was something new to us and was very interesting. On our way back we visited a nail factory. This was also very interesting. Ten or twelve machines were in operation and each machine spewed out nails of different sizes.

We were quite tired when we finally returned to the hotel. The afternoon was spent down by the pier, where it was very interesting for us landlubbers to watch the fishermen and the sailors. Fishing schooners arrived and departed constantly. It was a busy and colorful scene. The pungent smell of fish was everywhere. It was getting dusk before we returned to the hotel and the little room we had borrowed from the pretty waitress.

Next morning, we experienced the same courteous service by another waitress. Coming down in the assembly room, we were informed that our steamer was leaving at 10 o'clock that night. It would be a busy day for us as there were many things to attend to. First, we went to the Exchange Bank where we had our money exchanged into American currency. The rate was 3.80 crowns for a dollar and for 38 crowns I received two 5-dollar bills. This and a few Swedish coins were all the money I possessed at the start of my long journey.

Then we visited the office of the Cunard Line, where our contracts were signed, and we received instructions and valuable advice. From there to the Police Station, where our passports were examined and signed by the Chief of Police. Then, back to the office of the Cunard Line for final instructions.

We were advised to eat sparingly before we boarded the steamer in order to avoid seasickness, but the Norwegian lunches were so good that I boarded the steamer with a well filled stomach. It was 10 o'clock in the evening of May 14th. The "Tasso" was an old tramp steamer used to transport cattle from England to Norway and took passengers on its return voyage back to Hull, England. The hold, or bottom compartment, was cleaned out after unloading the cattle and the floor was covered with six inches of sawdust. Primitive bunks were erected along both sides for beds for the human load. When we walked up the gangplank, us men were directed to the hold in the bow of the boat. There were about twenty men in this room, and we were directed to sleep three in each bunk. There were no mattresses in the bunks, only an old blanket and a pillow. Two small portholes admitted light from the outside, one on each side of the three-cornered room, and as we would find out later, when the waves hit the water would seep through and run down on our suitcases which were stored below the portholes. Nobody could undress, so we all slept with our clothes on. The women had a similar cabin below deck in the rear part of the ship. This was going to be our quarters for the next three or four days and I resolved right there that I was not going to spend more time than I had to in this hell-hole. I left my bags and went on deck. A large crowd had assembled on the pier to bid us farewell, but the only one that we knew in the crowd was our acquaintance from the previous day, who had guided us around the city. Fully 75% of the passengers on the boat were Norwegians, and nearly all were emigrants like ourselves. The flower-decorated coats were evidence of that fact.

I stayed on deck until the city and its lights were out of sight, when I curled up in the bunk for a few hours sleep. I had not slept in such a crowded place since I was on the drive on Lake Helgesjön, when we slept twelve men on a bunk designed for four. At four o'clock in the morning, I was on deck again as the stifled air in the room below was almost unbearable.

At 5:30 we arrived in the harbor of Christiansund. As we would remain there for at least four hours loading fish boxes, I went ashore. The city is built on the bare cliffs. The streets are steep and crooked, and they all seemed to be paved with solid natural rock. However, small lawns and garden spots were visible here and there and I was informed that the soil had been brought by boats from distant islands for these gardens.

At 7 o'clock we were all called for breakfast. Each person received a tin bowl, a knife and a spoon. We were told to keep these as long as we were on the boat and take good care of them. If the tools were lost, we would be out of luck, as far as eating was concerned, unless we could borrow from somebody else. An hour later the steward appeared outside the galley door with a large kettle of soup. The passengers crowded around him, and each received a bowl of soup and two slices of black bread. There was not enough in the kettle to go around and those that were late had to eat their bread without soup that morning. Dinner and supper were served in the same manner, but we also received a couple of slices of raw, salted herring with the bread at those meals. the meals were not served at regular times. When the cook was ready, he called and everybody who felt like eating rushed out like hungry dogs to get their rations. Sometimes the dishes had disappeared, and we had to appropriate somebody else. At 4 o'clock in the afternoon, or thereabouts, we were called for coffee. Sometimes we had a slice of bread with it, but generally it was only coffee. It looked and tasted more like dirty dishwater, but our appetites were good, and we grinned and drank it.

Between our sumptuous meals we spent the time on deck viewing the rugged but beautiful coastline. In the afternoons and evenings, we danced on deck, to the tunes of two violins and a guitar.

We arrived in Aulesund the evening of the first day, and we laid there over an hour, loading fish. As soon as the boat left the harbor, I went to bed, as I had not slept more than a few hours the previous night. I awoke when we arrived in Bergen the next morning, May 16th. Bergen is one of Norway's largest seaports and the second largest city in Norway. When we were told that Tasso would lay in the harbor all day, we secured permission to go ashore. The first thing we did was to visit a restaurant, "Kaffe Stua" and have a good meal. In a group of four, we then went sightseeing in the city. There was no worry here that we would get lost, because from almost any point in the city we could see the harbor. Here for the first time, I had difficulty to understand the Norwegian language. I went into a store to purchase some loaf sugar, but it was only after showing me all the other kinds of sugar that the salesgirl at last understood what I wanted. There is a great difference on the dialect the people talk here, from what they talk further north.

One of the most interesting statues I have ever seen was here in Bergen. It was a statue of the great violinist Ole Bull, one of the worlds outstanding violin masters. A native of Norway, he is well known in all European Capitals and elsewhere, and Bergen has honored him with that beautiful statue. At the foot of the marble figure in life-size, a spring was pouring its water in a cascade and underneath the water cascade was the marble statue of "Necken" the God of the streams, seated in a listening position and holding his harp, learning the melodies from the master violinist. The arrangement, the sculpture, and the idea behind it is certainly a masterpiece of art, and for a long while we stood there almost spellbound.

It was 8 o'clock that evening before our steamer left Bergen. The air was warm, the sea smooth and we enjoyed dining on the afterdeck until 11:30. Then the steward appeared and ordered the ladies to bed. The men could remain on deck all night if they so desired, but soon one after another disappeared below. The deck was almost deserted when Andrew and I left it for our cramped bunk forwards.

The 17th of May is Norway's national day, and when we slowly steamed into the harbor at Stavanger, that morning, the whole city seemed to be dressed in Holy Day spirit. Flags were waving from every mast and the many people who had assembled on the pier in the early morning, were all dressed in their Sunday clothes. However, we were not allowed to go to shore here. The Norwegians on the boat joined with the crowd on shore in singing the National Anthem and other patriotic songs and hymns. It was quite impressive even for us Swedes to listen to it.

Stavanger was our last port along the Norwegian coast and when we left there, we were heading for England. Three hours later, the last glimpse of the Scandinavian Peninsula was out of sight. Nothing but sky and water wherever our eyes roam. A few gulls followed us for several hours after the coastline was out of sight, but they returned to the coast. We stood by the railing and watched the "springers", large fish who were playing around the boat and following it, probably looking for some waste food from the galley. The North Sea was unusually smooth, but the sailors predicted rough sea before we would reach England. The deck was crowded as everybody was up there. The music was tempting, but there was not much room to dance. Everybody seemed to be jolly and happy in spite of scanty food and accommodations. Every now and then our attention is called to a sail or a steamer on the horizon, which we watch as long as they can be seen.

Towards evening, we run into rough sea. It was not very windy, but large billows came rolling in and our boat commenced setting and pounding against the waves in a very unpleasant manner. One after another of the passengers made lunges to the railing and fed the fish. The girls, who a while earlier had been singing and laughing, turned pale and disappeared below. Soon the deck was almost deserted. Even my companion had vanished, and I went below to look for him. Our cabin forward was a stinking hovel. Only a few of the men were sitting up. Some had vomited in the sawdust making it slippery and among them was Andrew. When the bow of the boat met one of those great billows, it rose almost on end, only to set down again in the trough. If I had stayed down there for ten minutes, I would have been sick, so I returned to the deck. There I found a boy about my own age, Axel Smeths, from Sundsvall. Together we managed to reach the railing near the large chimney, where it was warm and where the waves did not reach us. There we remained all night. We could not get any sleep as it took all our effort at times, to hang on to the rail. We could not go below because a large canvas was nailed over the hatch where the stairway was. But we were both feeling good and did not suffer from seasickness like many of our fellow passengers and when morning came we were the only passengers at the galley door for breakfast.

Very few of the passengers appeared on deck the morning of May 18th. The ladies were all confined to their bunks. Those who did not suffer from the sickness decided to remain in their beds rather than stagger around like drunks on deck. Axel and I stayed together and after that night we had become very close friends. We were now approaching the coast of England, and shortly after dinner we saw the coastline. The wind and the waves calmed down and one after another the passengers appeared on deck. Some were pale and weakened, but everybody seemed happy that land was in sight.

At 2 o'clock in the afternoon we neared the city of Hull, where we were going to land. In the harbor we saw an interesting sight when we met and passed boats of many nations, sizes and descriptions. Our steamer docked close to the pier, but we were ordered to remain on board until next morning. However, we were allowed to go ashore in groups of three or more, with instructions not to separate. After four days and nights on Tasso, we were glad to leave it for a while, and in a group of four I soon found myself ashore.

Here we soon realized that we were in a foreign country. The people and the language was new to us. Our first contact with the population of Hull was not very pleasant. An army of beggars, bootblacks, fruit venders, and milk peddlers met us before we were a block away from the pier. Some of them had learned enough Swedish or Norwegian that they were able to offer us and tell us the price on what they had to sell or barter. For the first time in my life I saw a colored man. He came down the street, swinging a cane, well-dressed, smoking a cigarette like a typical gentleman. I must have stared at him because he gave me a broad smile when he passed us. His white teeth glistened against his dark face, and I thought it very peculiar that a human would have such black color.

We walked quite a few blocks from the pier, but our general impression of the city of Hull was narrow, crooked streets, old, dilapidated buildings, and dirty, ragged and poor people. We realized of course that there were other parts of the city where conditions perhaps were quite different.

Returning to the pier where our boat played, we found a spirited dance in full swing. We joined in and enjoyed that better than exploring the streets. It was after 12 o'clock midnight, before we turned in. Not having any sleep in 36 hours or more, I fell asleep as soon as I hit the bunk.

At 3:30 in the morning of May 19th we were awakened and ordered to go ashore. I was so sleepy that I did not know how I got off the boat. Agents from the different steamship lines were sorting us out, and we were separated in different groups as each agent gathered his own customers around him. Now we lost many new acquaintances whom we had met and traveled with and now considered good friends. Addresses were received and given with promises to write when we reached our destination. These promises and addresses were forgotten and lost.

From the pier we were taken to the railroad station in horse drawn busses. Here we were lined up and received our railroad tickets for the journey across England. We also had our breakfast here, which consisted of a cup of black coffee and a slice of bread. It was a good thing that we carried a little food with us in our bags, as the food received from the steamship company was very limited. Many who did not carry emergency rations had to go hungry, unless some more fortunate fellow traveler shared their supply with them.

There must have been close to a thousand emigrants gathered at the Railroad Depot in Hull that morning, and when I came into the great rotunda, I had lost my companions from the Tasso. I got my share of the lunch, but when I later met my friends, they had not been up to the lunch counter. I directed them there, but by that time everything was cleaned up. They had to go into their grips for breakfast.

At 7:45 a.m. we boarded the train for Liverpool. We were fortunate in getting together in a coach, all of us from the same part of Northern Sweden. The railroad coaches in England are quite different from those of the Scandinavian countries. They are divided into compartments, each with ample room for eight passengers. The seats face each other, so half of the passengers have to ride backwards. I had a seat next to the window, so I had a good view of the landscape that we passed through. We passed through several of the industrial centers of England, among them Manchester, a well-known textile factory town. The tall smokestacks in some of the cities resembled a great forest, and smoke and soot were evident everywhere. At times we went through long tunnels, then again over high trestles and bridges over rivers and ravines. In the rural districts we saw some really nice country. Prosperous farmsteads where horses and cattle grazed, and promising grain or hay fields. In several places we saw canals where long boats were being pulled by horses or mules from the canal bank. These boats were often loaded to within a few inches of the rail, but the water in the canals was calm and smooth and there was no danger of floundering.

It was exactly 1:10 p.m. when we arrived in Liverpool. The trip across England had taken only five hours and twenty-five minutes. However, this was a special emigrant train and did not stop at the regular stations along the route, except for fuel and water.

In Liverpool we were gathered together and driven like a herd of cattle, to the hotel of the Cunard Line. Here we were taken into a large dining room where we could sit down and eat a hearty meal, the best I had since I left home more than a week earlier. We were then directed to a large room on the second floor of the hotel. Our room had nine double beds, and as it was filled to capacity, we were 18 men in the room. All were Norwegians except Andrew and I who were the only Swedes. The hotel was quite comfortable in every respect. In the front was a large reading and writing room and there were facilities for bath and a large and sanitary toilet room.

After a refreshing bath and a shave, we went out on the street. We were warned to be careful and not to stroll too far from the hotel. Like in the city of Hull, we met beggars, both male and female, old and young. On the first street corner a four-year old boy was winding away on a hand organ while his mother was begging for money. Bootblacks, both black and white, offered their services. Fruit venders offered their wares very insistingly.

Outside the hotel we met two of our girl companions from Sweden and we induced them to accompany us, and together we set out in the direction of the harbor. We had received directions from the company interpreter, and we had only six blocks to walk so we were pretty certain that we would find the harbor and also find our way back to the hotel. The noise and the buzz was almost deafening. Newsboys, peddlers, streetcars, and steamboats together made a din that for us, who were not used to it, seemed like an inferno. The streetcars and omnibuses were rushing by and though it was only from 50 to 100 feet between them, they were all fully loaded with passengers. We realized now that we were in a large and busy metropolis.

Off the pier, majestically riding at anchor in the harbor, we saw three ocean liners. We thought we had seen large boats before, but never had we imagined that such great palatial monsters would float on the water. On the pier the rush was tremendous. Everybody seemed to be in a great hurry to get somewhere and we had to be very careful in keeping together. If we had lost each other in this maelstrom, we would never have found each other again.

When we decided to return to the hotel, we took the wrong street. Here the streets looked all alike. Great wholesale establishments and large warehouses everywhere. Instead of coming to our hotel, we came to a row of large factories. We retraced our way to the pier as we thought, but emerged among a lot of dirty hovels and hotels in a slum district. The girls began sniffling after several hours walking, and I do not blame them, I felt like crying myself. I had taken the initiative for the walk, and I was to blame. Now we realized that we were lost completely. We tried to inquire, but nobody understood us and we looked for a policeman to direct us, but could not find one anywhere. I thought that I knew a few English words, which I did, but now I realized that I did not know the pronunciation of those words. Finally, we came to a little restaurant, and we went inside for a rest more than anything else. We were not hungry but had to order something if we wanted to get a seat. We pointed on the words: "Steak" and "Coffee", the only two words that were similar to lunch. Fortunately, I had exchanged a dollar bill to English coins that morning, which gave us ready change for what we bought.

Back on the street I stopped dozens of people, including several policemen, but nobody could direct us to the Cunard Line Hotel. In desperation I entered a saloon filled with sailors and loudly asked if somebody understood Swedish. A middle-aged sailor got up from one of the tables and answered me in Norwegian. He accompanied me out to the street where he talked with a newsboy who knew where our hotel was. We were 28 blocks away from it. The boy directed us and we finally reached home quite late in the evening.

The night after we were lost in the city of Liverpool was the shortest night I know of. From the time I hit the pillow in our fresh clean bed, and until I awoke about 10 o'clock in the forenoon of May 20th, I had slept a dreamless sleep. When the others were called for breakfast, I had slept soundly. However, seldom have I been so fagged out as I was after that endless tramp for more than six hours. And for several previous nights I had only had short naps in uncomfortable, vermin infested bunks.

After dinner I joined a group who were going for a streetcar ride. This was my first ride on a streetcar or "tramcar" as they were called in England. As a guide we had a Norwegian who had been to the United States before and knew the English language. We rode for over an hour, and we began to realize how large Liverpool really was and the futility for a stranger to localize himself among these labyrinthical streets. In the evening we visited the Scandinavian Sailor Mission Church. The sermon was held in Norwegian, but songs were sung both in Norwegian and

Swedish. The church was quite large as there was amble seats for 1,200 people. The location is quite convenient to several of the steamship companies' hotels, and there was thousands of Scandinavian emigrants who stayed at those hotels every week at that time when emigration was at its height.

Back at our hotel, we enjoyed a dance in the hotel back yard. Our girlfriend adventurers from the previous day had rested all day and did not suffer any ill effects from the hike. Now they were happy over the adventure and told us that they would have something to write home about. We enjoyed the dance until 11 o'clock when the large portal was closed, and everybody was ordered to bed.

In the morning of May 21st, we awoke to more explorations of the great city of Liverpool. We visited the Railroad Station where we had arrived from Hull, but which we were not allowed to see much of at that time. This station is quite large. There is two large rotundas, each with twelve to fifteen tracks. There is a steady buzz of trains and people at all hours of the day or the night.

From there we visited a large palatial mansion, St. Georges Hall, which is a wonder of art and architecture. Near that palace is Queen Victoria's Museum. Here we spent many hours, but we could have spent days and still not have seen it all. It is certainly wonderful and almost unbelievable how human energy and intelligence can gather and preserve. I am only able to briefly mention some of the things I saw in that museum. As it covers a whole city block, there is plenty of space available inside, but both floors were occupied, and every room was filled.

In one room, (not ordinary rooms, but large halls) we saw birds of all descriptions and colors and from all parts of the world. They were of course mounted, but so lifelike that we several times thought that we saw them move. In another hall were the animals, from the great polar bear to the little house mouse. In many cases the male, female and young were represented. In another room were the insects, also mounted on cartons. In one great room were weapons, shields, and armor from the ancient age until the latest development in guns. In one room clothing and ornaments were kept and preserved, from the costumes of the Laplanders and the Eskimos to Indians and natives of Australia and the South Sea Islands. There were also wonderful works of art, unusual clocks and watches, paintings, and sculptures, all preserved and protected and displayed in sealed glass cases. In the center arena was a totem-pole, which must have been at least 35 or 40 feet long and reached from the ground floor up through the second story of the building.

What interested me more than anything else was the great aquarium hall where fish and sea animals were kept alive. Large aquariums were placed in rows through the room, or along the walls, where they could be viewed from all sides. In some, the fish were slow and lazy like. In others, they were quick and lively. Among those that I knew from the lakes and streams of northern Sweden were the trout, the pickerel, and the perch. There were also crabs, turtles, and lots of small sea animals that I never seen or heard of, and which were gathered here from all parts of the globe.

On our way back to the hotel, we visited a cemetery which seemed to be located right in the center of the city. It was surrounded with large trees, and we thought first that it was a park. Passing through the borderline of trees, we reached a little valley and here was a beautiful resting place for the dead.

When we reached the street the next morning, May 22nd, we met a cold, gloomy fog. While we knew that there were many interesting sights yet to be seen in Liverpool, we were anxious to be on our way. Nobody seemed to know when we were leaving, and if they knew they would not tell us. The day was spent at the hotel playing cards, reading, and visiting with our fellow emigrants in the other rooms of the hotel. One in the company had purchased a bottle of Italian wine. It was supposed to be non-intoxicating and we all had a taste of it. However, I noticed an alcoholic flavor to it, and I took only a swallow. The others, however, liked it and results were that they became gloriously drunk. For a while, pandemonium broke out in our room, and I fled to the reading room. Someone called the hotel police and two of the noisiest fellows were locked up until next morning when they had overcome the effects of the Italian temperance drink.

When we were eating our breakfast the next morning, May 23rd, we received orders to be ready to embark on the ocean liner. Again, we were examined by a doctor, had to show our emigration visas and had our bags checked and loaded for the pier. There we waited another two hours before we could get our handbags. Hungry, tired, and disgusted, we finally were directed aboard a small steamboat which took us out in the bay to where the liner Ultonia was waiting for us. It was 3 o'clock in the afternoon when we at last were aboard and were assigned to our quarters. We had not had anything to eat since 7 o'clock in the morning. If we thought that it would be something similar to the treatment aboard the Tasso, we were pleasantly surprised. Here everything was neat and clean. Andrew and I were given a nice cabin midship which we shared with two

Englishmen. We had plenty room for our baggage in our cabin. On each side of the cabin were two single steel beds, one over the other, each with a clean mattress, a pillow and a heavy wool blanket. In front of the lower beds was a bench to sit on and at the inner end was a washstand with a water pitcher and two glasses. In the aisle just outside our door was an electric light, burning night and day. If we wanted to darken our cabin, we just pulled the curtains for the door.

When everybody was aboard, we were called for dinner. The dining hall was quite large with two long tables where we could sit down and eat our meal in comfort. Our dinner consisted of fried fish, potatoes and gravy, sandwiches on white bread with marmalade. We had coffee to drink with the meal and we could eat all that we wanted. After nearly nine hours without food, I think wee done our duty at that table.

At 4 o'clock the anchors were lifted, and the big boat began moving. By the time our dinner was finished we were outside the bay and in the Irish Sea. We were heading straight westward, but all the rest of the evening we could see the English coastline to the south. Everybody was on deck. Some were sitting in groups conversing. Some were walking back and forth on the promenading deck. Others stood leaning on the railing, watching the coast and fishing schooners and yachts that we occasionally met or passed. As soon as the boat was outside the bay, the musicians tuned up and dancing was enjoyed on the aft deck until 9 o'clock. Then the ladies were ordered to their cabins. Soon the men also disappeared one after another and Andrew and I were among the last ones leaving for our bunks. The liner is gliding smoothly through the green water of the Irish Sea. Only a slight tremble is noticeable from the pounding of the engines below.

We were called for breakfast at 7:30 next morning, May 24th. The breakfast consisted of oatmeal and milk, meat and potatoes, bread, and tea. Coming out on deck a while later, I was rather confused in seeing the coastline on our right. When we went to bed it was on our left. Thinking that something had gone wrong and that we were on our way back to Liverpool, I inquired and was informed that we now had the Irish coast on our right. At 10:30 the anchors were dropped in the harbor of Queenstown, one of the principal cities of Ireland.

Soon a small steamer came out and unloaded about fifty emigrants from the "Emerald Isle". There was a lot of redheaded girls among them and most of them looked rather dirty and unkempt. They were continually chatting like magpies or laughing like hyenas, a screaming, hysterical laugh that was not at all attractive.

The members of the crew seemed kind and accommodating whenever we came in contact with them. Many of them could talk Swedish and many of them probably were Swedes by birth. They were not allowed to mingle with the passengers in games and dances, but the sailors often played games of their own, where we were glad that we did not take part. They were usually very rough. One of their games that we enjoyed watching was called "Who is it?". It resembled "Blind man's buff", but the blinded man was slapped with a piece of board and it must have hurt considerable, judging from the expressions on the culprits face. At any rate we had a very good time.

It was 12 o'clock noon when our liner left Queenstown. When we after dinner came out on deck, the Irish coast was slowly and apparently sinking in the ocean. It was our last glimpse of Europe and the Old World. When the last streak of land disappeared, nothing was seen but sky and water in all directions. The weather was favorable, and everybody seemed to enjoy themselves. Dancing, card playing, reading and conversation seemed to be the main diversion aboard. There was a large reading room on the Ultonia, but all the books and papers were in the English language and only a small percentage of the emigrants could avail themselves of the privilege of reading. Next to the reading room was a smoker, where the men generally assembled for conversation. It is very easy to make acquaintances on a boat. No formal introduction seems to be necessary. You make a casual remark about the weather to somebody near you and the ice is broken, and the next thing you know you are conversing like you had known each other for years. The reason for this apparently lies in the fact that everybody is on the same level, so to speak, and the craving of company does the rest. The first day out from England I met many whom I had not known before, and we became friends. Some of them had left Sweden four days later than I had, but they had not been delayed in Liverpool like we had who came from Norway. However, we had seen a lot of interesting things in Liverpool which they did not have a chance to see, and I for my part did not regret the delay.

May 25th and 26th passed without any special events. The weather could not have been any better on the ocean. It was warm and we did not need our overcoats, even in the evenings on deck. Very few of the passengers were seasick. The steamer was running steady and smooth, and only a slight setting now and then was noticeable. The 'setting' is caused when the bow dips down, causing the stern to raise and vice versa. The 'rolling' is the movement of the boat sideways.

The time was passed as usual, with dancing and card playing occupying the most interest. We have met the Irish redheads and even danced with some of them. They seem to be very friendly towards us Scandinavians, and the sign-language in all its variations is used to make us understand. However, we prefer the girls from our homeland.

I noticed on the third day out that my watch was two hours ahead of the big clock in the dining room.

I awoke on the morning of May 27th by one of our English roommates calling and gesticulating wildly. He was trying to get me out in a hurry and, sensing that something was up, I hurried after him on deck. There I saw a performance that can't be seen anywhere except on the ocean. To the left of us about a dozen large whales were swimming around, spurting streams of water high in the air. They did not seem to be the least afraid of the ship. Like a bunch of happy school kids, they were chasing each other across the water surface and at times someone raised himself in the water, giving us a glimpse of his entire body. One great bull whale came towards the boat. The girls screamed and everybody was prepared for a collision, but near the boat he dived and disappeared.

One man in the steerage died that morning and they were preparing for his funeral. He was from some south European country; I did not find out which. I do not think he had any relatives on the boat because there were no tears visible at the funeral. It was very simple. The corpse was placed in a wooden box. We were all summoned on deck where a Chaplain read, from a ritual, the funeral sermon. It was short and unintelligible. A gate on the railing was opened and the box disappeared in the ocean. Nobody talked about the funeral, but it seemed to put a solemnity on the passengers that did not wear off for several hours.

The beautiful weather held out and when we reached the deck on May 28th, we saw one of the most glorious sunrises that I ever seen. The clouds were reflecting the suns rays in every imaginable color. The solemnity from yesterday's funeral had now disappeared and as soon as dinner was over, the dance began. There was an abundance of jolly girls aboard the Ultonia, and in their company the time flew rapidly. A stately matron was always around watching the lady passengers to prevent the flirt from going too far. If anybody as much as tried to steal a kiss from his lady friend, the old lady, "Snok-lisa" we called her, was always on hand. At 9 o'clock sharp every evening, curfew was called for the women, and it did not take long before they were chased from the deck. One night a young Norwegian played a trick on the matron and the orderly. He had borrowed a skirt from a girlfriend and went below in the woman's quarters. However, he was caught and spent the rest of the journey in solitary confinement in jail. We saw him again in Boston, and he was given the choice of either marrying the girl or be sent back to Norway. I do not know what his choice was.

May 29th was our sixth day on the ocean and the weather remains the same. A sailor told me that it is very seldom that they have so long steady weather. We were then getting close to New Foundling, and he predicted change in the temperature if not stormy weather during the last days of the journey.

We were not alone on the ocean, though it sometimes seems so when we do not see anything but sky and water. That day, however, we passed a large sailing vessel, but as there was very little wind, they did not seem to move at all. We also met another of the Cunard Liners, Aquatania, on its way to England. The steamers exchanged signals as long as they were in sight of each other.

Orders were given that all men were to be vaccinated that day. Every man was ordered on deck, and all the cabins were searched for possible hiders. One stairway was closed, and at the foot of the other stairway we had to pass the doctor and the chief steward with our left arms bared. The steward dipped a stick in vaccine and planted two drops on the arm about two inches apart. The doctor, with a small penknife, disinfected over a burning flame, scratched the skin until the vaccine mixed with the blood. It took about two hours before every man had passed by the doctor. Then the stairways were opened again, and we could return to the deck. At the dance that evening, the girls seemed to find much pleasure in squeezing and pinching our sore arms. The vaccination did not cause any blisters or sores on my arms, so consequently I must be immune.

In the morning of May 30th, I woke up with a very unpleasant noise in my ears. It was the foghorn screaming at regular intervals. It was the first time that I ever heard the foghorn, and every time it screeched, it sent cold shivers down my back. Before I reached the deck, I could smell the raw, damp air of the fog and on deck we could not see ten feet outside the rail. The deck was deserted that morning. Everybody stayed below in the reading room and the smoker, reading, and playing cards. Towards noon the noise from the foghorn ceased, and when we came on the deck, the sun was breaking through the fog. However, the fog only lifted and formed clouds and in the afternoon, it commenced to rain. For the first time since we left Liverpool, there was no dancing in the evening. The deck was wet and slippery, and very few of the passengers ventured out.

May 31st was another gloomy day. The rain was pouring down and besides it was quite windy. The waves went high and lifted the ship up and down, up, and down. The boat was also rolling considerably and there was many empty seats at the breakfast table. Two thirds of the passengers stayed in their rooms that day. The others assembled in the smoking room, and there we listened to sailor stories told by a Norwegian sailor who, according to his own words, had been around the world several times. It was not all true stories that he was telling, but who cared as long as we enjoyed them. And as he had a natural talent for storytelling, we could have listened to him all day. Our girl companions were out of sight all that day. We missed them and hoped for better weather.

June 1st was a Sunday, and when I came on deck the sun was shining. On the aft deck, where we used to dance, I saw a group of Irish having their Sunday sermon. One of them must have been a priest. He was reading in a sin-song voice, while the others knelt around him in holy reverence. A few minutes later it was over, and they were all jolly and gay again. The redheaded girls were giggling and throwing kisses at us whenever they had a chance.

It was a welcome sight when a flock of seagulls met us. It was the first greeting from another continent, from America, which we came nearer every hour. On the horizon we saw sails, another sign that we are approaching land.

In the evening our steward came to our cabin and asked for "tips". He told us in faltering Norwegian, that their salary is very small and that they have to depend on tips from the passengers. We each contributed a few pence in appreciation of his kindness and services.

In the evening a special farewell party was arranged in the dining room. The tables and seats had been removed and there was ample room to dance. Speeches were held, but as this was in English, I did not get much benefit from it. Singing followed and I enjoyed that better, but when an orchestra appeared and commenced playing dance music, I was one of the first on the floor. Everybody was happy that night, and I heard many exclaim that they would not have objected to have the trip last another week.

"AMERICA", This was the only word I heard when I awoke in the morning of June 2nd, 1902. Nearly all the passengers of the Ultonia were on deck when I reached there, and all were scanning the horizon to the west, where a dark streak was visible, which we knew was land.

After ten days on the ocean, even though we had excellent weather most of the time, it surely was a welcome sight. And this was the land of our dreams, the land of opportunities that we had heard and read so much about back there in our homeland. What did it have in store for us who stood there at the rail, watching it raise on the horizon? For many it perhaps meant prosperity and happiness, for others perhaps endless hard labor and poverty.

Soon we entered Massachusetts Bay where we met and passed boats of all descriptions and nationalities. There was a large sailing vessel with six large masts, all of the same length or height. It seemed to be manned by young lads and was perhaps a training vessel for student mariners or navigators. An American warship passed us at a close distance, probably a Government Patrol ship. Doctor and emigration officials came aboard, and all the passengers were lined up for examination and inspection.

At 10:30 a.m. we were in the harbor of Boston. Nobody but American citizens were allowed to go ashore, however. We had to wait until after dinner before our turn came to leave the boat. While we were waiting, we had an excellent chance to study life in the harbor. Close to the Ultonia, a large schooner was anchored. The crew, and they were all colored, were painting and cleaning the ship. It was quite interesting to see how expertly and cleverly they worked in all possible positions, hanging to a hawser or a ladder made from rope.

When we finally were allowed to disembark, we were taken to a large rotunda called Castle Garden. There we had to display our traveling cards or visas and were directed into long aisles separated by ropes. At the far end of each aisle sat an official of the emigration bureau. Here we were closely examined again. We had to relate our past, present, and future in close details, where we came from and where we were going, if we had bought our own ticket or if somebody else had bought it for us, if we had work at our destination or if we were looking for work and what kind of work we were seeking. We had to tell him our financial status and satisfy the official that we had money enough to take care of ourselves until we were at our destination. I showed a five-dollar bill and he was satisfied. One man had only 25 cents to show, and he got by, although the officer shook his head.

All the cash I had was six dollars, and before leaving the boat I had lent one dollar to a boy who had spent his last cent aboard. He had promised to wait for me at the exit of Castle Garden and return the dollar bill. He showed his appreciation by disappearing up the street. This was called to my attention by another fellow who knew that I had helped him, and together we took after the culprit. We chased him for several blocks before we caught up with him and I recovered my money.

Returning to the Garden, I found my companions. We visited the detaining room or jail, where a group of our fellow travelers were detained and going to be sent back to Norway. Others were detained for further information from relatives in America.

When I found my handbags at the custom office, they were checked without inspection. I might have smuggled a million dollars' worth of diamonds on that trip without being detected. The custom officers in Boston were not so particular in those days.

Next, we were lined up to receive our railroad tickets. This was proceeding very slow, and we were both hungry and tired before we were waited upon and received the long strips that entitled us to ride to our destination in Minnesota. The day was very warm and being on our feet all afternoon without a chance to sit down for a minute, it was without doubt the hardest and most tiresome day of the entire journey.

Here we bid goodbye to nearly all of our traveling companions from the northern part of Sweden. My close friend and companion, Andrew Persson, was going to Naugatuck, Connecticut on a different train and now we had to part company. Others, whom we had traveled with all the way, were going to parts in Canada and left Boston on a different railroad. Again, we exchanged addresses, promising to keep in contact with each other. Those promises were later forgotten.

18
From Boston to Minnesota

It was 6 o'clock p.m. on June 2nd, 1902, the day we landed in America, when we boarded the special emigrant train that was going to take us to Chicago, Illinois. My traveling companion now was a girl, Bertha Holm, from a neighbor parish in Jämtland, and who was going to the same place as myself in Minnesota. My watch was now even six hours ahead and I set it back to correspond with the Eastern Standard Time of Boston. The railroad coaches were quite different here from any we had traveled on before. Another thing that we remarked on was that here was not class distinction like in the old world. Over there they had different coaches for the poor and the rich travelers. Here they were all riding together. Our first contact with the democracy of America.

Passing through Boston, while it yet was daylight, we noticed the great difference from the European cities we had traveled through. The streets were wider and cleaner, the buildings higher and more businesslike. At 7 o'clock it suddenly turned dark. There was no twilight here like it is in the Scandinavian countries.

It had been a wearisome day, and soon we dozed off in sleep.

There was no steward calling us in the morning of June 3rd. I felt, however, that I had been awakened fifty times during the night. At Syracuse, New York the train stopped for twenty minutes, giving the passengers a chance to have breakfast. Until now we had received our meals free on our ticket, but from now on we had to pay for what we ate. It felt good to get out and stretch our legs after the cramped-up positions in our seats all night. Bertha and I joined the others in a large restaurant in the basement of the large depot. The waitress understood Swedish and served us a good, refreshing breakfast for 25 cents.

Soon the Conductor was shouting, "All aboard" and back we went to our seat in the train. We were on our way again. If I should describe everything, I saw that was unusual to my eyes, I would be constantly writing. However, I had my notebook in my lap and now and then I jotted down something that I found interesting.

Traveling through the great state of New York is somewhat similar to parts of England. Large industrial cities with factories were seen and passed. Our train, being a special, it stopped only occasionally for fuel and water and to allow the emigrants to get their meals. At 1 o'clock we left Buffalo, New York and following the south shore of Lake Erie, we passed through the cities Erie and Ashtabula and reached Cleveland, Ohio at 4:40 in the afternoon. We had our dinner in Buffalo and in Cleveland we had our supper. Wherever we stopped for lunch, there was always some interpreter who understood several languages and who helped us order what we wanted. Some of these were women.

At 5 o'clock we left Cleveland, went through Toledo, Ohio and Elkhart, Indiana and arrived in Chicago at 2 o'clock a.m. We were both sleeping, and it seemed very cruel indeed to wake us up at that time of the night. But we were in Chicago, the metropolis of the middle west, and which we had heard so much about.

Large omnibuses were waiting for us. We were directed to leave our baggage in a large van which was there for that purpose. I jumped up beside the teamster of the omnibus, in order that I might see as much as possible of the city, or the part of it that we were riding through. We passed some great buildings, one of them fifteen stories high. I had heard and read about the skyscrapers of New York and Chicago, but this was my first view of one. Above the street on which we rode was an electric railway where electric trains were constantly running, even at that time of the night. Soon our horses stopped near a large depot, and we were unloaded. Here we had roll call and, as our names were called, we were allowed to enter large waiting room. We must give the railroad company credit for being very careful about their human cargo. There was always somebody on hand, watching that nobody would get lost. They warned us from listening to or accompanying any strangers. These warnings were not always adhered to, as our own experience showed.

We were allowed to go out on the street, with admonitions not to stroll too far from the depot. After a while we spied a Swedish restaurant where we obtained a good meal consisting of meat stew, potatoes, bread and butter and coffee, all for the sum of 10 cents. It was the cheapest meal I ever had since in an American restaurant. When we came out from the restaurant, we met a well-dressed young man, who addressed us in Swedish, and asked if we wanted to send a telegram ahead to our destination. One of the girls in the group said that she would like to notify an aunt, who lived somewhere in Wisconsin, and to whom she was going. The stranger offered to show us "a cheap telegraph station which was owned by his sister" as his words fell. It was only a block or two from where we were. Unwittingly, we followed him down the street. However, after walking three blocks, I stopped and told the girls that I would not go any further. The stranger got peeved and told me to go back to the depot but insisted that the girl who wanted the telegram sent accompany him to his sister's office. When she hesitated, I hit on a bright idea. I saw a policeman on the opposite street corner, and I told them that I would go over and ask him about the telegraph office. The bluff worked immediately. The stranger stalked away through the alley, and we returned to the depot. Realizing that we had been following one of the numerous sharks who prey on the unsuspecting emigrants, the girls thanked me for outwitting him. The fact was that I would have been unable to get any information from the police, unless he had been a Scandinavian, which was doubtful. Back at the depot we learned that a telegram could be sent to any part of the country from an adjoining room.

There happened to be a strike in Chicago at the time we were there, and from our observation place near the depot, we saw a rather unusual scene. A well-dressed man came riding down the street in a swell buggy drawn by two spirited horses. In front of the Swedish restaurant, a group of workmen had gathered, and when they saw the buggy, they ran out in the street and stopped the horses. Somebody was demonstrating or arguing with the driver first. Then they unhitched the team and grabbing the buggy, they overturned it in the middle of the muddy street. Quite a crowd was gathering around the scene and a policeman arrived, blowing his whistle for help. We were interested to see how it would end, but our watchman came hurrying us out and ordered us all back into the waiting room. He told us that bullets might be flying, and he did not want any of us to get hurt.

It was also time for us to board our train. We left Chicago at 9 o'clock, and this was June 4th. As before mentioned, we had a special train, for emigrants only, from Boston to Chicago. Now we were sent with the regular train, which made stops at all stations along the route. At Elroy, Wisconsin we changed trains. The number of our companions were rapidly dwindling. Those going to Minneapolis and St. Paul, Minnesota stayed on the Chicago train.

We left Elroy at 8 o'clock p.m. and an hour later we passed the great Mississippi River. At midnight we arrived in Mankato, Minnesota where we again had to change trains. There we boarded a train coming from St. Paul which was crowded with passengers. I found a seat beside an old gentleman. Noticing that I was an emigrant, he immediately spoke to me in Norwegian. He told me that he had been in America over 30 years, and now owned a section of land in South Dakota. He offered me a job and gave me his address.

It was 3:30 in the morning of June 5th when we arrived at Worthington, Minnesota, our destination. At last, we had reached the end of the long journey. From Sweden, we had crossed the North Sea, then across the entire country of England, spanned the great Atlantic Ocean, traveled through eight states, namely: Massachusetts, New York, Pennsylvania, Ohio, Indiana, Illinois, Wisconsin, and Minnesota.

PART 3 -
"The 'Dog' Years"

My first three years in America, commonly called the "dog years", where I had many adventures and often quite narrow escapes, during my eighteenth to my twenty-first year.

19
Working for Mr. Wickstrom

I arrived from Sweden to Worthington, Minnesota at 3:30 in the morning of June 5th, 1902. There was of course not anybody at the depot to meet me at that unearthly hour of the night. The waiting room at the depot was open, but there were no lights. The full moon, however, spread enough light through the windows so we could find seats and make ourselves as comfortable as possible while waiting for morning and daylight. As companion, I had Miss Brita Holm, who was from a neighbor parish in Norther Sweden.

At daybreak an old Negro came into the waiting room and spoke to us. Unable to understand him, I spoke Swedish to him, which made him understand that we were immigrants. Without another word he left. At 6 o'clock another man came in. He was a Norwegian, whom we could talk with, and he immediately took us to his boarding house, O. Noreen's Place, near the depot. There we were welcomed like members of the family. We were invited to the breakfast table and, while we were eating, somebody called Peter Wickstrom, the son to the farmer who had advanced my ticket, and he soon came over and took us to his home in the city.

Later, he rented a team of horses and a buggy and took us out to his father's farm, which was located six miles from the city of Worthington.

I'll never forget the first week on the farm. Everything was new to me and so confusing. The language, for one thing, was very peculiar. The family I was working for were Swedish, and they talked, what they thought was Swedish, but it was very difficult to understand for me. It is true that I understood the most words, but the ending of some words and the Americanization of others made it all very confusing. Especially at meals, this was very annoying. Somebody would ask me to pass something and while they thought that I understood their request, I sat there like a dumbbell trying to figure out what they wanted. However, it did not take me long to learn those everyday phrases, and soon I was using them myself. However, a lot of other words and phrases were harder to understand and learn. Many Swedish words have gradually been changed or americanized, until they are completely unrecognizable, and the same applies for many English words. Thus, the Swedish-American language is a confusing mixture of the two languages. In fact, it is a language by itself.

The general work on the farm was quite different from what I was used to, but this was learned and overcome within a short time. In fact, I have often wondered afterwards how easy it was for me to familiarize myself to the conditions in America. Perhaps the fact that I was accepted and treated as a member of the family helped me to overcome the difficulties that I met in the new and strange conditions in which I was placed.

The first day on the farm, the old farmer took me out himself and showed me the machinery, the cattle the horses and other animals on the farm, explaining everything the best he knew, and I kept my eyes and ears open and learned a lot.

The second day, I was told to go out in a grain field and pull mustard weed. I did not think that this work was worthwhile, but I learned later that if the threshed grain was mixed with weeds, they would have to take a great deduction both in grade and price.

After a few days in the grain fields, I was promoted to drive a team and cultivate corn, and this I liked better. I had never driven a team before, but I did not experience any difficulty when I once learned to harness the horses.

Then haying commenced. This was very interesting work, and quite different from the way it was done in Sweden.

One thing that I was required to do was milking. This I had never done, and I pretended that I could not learn it. So, I was allowed to feed and care for the horses and the hogs while the other boys done the milking.

Besides me, there were four men on the farm. The old farmer himself did not do any work in the fields, but he cared for the chickens and the turkeys. The three boys, William, Alfred and Joseph, were all older than me, and they were all good workers. Mrs. Wickstrom, who was considerable younger than her husband, was his second wife and a stepmother to the boys. She done all the cooking, while Brita Holm, or Bertha as she was called here, was the hired girl and took care of the house, done the family washing and sometimes helped with the milking and other chores. Besides the three boys mentioned, Mr. Wickstrom had one son, Peter, who was married and lived in the city of Worthington, and one daughter, Emma, married and resided in Davenport, Iowa.

The first Sunday I was there, the family were invited to a neighbor, John Nostrum's for dinner. They asked me to come along but I excused myself saying that I had to write some letters. While they insisted that I should go, I did not feel that I belonged in the family, and I persisted in staying home. A short while later a team drove into the yard, and there was Mr. Nystrom, urging me to come for dinner. "We are waiting for you", he said, "and we will be very disappointed if you don't come." I explained that I felt that the invitation did not include me, as I was only the hired man, and it was not customary where I come from to include the servants in the social gatherings. He then informed me that this was America, and that no such class distinction is tolerated here. So, I went with him and I found to my pleasure, that I was considered just as much as anybody else in the party, in fact at that time a little more, as everybody liked to hear about the journey, about conditions in the old country at the time I left there and how it felt to be in America. They were all friendly and I spent a very enjoyable afternoon in their home.

A few days later I was called into the house in the middle of the afternoon and informed that the Minister was there and wanted to see me. After the usual introduction, the Reverend Palmborg, as his name was, informed me that he knew my parents and that he several times had visited and stayed at our house in Järpen. I did not recognize, nor remember him in particular, but I had a vision of us children sleeping on the cold floor while a well-fed preacher occupied our bed.

After asking a few questions in regard to my father and conditions in Sweden, he told me that he would be glad to accept my application for membership in the Baptist congregation. He told me that all the young people in the community were members and that I would feel more at home in the community if I also belonged to the "Church of God". He told me about the good times had by the members, about parties and picnics and youth's meetings, but he never mentioned that I would have to confess faith in God and be baptized, which is the doctrine of that church.

This puzzled me, and I asked him if there weren't the same requirements here as in Sweden.

He answered that it was, but as I had been brought up in a religious family, he took it for granted that I believed in God and had accepted the faith of the Baptist's in the old country.

I was not bold enough at that time to inform the reverend that I was a freethinker, but I told him that I wanted time to think it over. One night about a week later, I got into an argument with Mr. Wickstrom in regard to religion, and I expressed my view, which he considered heresy. He must have told Mr. Palmborg, as that gentleman never mentioned that he wished me to become a member of the church again as long as I was there.

There was one thing that I resented very much, and that was when the Swedes were talking English in my presence. I always imagined that they were talking about me and that they said something about me that they did not want me to understand. I did not realize then that they found it more convenient to express themselves in the American language. This experience taught me to be more considerate and not persist in talking one language when there is somebody present who does not understand it, however, I made up my mind that I would try to learn the language of my new country as soon as possible.

In that summer of 1902, the emigration was at its height and young men and women arrived constantly from the Scandinavian countries. On several farms in the neighborhood the hired men were immigrants, or new arrivals from the old country. We were called "greenhorns" by the natives. We greenhorns quite naturally found more pleasure in each other's company than in company with the English speaking farmer boys and we met each other regularly every Sunday. If one had received news from home during the week, we all enjoyed it, and if one had been in trouble of some kind, we were all concerned about it. Gradually we drew away from the other boys of our age and formed a clan of our own.

The usual, and I might say, the only recreation or pastime we had was to attend church Thursday and Sunday evenings where we met the young people from neighborhood farms. This was before the automobile era, and folks either walked or rode after horses. In the road, outside the row of horse stables, the young people gathered, before or after the service, and here was the trysting place where the young men dated the girls, and sometimes vice versa. Many of the youngsters did not even go inside the church. They sat out by the stables smoking their pipes, or strolled about, waiting for the service to be over.

It happened sometimes that some girl smiled sweeter at one of us greenhorns, and that we took advantage of the smile, and took her home from church. Then her regular beau would get jealous and threaten bloody revenge. The word was passed around and next time the rest of us acted as bodyguard until the vengeful party cooled down. A couple times it happened that a good thrashing was necessary before the jealous part cooled down.

Very few of the older people attended church in the evenings. Their meeting was at 11 o'clock on Sunday forenoon. Often when we came home after church, old Mr. Wickstrom would ask us about the subject of the sermon. Nobody seemed to know because they had not listened to the preacher. After the first two or three meetings that I attended, I took it upon myself to inform the old gentleman about the contents of the sermon. I listened attentively, and as I had a good memory, I could almost bring the sermon home with me. Mr. Wickstrom appreciated this and I was always a favorite with him.

When the harvest was over, threshing commenced. About half a dozen farmers owned a threshing rig together, and the crew went from one place to the next, until everybody were done threshing. When away from home I generally slept in the haymow, and I enjoyed it. The feed was excellent during threshing time, and it was just like sitting down to a banquet every meal.

The threshing was generally done from shucks, and it took many men and many teams. One evening I come rather close in having a serious accident. We were done in the field and were driving home for supper. I was riding in an empty grain wagon and was sitting on the edge of the sideboard. The team shied at something and suddenly lurched to one side, throwing me backwards out of the wagon. Headfirst I struck the road but had presence of mind to roll myself towards the ditch. If I had not been able to do that, I would have been trampled by the following team. Now I just felt the hoofs graze me as I rolled myself out of their way. I did not utter a sound as I fell, but the boys missed me and came back expecting to find my mutilated body in the road. It was a wonder that I did not break my neck or my back in the fall, but all the harm it done was a great lump on my head and scratches on my arm from the horse's hoofs.

We did considerable plowing that fall. One field contained eighty acres and we plowed with two riding gang plows and eight horses in this field for nearly two weeks. It was monotonous work, and many times I almost went to sleep. The furrows were half a mile long and there was nothing to do but ride and watch the grasshoppers and the gophers. I became so lazy that I resented harnessing the teams in the morning and unharnessing them at night.

When we were through with the plowing, we commenced husking corn. Then I had to limber up again. Fifty bushels of corn a day was considered a man's works. I did not make it the first week, but after I got accustomed to the husking hook, I filled my wagon box twice a day, which was all that was required of a good husker. When through on the home farm, I was sent to a neighbor, Jacob Seline, to help with the cornhusking. By that time, it was getting cold and unpleasant in the cornfields, as it was the month of November. I was happy when the last rows were cleaned up and I could return to Wickstrom's place.

It was getting close to Christmas, and I was wondering if it would be anything like it was in Sweden. There was no snow on the ground that year, but it was quite cold and a biting wind was sweeping across the prairie. Well, I found out that Christmas here was like any ordinary Sunday. There was no Lutefisk, no rice porridge, and no Christmas tree like I had been used to in Sweden. I received a necktie and three cigars as Christmas presents, however. In the afternoon the turkeys had gone visiting and Joe and I were sent after them. It was below zero and outside the windbreak the wind went right through us. I froze my nose and both ears, and they peeled and were sore the rest of the winter.

We had stacked a considerable amount of wild prairie hay, and, during January and part of February 1903, this was baled and shipped. It was no pleasure to be out on the open prairie and work in zero temperature. There was always wind, and no matter how heavy we dressed, that wind found its way into our body. Never in my life have I experienced and felt the cold as I did that winter.

At times when we worked together in the garden, or sat together in the house, Mr. Wickstrom told me many of his early experiences from the time when he first settled on the prairie about the year 1875. The land had then recently been surveyed and the nearest railroad was 60 miles away. There were no roads of any kind across the prairie, only buffalo trails here and there. There were no trees of any kind for miles and miles, just open, flat, and bare prairie.

He was one of the first settlers in Indian Lake Township. With him was his brother and two others, all from the same parish in northern Sweden. They built dugouts on their land in which they lived the first years. After they had harvested their first crop of grain, they built straw barns for their cattle. Their worst experience was the blizzards in the winters when the snow was whipped across the open prairie. Many times, for days, they did not dare to leave their dugouts to feed their cattle for fear of getting lost between the dugout and the barn.

As soon as they had their first houses built, they sent for their sweethearts in Sweden. There were no big steamships crossing the ocean in those days. There was only sail vessels, and as they had to depend on the wind for progress, there was no prediction when they would arrive in port. So, he told how these four settlers took turns to watch at the nearest railroad station, and how they waited for months before the girls finally arrived.

The old pioneer was broadminded and very considerate, and after our first clash on religion, he never brought the matter up during the year

84

and a half that I worked for them. He was one of the most broadminded Christians that I have ever met during my life. He respected my opinions as I respected his, and we were always very good friends.

1902 - This is first portrait taken of John Ostlund in America. He was 18 years old and working for farmer, William Wickstrom, in Worthington, Minnesota to pay off the ticket he bought for John to come from Sweden.

John Ostlund collection

20
My First Fourth of July in America

I had only been in the United States a few weeks July 4th, 1902. On the farm where I worked, the youngest son, Joseph, was about my age. We roomed together and generally worked together and became pretty good chums. On the above mentioned day he suggested that we should take a bicycle trip to the city of Ocheydan, Iowa, about 12 miles south from the farm. This would give me an idea of how a July 4th celebration was.

It was a clear bright morning when we rode our bikes to Ocheydan, the road was dry and hard and level as it usually is on the prairie. We passed the state line between Minnesota and Iowa and rode through a seemingly prosperous farm area settled by Germans. By the time we approached the city, a lot of people were on the road on their way to the celebration. We passed many teams of horses pulling buggies or lumber wagons filled with men, women and children waving small American flags. Everybody seemed to be in a festive mood, and some were singing and shouting when we passed them.

Near the outskirts of the town, we stopped and hid our bikes beside the road and walked up the main street. A parade was just forming, and we arrived just in time to view it. It was all new and interesting to me. An elderly gentleman, dressed entirely in white and riding a beautiful white horse, let the parade. Behind him came several teams pulling shining surreys decorated in red, white and blue bunting, where the city honoratories rode pompously. Next came a great cannon pulled by eight horses and followed by civil war veterans marching four abreast. A brass band followed the veterans, playing martial music, and closely followed by members of fraternal organizations wearing their regalia's. Toward the rear came what interested us most, clowns, hooligans, bagpipe players, boys riding ponies, cowboys, and chimney sweeps. All very fascinating, particularly for me who never saw anything like this before.

Along the street, wherever there were any vacant lots, nicely decorated stands were erected. They were shooting galleries, sideshows, fortune tellers, coffee stands and hot dog dispensaries. The smell of hot dogs made us hungry, and we joined the crowd packed around the stands. Over and above everything else was the continuous bang, bang of exploding firecrackers which almost gave an impression of that we were in the midst of war.

Later we left the throng on the main street and walked out to a high hill outside town called Ocheyedan Mound. We climbed it about 150 feet and had a nice view of the city and the surrounding farm area, all level prairie as far as the eye could reach.

Back in town and after another visit to the hot-dog stand, we decided to start for home. It was hot and sultry, and Joseph predicted a rainstorm. We found our bikes and treaded towards Minnesota and home. We had not gone more than a couple miles before we noticed a black cloud on the horizon ahead of us. We raced along as fast as we could but before we reached home the rain came. The road became so slippery and sticky that we could not ride our bikes on it. Leading the bikes we reached home soaked to the skin.

21
Adventure with a Skunk

I had been in the United States only about a month and while I had heard about the stinking animals called "skunks" I had never seen or smelled one.

It was Saturday evening on the farm, and we had just enjoyed a good supper. We were sitting contended on the front porch when we heard the dogs barking furiously over by the barns. One of the boys went over to investigate and returned and told us that there was a skunk under the granary.

Armed with a shotgun we all went down to the granary. I was interested in seeing the animal I heard so much about and it did not take long before I knew what it smelled like. But the skunk was hidden under the building and refused to come out. Joe peeked under the granary and saw the animal sitting on top of one of the sills by the opposite wall. Next to the granary on that side was the machine shed. I offered to crawl in there and try to chase the animal out and donning a pair of heavy leather gloves and a short stick I tried to poke around where I thought the skunk sat, trying to dislodge it from the sill. I could feel it with the stick, but I was quite unable to get it to move. Discarding the stick, I reached under the sill and grabbed one leg. I shouted to the boys, telling them that I had him and to be ready to dispose of him when I tossed him out to them. So, I pulled him down under the sill and out in front of me. Wheee! I was sprayed from top to toe and even got some of the vile stuff in my mouth. However, I hung on to it and tossed the animal out of the shed in front of the boys. I heard a shot, but how I came out from under the machinery, I don't know. I was too dizzy to know where I went but one of the boys led me to the barn where I undressed every stitch I had on, even my shoes. Joe brought me a tub of warm water and I scrubbed myself until I was aching all over. I vomited until I thought everything in my stomach was coming loose. When I finally came up to the house the women held their noses, so I presume I still was stinking. I stumbled in bed but did not sleep a wink all night.

The next day was Sunday and I stayed in bed all day and I could not eat though Mrs. Wickstrom brought a tray of tempting food to my room. The family were worried and wanted to call a doctor. I told them to wait until Monday and if I did not feel better, I would appreciate if someone brought me to town to a doctor. I slept good that night and Monday morning I was able to get up, dress and come down to the breakfast table. However, I was so weak that I could not do much that day. I gradually improved but it took a whole week before I got my appetite back and two weeks before that smell left my body. My clothes were buried in the ground for a week but still they smelled skunk. And I gained a wholesome respect for those animals and when I have an opportunity to kill one of them, I feel no remorse.

22
Forbidden Fruit

In the community where I was raised in Sweden, apples were a luxury as they did not grow but had to be imported to northern Sweden. Consequently, when I arrived in America and saw the long rows of apple trees in the orchard owned by the farmer that I worked for, I looked forward to the day when I could eat as much as I wanted of this delicious fruit. Once when Mr. Wickstrom saw me in the orchard, he warned me from eating apples until they were ripe. "You may have all you want," he said, "but wait until they are red and ready to eat."

One day when we were harvesting wheat, I walked through the orchard on my way to the field. The apples were beginning to ripen, and I put some in my pocket and ate one on my way to the field where I was shucking grain. The apple tasted good and quenched my thirst and I soon ate another one. I had worked perhaps an hour and made a round of the field when I commenced to feel pains in my stomach. Suddenly I became very sick. Cramps tortured me and I thought my stomach would explode. I vomited and then felt better for a few minutes, but the cramps again doubled me up. When I almost fainted, I fell over a grain shuck and there Will found me when he came around on the grain binder. He told me to go home but I was unable to even stand up. Leaving his four-horse span tied up, William ran home and returned with a horse and buggy and his dad. They helped me into the buggy and the old man drove me to town, six miles to the doctor. There I received medicine that soon cleaned out my stomach and relieved the almost unbearable pains and cramps.

However, the ordeal left me so weak that when we returned home, I immediately had to go to bed. I remained in bed the rest of the day and was unable to partake of any food, though Mrs. Wickstrom came to my room with specially prepared soup for me. As it was a very warm day, they had worried thinking that I had an attack of malaria, as I had not told anyone of the apples I had eaten. When I told Mrs. Wickstrom she said it was a relief for her, as now she knew that I would soon get well again.

The next morning, I felt good and was able to eat a good breakfast. However, I was still quite weak. And the peculiar fact was that I had an aversion for apples that stayed with me for more than twenty-five years afterwards. I never tasted an apple in Wickstrom's orchard during the two years I was there, and when I saw other people eat raw apples, I turned away. It reminded me too much of the sufferings I went through when I ate those FORBIDDEN FRUITS.

23
In a Cyclone

If I live to be a hundred, I will never forget my frightening experience with a cyclone. It was July 20th, 1903, and I was working on a farm in Worthington, Minn. It was a sultry day, and we were busy hauling hay from an adjoining forty to the barn. We had unloaded our wagon just before dinner and put the team in the barn, and when we walked up to the house, my boss said; "I would not be surprised if we have a storm tonight."

After dinner I went out to hitch up the team and was watering them when Bill, my boss, called from the house, "Put the team in the barn, John and come to the house as soon as you can. And hurry!" I did and when I came out from the barn, the air was filled with straw and leaves, but there was not much wind. I hurried up towards the house but before I reached it the wind came and lifted me off my feet. I was near a huge elm tree, and I grabbed it and threw myself on the ground embracing the tree. There I layed thinking that this must be the end of the world. It roared and whistled around me when branches from the trees were broken off and carried away. Several trees near me were torn out with their roots, other trees were broken off and tossed long distances. If the tree that I held on to would have broke, I would most likely be crushed and killed. The cyclone did not last more than a few minutes, but it was long minutes for me and when it was over, I still layed there holding on to the tree.

Suddenly, I heard voices, and I sat up. The family was coming out from the storm cellar and were all coming down to the barnyard to view the damage. Everything that had been loose, had been picked up and carried away. Our hay wagon had been carried about four hundred feet and was laying upside down against a fence. The rack was broken to pieces and could not be repaired. A grain binder had been carried in between the trees in the orchard and part of it was hanging on a branch of an apple tree. The poultry house had been lifted off its foundation and even the large cattle barn had been twisted by the enormous power of the wind. But the damage on our farm was not bad compared to damages done on other farms in the neighborhood. Six miles to the northwest was the little village of Org. There almost every house was razed or had roofs lifted off and carried away. Near the railroad depot, four railroad cars had been standing on a siding. All four cars were picked up by the cyclone and turned over into the slough beside the track. On a farm nearby, the large barn was torn down entirely and about a dozen young stock in the barn were killed or wounded so bad that they had to be slaughtered.

For several weeks after the storm everybody talked about it. In the village of Org several persons had received injuries and were brought to the hospitals in Worthington, but as far as I know there were no deaths in our immediate vicinity. It was my first, and so far my only experience with a cyclone, and one experience like that in a lifetime is enough for anybody.

24
Adventure with a Mad Dog

I had been in the United States about five months and worked on the farm in Worthington. The harvest season was over, and we had filled the granaries with thousands of bushels of golden wheat. For two weeks we were busy hauling it into the elevators in the city. Usually, we hauled with two or three teams and wagons but when the boys were busy with something else I hauled alone. We usually were up at five o' clock in the morning and loaded up the wagons before breakfast. After we and the horses were fed, we set off and one load was an all day job as sometimes when we were held up at the elevator, we did not return home until after dark.

One day when I was alone, I had an experience that set my usually good temper up to the boiling point. About halfway to town I passed the farm of a German bachelor. He owned a large aggressive Airedale dog, who always was a pest to the people passing by the place. Never thinking of the dog, I sat carelessly holding the lines of the team when the dog jumped out of the ditch in front of them and scared them. They made a side jump for the ditch on the opposite roadside and before I had a chance to gather in the reins, the team crossed the ditch and almost upset the load of grain in the wagon. A barbwire fence stopped them where they tangled up their forelegs and cut themselves quite badly. I jumped for their heads and held them while I shouted for help. The owner of the dog came down and in my broken English I tried to tell him that it was his dog that scared my team. I asked him to help me unhitch the team, but he just stood there and laughed. Then he went back home.

Finally, I was able to unhitch and get the horses away from the fence. About a quarter of a mile from the place lived a Swedish farmer whom I knew, and I drove the team over there. He helped me bandage up the bleeding cuts in the horse's legs, lent me a chain and came back and helped me get the load back on the road. Finally, I was on my way again but several bushels of wheat were left for the birds on the roadside. I reached the elevator late in the afternoon and when I returned home, everybody was in bed.

I was hungry and tired, but I woke up the boss and told him all about it. I asked him if I could use his shotgun and I intended to go back and dispose of the dog that night. But he persuaded me to wait until the German had forgotten about the incident. Two weeks later on a dark evening, Will and I left the house after everyone was asleep. Armed with a shotgun each we mounted two of the fastest horses and rode north to where the bachelor lived. We met the dog at the gate and finished him with two well aimed shots. The owner woke up, jumped on a horse, and came after us. We rode as fast as our horses could go but he was gaining on us. Will was ahead and at the first crossroad he turned west, and I followed. We continued that direction for about five miles when we realized that we were not followed any longer. We rode off the road and waited for about twenty minutes, resting our horses, before we returned home. A few days later we saw an ad in the local paper offering $100.00 reward to anybody who could tell who the culprits were that killed his valuable dog. But nobody had seen us, and we never heard any more about it.

25
Haying on the Prairie

The farmer I worked for during the first year I was in America had leased eighty acres of virgin prairie land where a luxuriant crop of prairie grass was ready for the mower. We were four men on the farm and one morning in the middle of the month of June we commenced haying. Will and Alfred with four horses and two mowers began cutting, while Joe and I brought the rakes and hay gatherers and the stacker over to Section 13 from the home farm in Section 24.

When we had everything assembled, we prepared a stack bottom in the center of the already mowed hay. Then at 12 o'clock the old man, Mr. Wickstrom came out with our dinner. The teams were fed while we ate and rested a while. Will and Alfred resumed their mowing while Joe and I commenced raking what had been mowed down during the forenoon. The prairie grass was already dried out and its delicate smell filled the air. By 4 o'clock when Mrs. Wickstrom arrived with afternoon lunch for us, we had raked all the hay that had been cut in the forenoon and were ready for stacking it. The two teams were hitched to the hay gatherers, old Nell was hitched to the stacker rope, and I was placed in charge of her. Alfred was to do the stacking and Will and Joe were driving the hay gatherers. When one of them brought in a load on the stacker, and had backed off, I and the mare pulled it up and dumped it over the stack where Alfred spread it out forming a square stack of about the size 16 X 26 feet.

I have always liked to see fast work, and here it really surprised me to see that hay could be cut, cured, and taken care of so fast. In Sweden where I was brought up, the farmers cut their hay and hung it up on racks (hassjor) where it was left for several weeks to cure before it could be hauled in the haymow. Here the main part of the work was done with horses and machinery, the only man with a pitchfork was the man on the stack.

We finished a stack containing about 8 ton before supper, and Joe and I raked the rest of the newly mown hay before we returned home. It was getting pretty late but Alfred and Will had finished milking before we came, so after a late supper we went to bed pretty tired after a long day's work.

The weather held and we worked with the haying on Sec. 13 the whole week when it was estimated that we had put up about 100 ton. The last three days we took a big load of hay with us home every evening, which we unloaded in the dark after supper.

During the month of January, the following winter all that stacked hay was baled and shipped to Chicago. They had a horse drawn baler and old Nell was trained so she did not need a driver when the baling was done. We were only three men then as Alfred had married and left the farm. I pitched the hay from the stack into the baler, Will tied the bales and Joe weighed and piled up the hay bales. When all the hay was baled, we loaded the bales on wagons and drove it to the town of Worthington, a distance of about six miles, where it was loaded onto railroad cars and shipped. I received a dollar per day that winter for the days we worked but otherwise I worked just for my room and board.

26
School Days Again

During the winter of 1902-03 I remained on the farm where I had worked during the summer, and just worked for my board helping with the chores. During the month of January 1903 we baled about 100 ton of wild prairie hay and during the days we baled, I received a dollar a day.

We finished baling on the 10th of February, and a couple of days later the old man asked me if I wanted to attend the country school a few weeks until the beginning of spring work. It was on Feb. 15th. I reported my presence at the little Indian Lake Town school, about two miles from where I lived, and was registered as a pupil by the young teacher.

Besides the regular school class of about 15 children, we were four greenhorns, 18 to 20 years old, who had recently arrived from Sweden and quite unable to understand or talk American. Our teacher was unable to speak Swedish, which made it indisputable that here we had to speak American whether we could or not. We commenced by reading with the first grade pupils but we soon passed them and before the week ended we advanced to third grade. The second week we advanced another grade and were studying with the 4th graders.

Besides spelling and reading we took lessons in arithmetic and as that had been my favorite subject when I attended school in Sweden, I was rather surprised to learn that I had advanced farther in arithmetic in Sweden than our teacher had here. When she noticed this fact, she seemed to have more respect for us and she paid more attention to us.

One hour every week we had spelling down exercises. The teacher pronounced a word and the one she pointed to had to spell it. It was interesting and educational but when some of us greenhorns made mistakes in the spelling, it could become laughable. The youngsters commenced to fnitter (giggle) and when sometimes even the teacher could not hold back a smile, we all joined in the fun, except of course the one who had made the laughable mistake. But we learned from our mistakes and those weeks in the country school were worth a lot to me.

Out teacher was a young girl about 20 years old and she was very pretty. We boys were in the romantic age when the opposite sex is interesting and many times, we could not help that we admired her pretty face and her rounded bosom. When she caught us staring at her instead of our books, she often blushed, but we always tried to act as gentlemen towards our pretty teacher and never done anything to lose the respect we had for her. When sometimes the younger pupils misbehaved themselves, we helped the teacher restore order and discipline and she seemed to appreciate this.

I had hired out on the same farm for the summer and should begin work on April 1st. So on March 30th I said good-bye to the teacher and thanked her for the education she had given me. It was the first time I held her little hand, and perhaps I held it longer than I should, but she didn't seem to mind. We parted and I never saw her again.

27
Shotgun Fishing

On the first of April 1903 I hired out for another season on the farm of Wickstrom in Worthington, Minnesota. The old man had now retired, and his son William was the boss on the farm. I had worked for my board and keep during the winter and had opportunity to go to school a few weeks during February and March.

At the breakfast table that first morning Will said, "Now that we hired you back for the summer, John, let us celebrate by going fishing today." He brought out two pair of hip boots and two shotguns and told me to hitch up Fanny to the top buggy. When I asked him about rods and lines, he said we were going to use the guns. I thought this was just an April fool's joke, but while we were driving east towards the little town of Round Lake, he explained our fishing methods. It was a sunny and warm day and when we came to the lake, we drove off the road and in under some bushy oak trees where we tied the horse. Then we pulled on our hip boots, loaded our shotguns, and walked down to the shore. Will meanwhile advised me what to do. The large pickerels come up close to the shore where they bask in the sunshine. When I saw one sunning itself, he told me to aim just below the fish and I would get them every time. However, he told me to be careful that no person was in line with my shot as sometimes the lead pellets glance off the water and go long distances.

We parted and went in different directions. In a little while I heard Will shoot and saw him walk out in the water and pick up a large fish. A while later he shot again and bagged another pickerel. I was just wondering if all the fish were at his side of the lake when a big splash occurred just in front of me, almost scaring me. I saw a great pickerel go for deep water but before I had time to aim at it, it disappeared. It now dawned on me that I was walking against the sun and its reflection from the water made it hard to see the fish. I left the shore, walked through a field and came down to the shore again now walking with the sun on my back. Suddenly I noticed a dark object in the water ahead of me. Carefully I raised my gun and fired. The shot just stunned the fish and there it laid on the surface of the water. I picked it up and it was a beauty and weighed well over eleven pounds. In about an hour I bagged three more but none as big as the first one. Proudly I carried my catch over to where our buggy was and put the fish in a gunny sack under the seat. I was eating a sandwich from our lunch basket when Will also arrived. He had shot six pickerels but none of them were as big as my first one. I heard later that my fish was the largest ever caught in Round Lake, that anybody could remember. Together Will and I had almost sixty pounds of fish.

We drove into town to a butcher shop where we had the fish weighed and cleaned, and Will treated me on a good steak dinner at a restaurant. It was two happy fishermen that drove home that evening to the farm, and I was dreaming about large pickerels for several nights afterwards.

28
Basket Social

Working on a farm in the prairie country and far from the city can be a monotonous existence, particularly for young people. I had been in the United States a little over a year and during all that time I had not attended a dance or other gathering of young people. I was never free to go any place, as there was work every day, including Sundays. The youngest son on the farm, Joseph, was my chum and roommate and our only recreation was to take a ride on our bicycles over to some neighbor after supper once in a great while, or we sat in our room and played five-cards for pastime before we hit our bed.

One Saturday evening Joe had heard in town that it was going to be a basket social and dance in a schoolhouse about six miles from our farm. We decided to ride over there and take it in. After supper and evening chores were done, we dressed up and pedaled away happy and spry as a couple young calves just let out of the pasture. When we reached the schoolhouse, it was quite late. The usual program was over, and they were auctioning off the women's baskets. We stood by the door as there were no available seats. When a basket was lifted up by the auctioneer, I immediately bid a dollar. I did not think I would get it and I was rather surprised when nobody bid over me and it was sold and handed to me. I paid my dollar and Joe told me to look inside for the name of the woman who had brought it. It was a girl's name and while I did not know who she was, as neither Joe nor I knew anybody here, I soon found out. She was one of the prettiest girls in the room, and did I feel embarrassed holding that girl's basket.

When all the baskets were sold, I walked over and introduced myself. While I knew every day English to some extent, I was not a very good conversationalist in it, but I did my best and we understood each other fairly good. She did not understand Swedish, however. Before we were through eating and drinking coffee, which was served by some elderly ladies free to holders of baskets, I had fallen in love with my beautiful partner. Her name was Ellen and she called me John.

Then the musicians played up for dancing and we mingled with the other dancers on the floor. It was a waltz, my favorite dance, the girl was like a feather in my arms, and I was in dreamland. But it ended all too soon and when I led her back to her seat, I was bold enough to ask for the next dance too. She smiled and promised yes. When a polka sounded,

I was the first one on the floor and we took the lead on the floor. We circled the room once and close to the door I was grasped by two strong arms and jerked away from the girl. Two men pushed me through the door faster than I can describe it, and out in the yard I received several slaps to my face by one man, while the other held my arms so that I could not defend myself or dodge the other man's fists. I was knocked out and left lying on the ground and did not know any more until I woke up and saw Joe standing over me swatting my head with cold water. My nose was bleeding, and my lips were cracked open. To return to the dance was out of the question and we found our bikes and rode home. It was the last time I attended a dance in that schoolhouse, and I never saw Ellen any more. My ardent affections toward her cooled off after a while. But I still remember her soft voice and endearing smile.

29
My First Sweetheart

When a person is at the age of 20, life is before him and the opposite sex is attractive to him. In other words, it is easy to fall in love. When I first met Mary Nordstrom, I became charmed by her beauty and attractiveness instantly. She had just arrived to this country from Sweden and she had the prettiest blue eyes and a body like Venus. I felt that I would do anything for her if only to get a smile from her rosy lips.

This was in the spring of 1903, and I worked on a farm. Mary was employed as a maid on a nearby farm and we met occasionally. At first, I only adored her in my mind and in my dreams, as we very seldom had an opportunity to be alone. Evidently, Mary noticed my admiration for her and it seemed to please her, which she sometimes showed by gentle gestures and smiles when we happened to be near each other.

When the threshing commenced, I had an opportunity to see Mary every day. Several farmers owned a threshing rig together and each owner of a share furnished a man for the threshing crew. I was selected from our farm to follow the thresher. Mary was hired to help with the serving of meals by all the farmers, so she also followed the rig from farm to farm.

One evening when we had had our supper at the John Nystrom farm, I went out on the porch and was looking through some magazines while hoping Mary would come out when she was through with the dishes. She evidently saw me and came, telling me that she was going to take a walk and get some fresh air before she went to bed. I went out with her and we took a walk towards the apple orchard. We had a lot to talk about and we were alone. She walked close to me and I put my arm around her. It felt like an electric spark hit my body when I touched her. She did not withdraw, and we walked without talking for a while. Finally, we stopped under a large apple tree and stood embracing each other. I kissed her and she returned my kiss. Here she became my sweetheart, and we pledged our love for life. It was late before we returned to the house and all of the lights were out. Another kiss and she sneaked into the house while I went to the hay barn to sleep with the rest of the hired men. However, I did not sleep much that night. I was too happy to sleep.

I saw Mary many times after the threshing was over and sometimes, we managed to meet alone. Near the farm where she worked was the schoolhouse, and there we met sitting on the front steps. But I soon found out that somebody else was also courting Mary. He was a well-to-do farmer boy. Mary told me about it but assured me that I was the only one in her heart.

I was leaving the farm in the fall and Mary also left and stayed with a married sister in town. The last evening, I was there I took her for a buggy ride out in the country. On our way home we almost had an accident. A train scared our team, and we had a runaway ride. When I finally was able to control the horses, Mary had fainted. I tied the team and after a while she came to, but the pleasure of the ride was spoiled. When I brought her to her sister's place she complained of a bad headache, and we said goodbye and parted. She promised not to forget me, and I said that I would be back and claim her.

But promises are made to be forgotten and the following spring I learned that she was engaged to be married to the farmer boy that had been my rival.

30
A Near Accident

My summer contract as a farmhand in Worthington was finished and I was leaving for the Twin Cities to look for employment during the winter. I was in no hurry to leave Worthington as I intended to apply for my first citizen papers before going north. Another reason for lingering was that my girlfriend Mary Nordstrom was in town and was staying with her married sister there. I rented a room at a hotel and took my meals at a restaurant across the street. I was free and felt independent as I had about $150.00 in my pocket.

The second day I went to the courthouse and saw the clerk of court and without many formalities I received my papers. I then called on Mary and made a date with her that evening to take her out to the country church, about seven miles from town, where they had a social that evening.

I rented a young, lively team from a livery barn after supper, picked up my date and we had a pleasant ride through the countryside in a light buggy with top. It was the last days of October but the weather was warm and nice and clear, just perfect for a buggy ride. When we reached the church, it was too early for the social, and we drove right by and continued out to the little town of Round Lake, where we stopped for an ice cream sundae before we drove back to the church. I found an empty barn and put the team in.

It was quite late before the social was over and I hitched up my team for the ride back to town. The full moon lit up the landscape and Mary and I drove slowly and leisurely along the lonely road chatting as two young lovers naturally would, more occupied with each other than with the team. Least of all did we expect anything dangerous that peaceful evening. We were nearing Worthington when suddenly the midnight train came up behind us on the railroad running parallel with the road we were on. The engineer blew the approach whistle for the crossing just ahead a few hundred feet, and the team bolted and raced off in a runaway flight. In the excitement I lost one of the reins and was unable to hold the horses back. We were now even with the train and the crossing dangerously close. An accident seemed unavoidable. Shouting to Mary to hang on, I climbed over the front of the buggy and onto the tongue. Leaning down between the flying hoofs I reached the dragging rein and clambered back into the buggy. If I had slipped, or if the team had left the road, it would perhaps have been a serious accident for me and my companion and also for the horses. Back in the seat I was able to hold the team until the train had passed and the horses calmed down.

Looking at Mary, I saw that she had fainted. The excitement had been too sudden for her. I stopped by a farm gate, tied the horses and after a while the girl came to. The danger was over but we were both shaken up and we sat there for a long time talking it over before I untied the team and we continued to town. I took Mary home as she complained of a serious headache. I returned the team to the livery stable and went to my room. But for several hours I lay awake brooding on what could have happened in the runaway.

John Ostlund and friends in Minneapolis, Minnesota. John is standing on the right. He has his hand on the shoulder of his good friend, William Carlson. They were from the same town in Sweden, worked together for years and built farms next to each other in the town of Gheen, Minnesota.

John Ostlund collection

31
In the Twin Cities

I had fulfilled my contract as hired man on William Wickstrom's farm in Worthington. I had saved up about $150.00 during the summer and it was with a feeling of independence I packed up my few articles of personal possessions and rode with Will to the city from where I took the train to St. Paul. I had corresponded with a fellow worker from Sweden, by the name of Olaf Bredesen, who owned property in St. Paul, and had invited me to come and live with him in the city until I found work there.

A neighbor farm worker, Stefan Stefanson, also left Worthington at the same time and we traveled together. On our arrival, we were met at the depot by Bredesen who took us to his home. This consisted of a small tent on a lot purchased by Bredesen in a suburb to St. Paul on Curfew Avenue near St. Anthony Park. Here we were invited to share his accommodations. We all slept on a cot, and it was not as comfortable as we had expected those cold November nights. Bredesen had a small kerosene heater beside the cot which smoked a lot but heated less and during the night it usually went out, leaving the tent so cold that water standing in a pail beside the heater was frozen in the morning. On the kerosene stove we also prepared our meals, and it was not the sumptuous home-cooked meals we had been used to eating on the farm. Bredesen lived like a recluse and a hermit and was satisfied with the barest necessities and Stefan and I could not get used to it. We spent the first week sightseeing in St. Paul and Minneapolis and we generally ate a good meal at a restaurant every day. At night we slept with all our clothes on and never undressed.

One day we visited an employment bureau and hired out to load dump cars for an excavation contractor near Midway, only five blocks from where we lived. We worked ten hours a day for which we received $2.00 it was very hard work, picking and shoveling gravel and clay into those dump cars and when evening came, we were almost played out. Living in the tent and preparing our own meals became unbearable and we were able to rent a room from a new neighbor who had just moved into his new home on the same avenue. We also arranged to board there. His name was Robert Glyer and we found them to be very friendly people and Stefan and I were accepted almost as members of the family.

Our job did not last long and at Thanksgiving we were laid off. The contractor, Mr. R.J. Lizce, offered us to accompany him and his outfit to Kansas City, Missouri, where he promised us steady work all winter. He offered us free transportation and told us how pleasant it would be in the sunny south where they seldom see snow. It sounded so good that we promised to accept his offer. He accompanied us to the office where we received our tickets, we packed our trunks and brought them to the depot where we checked them on our tickets, and we decided to leave St. Paul for Kansas City early the next morning.

That afternoon, we went back to Glyer's to bid them goodbye, and there we met William Carlson and Hugo Wallin who had just arrived from Worthington. When they heard about our plans, they did not approve of them at all, and neither did Mr. Glyer. He had been in Kansas City and froze more there than in Minnesota. Then we changed our minds about going south. We went back to the depot and had considerable difficulty in reclaiming our trunks, and only after we had threatened to notify the police, did they give us the trunks back. We stayed in St. Paul and now we had to show the boys the sights of the city, which we did until we were all nearly broke.

32
As a Greenhorn Lumberjack

We were four young men together in St. Paul, who during the summer had worked as hired men on adjoining farms in southern Minnesota. Now we were in the city looking for winter work. This was in the fall of 1903. We were advised to go to Stillwater, and hire out to some large logging company, where we would get into better camps and receive better pay than if we hired out from Minneapolis. We found out later that we made a great mistake.

One day we boarded the streetcar that at that time was running between St. Paul and Stillwater. The logging firm of James McGrath, in Stillwater, had been recommended to us, and we were fortunate to hire out to the chief himself. We were to receive free board and $28.00 per month for common labor. If we'd done more skilled work, we would be paid accordingly.

We left Stillwater on the train that evening at 10:45 and arrived in Finlayson, about 100 miles north, at 3:30 a.m. There we were driven like cattle into a large shed near the depot where we parked on the floor for a few hours sleep. After a slim breakfast we donned our packs and followed a boss into the wilderness. We walked some 25 miles to an old logging camp located on Snake River in Pine County. It was the most primitive camp that I had ever seen. We entered a dirty and dark log cabin, which must have been at least thirty years old. There was no other floor in the sleeping compartment than the bare ground. On both sides were double bunks, in the center of the floor was a large box stove, a kerosene lamp was hanging from the roof, by the little window stood a grindstone and a bench and this completed the furniture. There was no ceiling and the stars were visible through the roof boards. A thin board partition divided the sleeping quarters from the combined kitchen and dining room. Here was a board floor but the boards had cracks wide enough to take care of all sweepings, breadcrumbs and dirt that accumulated in the room.

The principal fare was beef and baked beans. Potatoes were not served; the reason was that there was not any root cellar so perishable food could not be kept.

We had a three mile walk to reach the place where we worked. At five in the morning, we were awakened and breakfast was served. At 6 o'clock we left camp in order to reach the place where we worked at daybreak. At noon the bull cook brought our noonday lunch and built a fire around which we ate. We picked up a tin plate, a knife and a fork and helped ourselves to what was dished up. As soon as we had gulped down our food we returned to our work. At 5 o'clock we generally headed back to camp to get there in time for supper which was served at six.

The evenings were usually spent in grinding axes, darning socks and patching worn or torn clothes. Sometimes we found time to play a game of cards or listen to stories told by some old timer. At 9 o'clock sharp the lights were turned out and we crawled into our bunks to sleep and feed the lice. Yes, that camp was infested with vermin of all descriptions. Every Sunday morning, we washed and boiled our underwear and shirts, but some lazy jacks were using another system in exterminating the vermin. They just hung out their underwear to freeze.

The camp foreman was a husky French-Canadian, whose first name was Larry. The crew was a mixture of many nationalities. Nearly 50% were Indians from a nearby reservation. Others were French, Irish, Scotch, German, and a few of us were Scandinavians. The entire crew consisted of about 40 men.

I was a jack of all trades that winter. The first week I was clearing and cutting out roads, then I was swamping a few weeks, then I was bull cook and cookee about three weeks, and in the spring, I was a sawyer, and this I liked the best.

When the camp broke up in the spring, I had just 80 days wages coming. All four of us boys had been doing skilled work during the entire winter and we expected that we would be paid off at $35.00 per month. But we had no written contract and they paid us off at only $22.00 in spite of our protests. We were "greenhorns" and we were treated as such and had to take what they offered us.

The following two pages are a poem or song written by John Ostlund about the experience recorded in his diary entry "As a Greenhorn Lumberjack". It is from one of John's handwritten journals in Swedish.

Words by John Ostlund

Skogsresan. 1903-1904.

Wm Carlson.
Hugo Wallin.
Steph Stephenson.
John Östlund.

December den första vi till Stillwater kom
För att efter arbete höra oss om
Vi gingo och sökte så glader och kvick
Men allting var lönlöst vi ej arbete gick.

Sen styrde vi kosan till Berglunds saloon
Där träffade vi på en trevlig person
Det var en sadelmakare en svenske jag tror
Han viste oss James Mc Grahs hufvudkontor.

Där började gubben att språka om skog
Och genast vi honom på ordena tog
För tjugorex dollar vi hyrde oss ut
Från månadens början till månadens slut

Klockan 10 på kvällen till depon vi gick
Och nyss före tåget billjetter vi fick
En flaska af "brandy" vi hade pr man
Jag tänker det räcker tills vi kommer fram

På tåget vi sjöjs och skratta och sjöng
Och den natten blef det då ej mycket sömn
Klockan tjsaa på morgon vi i Finlayson var
En half mil från depon de lämna oss kvar

Vi blefvo förargade vi skreko och svor
Men det hjälpte inte i diket vi for
Vi kraflade oss opp och till depon vi kom
Men till vår förvåning stod den öde och tom.

17

Ej långt ifrån degrou vi sågo ett ljus
Vi tänkte hvad kan det väl vara för hus
Och tur vi då hade hotellet det var
Och där fingo busarna då stanna kvar.

Klockan half sex på morgonen väcktes vi opp
För att tillfredställa vår hungriga kropp
Det smakade fogel att få sig en bit,
Af färskt hvetebröd och ett stort stycke meat

Tjugosex mil vi hade den dagen att gå
För att Larrys campen vid Snake river nå
Ju längre vi kommo ju bättre det var
För bolaget att få behålla oss kvar

Nog var det besvärligt det kan ni förstå
Att hela den dagen få traska och gå
Vi voro så trötta vi kunde knappt stå
Vi trodde då alldrig att campen uppnå

Men sent uppå kvällen vi dock kommo fram
Om det ej vart för skams skull vi genast vändt om
En koja så liten framför oss vi såg
Vi måste oss kröka ty dörren var så låg

Men nu för att ej göra visan för lång
Så vill vi här sluta vår långrinna sång
Skogsrisan den vintern den glömmer vi ej
Och alldrig vill vi göra om den. O nej.   John Dörling

33
Beating the Train

I had been working in a logging camp on Snake River during the winter of 1903 - 04 and when the camp broke up in the spring, I found myself with about ten other lumberjacks on the depot in Finlayson waiting for a train to take us to the Twin Cities.

After waiting for a while, a long freight train from Duluth arrived and our leader, a tall Norwegian suggested that we should beat our ride and save the train fare. There was a long string of flatcars loaded with lumber and when the train stopped, we climbed aboard and hid ourselves among the lumber piles. However, someone must have seen us board the train as when we reached the next station, which was Hinkley, several railroad men came along the train and chased us all off. They watched us until the train started up, then they jumped aboard and left us stranded in the railroad yard.

Across the street from the depot in Hinckley stood a saloon and everybody in our gang, except myself and my partner William Carlson, rushed over to the saloon. As they had not tasted whiskey for several months, it did not take long before some of them were getting intoxicated. Another freight pulled in and William and I rushed over to the saloon and herded the gang back to the railroad yard. This train consisted mostly of locked boxcars and our leader suggested that we find the conductor and perhaps he would let us ride in the caboose. When we agreed he left and returned with the conductor, who agreed to let us ride to St. Paul by paying him $1.50 each. We all paid and were ushered over to the caboose where we huddled around the warm coal stove, thinking that now our transportation troubles were over.

Five minutes later, three railroad men entered the caboose and wondered what in heck we were doing in their caboose. Our leader explained that we had paid for our transportation to St. Paul and they seemed to get a big thrill out of his story. We had paid the conductor of another train and he had played a joke on us by letting us in here in their caboose. If we wanted to ride along, we had to fork over another $1.50 to them. As this was out of the question, we were chased off.

Enraged, we marched up to the depot and reported the incident to the depot agent. He promised to report to the proper authorities, but I could see that he took it as a joke on us foolish lumberjacks as he had a hard time to conceal a laugh when we cussed the conductor. We could not prove that we had paid the conductor, and nobody would believe our story.

An hour later a passenger train arrived and some of us purchased tickets and rode like gentlemen to St. Paul. We had enough of the game of beating the train and we had learned a lesson. I bet that conductor greatly enjoyed when he was able to swindle a group of fool lumberjacks of their hard-earned money.

Young John Ostlund in Northern Minnesota.
After he left Worthington, Minnesota, John went up to the Iron Range to work in the mines. He wanted to make enough money to bring his two sisters, a brother, and his father to America. At that time, the mines were the best place to earn good money.

34
In Search of Work

After spending the winter in a logging camp on Snake River in Pine County, I returned to St. Paul in the last part of March 1904. With my companion, William Carlson, we decided to go up on the Mesabi Iron Range and look for summer work in the mines. We took the train to Duluth and from there to Mountain Iron, where William's brother, Joel Carlson, was supposed to be working. We arrived in Duluth for the first time, and while the lawns were green in Minneapolis, here the streets were icy and the bay was frozen. Climbing up the hilly streets to get a view of the city, we were disappointed. We wondered what people could find attractive in the city of Duluth.

It was a late spring and when we arrived in Mountain Iron, we found that everything was shut down, even in the underground mines. We were broke almost. We made arrangements with the owner of the boarding house, Mr. John Takala, to let us have board and room until we could find a job. We slept in the attic and were eaten alive by bedbugs. When the lamp was blown out and we had retired, it actually rained bedbugs over us. Nobody had slept here for some time and the bugs were starved. However, we lived through this experience, too.

The cold weather continued, and the opening of the stripping work was postponed from day to day. Every morning we walked out to the Iroquis mine where we were promised work as soon as they opened up, but we always met the same answer, "Nothing doing yet!"

Two weeks we stayed in Mountain Iron waiting for the stripping work to open up. With only a few cents in our pockets we finally decided to hit the road and try our luck in some of the other towns along the Mesabi Range. Leaving our trunks with Mr. Takala, we walked one morning to Virginia. We visited several mines, but without any result. In the evening we walked to Eveleth. We were wondering where to sleep that night and mustered up enough courage to walk up to the proprietor of a Scandinavian hotel, whom we told that we were going to work the next morning and asked for board and lodging. He evidently thought we looked honest and gave us a room. The next morning we had breakfast and a dinner pail each and went in search for work. We hid the dinner pails under a railroad tressel outside the city, as we could not very well carry them with us all day. The Butler Bros. Stripping Company was going to commence work in a few days, and their foreman told us to come back in two days. Happy, we returned to the city, but we did not dare to go to our hotel until suppertime. We found our dinner pails and ate our dinner under the tressel and sat there all afternoon. In the evening we returned to the Scandia Hotel, had our supper, and went to bed.

The next morning, we decided to go back to Mountain Iron for our suitcases. We picked up our dinner pails and took them along until we found a good hiding place for them. In Mountain Iron we met the foreman for Winston-Dear Company and were told to come to work the next morning. We never returned to Eveleth.

35
Fired and Robbed

In the spring of 1904, when I first came to the Mesabi Range, it was hard to obtain any work. My companion, William Carlson, and I combed the villages of Mountain Iron, Virginia, and Eveleth in search for any kind of work, even underground mining work, but wherever we came we met the same answer, "Not yet, but perhaps in a week or two." We had spent our meager winter wages in the Twin Cities and were almost broke, both of us. We were fortunate to get room and board at a Finlander boarding house in Mountain Iron on credit while waiting for an opportunity to get a job.

Finally, we obtained work for the Winston Dear Stripping Company in the Iroquis mine outside of Mountain Iron. There we had to live and board in the company's camps near the mining pit. I was at first placed in a track gang, laying ties and rails. Later I joined the blasting crew, drilling and blasting the frozen clay bank in front of the steam shovel. We worked every day, even Sundays, and we were driven like slaves. Every morning a long line of men looking for work stood in front of the company office, and if the foreman or superintendent caught a worker leaning on his shovel during work hours, he was immediately replaced.

After six weeks we finally had a payday, and by that time I had almost forgotten what money looked like. I squared up my bill at the boarding house in town and had a few dollars left for clothes.

I had worked for about two months, had done my best and was well liked by the foreman, John Clareen, when one afternoon he came over to where I and my partner were drilling a hole, and told us that he had orders from the superintendent to lay us both off. He did not know the reason why, and he told us that he was well satisfied with our work. He told us to see the super. At the office we were told that the super had left for home, but we could see him the next morning. My partner, Bill Warwick, told me that it was no use. "When we are fired once, we are fired." he said. However, I had never been discharged before without cause, and I wanted to find out, so I waited for the super the next morning until he arrived at the office. When I politely asked if I could talk to him and inquired why I had been discharged, he gave me a hard stare and turned his back to me. "I can fire anybody I want," he said, "and I don't need to give reasons for it." I received my check amounting to about 30 dollars and left. In town I met Warwick, and we cashed our checks in Oakman's Saloon and decided to walk to Virginia and look for work.

Before we started out, I put a twenty-dollar gold coin under the sweatband of my hat, because we had been warned that people had been held up along the roads. The Mesabi Range was a regular wild west in those days. Hundreds of people were without work, and some had resorted to highway robbery in desperation. About two miles out from town, two rough looking men jumped out from the side of the road and leveled revolvers at us. One of them went through our pockets and took everything they could find our watches and our money. They did not look in my hat. Bill lost every cent he had, and I lost about seven dollars and my watch. The men disappeared into the woods and left us, and we continued our walk to Virginia. When there, I took off my hat and showed Warwick the gold piece and he almost fell over. I paid for our supper and room that night and the next morning I gave Bill five dollars and we parted.

36
Looking for Homestead

One of the more memorable episodes in my life was in the spring of 1904 when I and my partner, William Carlson, accompanied Ole Ronning, a land cruiser from Virginia, on a trip through part of northern Minnesota, searching for a homestead. The country north of the Mesabi Range was at that time unsettled but had recently been surveyed and was open for settlers under the homestead entry laws.

A railroad was built from Virginia to Ashawa, about 25 miles, and was staked out, graded and corduroyed further north another fifteen miles. We boarded a logging train on June 13th and rode as far as to the end of the line. Then we followed the grade, walking on corduroy for many miles across great swamps, and reached Camp 14, just north of where Gheen now is. In this camp we found two white men who were married to squaws, or Indian women. There we stayed overnight.

One of the squaw men, whose name was Billy King, had lived here in the wilderness many years and was quite talkative. He told us many interesting tales from his experiences with and among the Chippewa Indians. When we awoke the next morning, the men had shot a nice deer buck and we had fresh venison for breakfast. After breakfast we strapped our packsacks on our backs and set out on a tote road, which would bring us near Pelican Lake. In the middle of the forenoon, we reached the lake. Leaving the tote road, we now followed an Indian trail along the south shore of the lake, where Ole thought we would find an Indian willing to take us across. We did not find anybody, so we walked west following the south shore of the lake, through cedar swamps where we sometimes sank down to our knees in mud and water. When we finally reached higher land, we camped for the night under a great pine tree near the shore. We were fighting mosquitoes most of the night and did not get much sleep.

When we resumed our hike, we soon found a good trail which we followed and in the middle of the forenoon we reached the shore of Nett Lake. Across the bay from where we were we could see an Indian village and we rested a couple hours and hoped that some Indian would see us and come out with a canoe. When nobody showed up, we built a raft from driftwood and crossed the bay on it. It was now quite late in the evening, and we camped on the lakeshore below the village. We were tired that night, so in spite of mosquitoes and Indians, we slept fairly good.

In the morning I went fishing, and by the time Ole and William awoke, I had caught a mess of fish for breakfast. While we were preparing our meal, the natives came down to the shore and watched us. Ole, who could speak the Chippewa language, dickered with some of the men for the purchase of a canoe, as we intended to cross the lake that day. They brought the chief and after considerable dickering, we bought a good birchbark canoe for the small sum of $3.00. We loaded ourselves and our packs in the frail boat and shoved off, and I believe the entire Nett Lake Indian population were on the shore seeing us off.

We loaded our packs in the frail craft and after considerable difficulty in balancing ourselves and our packsacks in it, we took off. We did not dare to go very far from land, however, because William and I were having our first experience in a boat of this kind, and Ole was afraid that we might upset it any time.

In the late afternoon, we reached the outlet of Nett Lake and paddled down the river a couple miles to look at some claims that Ole described as "the best land in the United States". Before we reached the land we were looking for, we came to a rapids in the river and we had to beach our canoe and proceed on foot for another mile or so. The land here was sandy loam and looked fertile indeed. The wild grass was knee high wherever there was an open space. The trees were mostly slender poplars with a jack pine grove here and there. The river ran through it and if it had been closer to civilization, we could not have picked anything better for a home site. We built a shelter, made a fire, ate our supper, and settled for the night.

We woke up around midnight from thunder and lightning. The rain came, a regular cloudburst, which put out our fire and drenched us to the skin. If we had had the canoe, we could have used it as a roof, but it was too far away. There we stood shivering for several hours while the rain poured down in torrents. It was a long, long night, but the dawn came at last and then the storm was over. We were fortunate in having dry matches to rekindle our fire and dry our clothes.

Our worst calamity was that all of our food was spoiled. The rain had seeped through the pack sacks. The sugar, salt, rice, and bread were mixed into a mush unfit to eat. And here we were a hundred miles from civilization.

After the rain let up and drying out somewhat, we spent the day following Ole around, looking up quarter posts and government blazing's. In the evening we found a spruce grove and we built a substantial shelter with a bed of soft boughs and slept peacefully all night. For supper we had killed a rabbit and roasted it on the fire. It tasted just fine. Though the land there on the river was as good as we could ever expect to find anywhere, we thought that it was too far from civilization, and we would prefer to take land closer to the railroad.

The next morning, we were up before dawn and returned to where we had left the canoe. We paddled up the river and across Nett Lake, carried the canoe four miles over the portage between Nett and Pelican and paddled across the whole length of Pelican Lake and down Pelican River until at dusk we reached Joe Fisher's cabin. We had not eaten anything all day except chewing on salted, raw rice. We stayed overnight with Fisher, and I'll never forget that supper. We were actually starved, and Joe had baked bread that day and prepared a good venison supper for us.

In the morning of June 19th, we left the canoe after paddling into Mud Lake. We stopped at Camp 14 where we had a second breakfast with Billy King and his squaw. She also made a couple of sandwiches for each of us with thick slices of smoked venison. We were still looking for homestead and Ole took us westward along an old tote road. We came to an old log dam where we crossed the Willow River and passed through a thick stand of spruce timber and occasional Pine trees. This was marked vacant on Ole's map, and I decided to file on it. I figured that the ownership of this valuable timber would be well worth what it would cost me. According to the map it would be within four miles of the railroad when that was built through.

We now crossed the country by compass due east to where we saw a large group of stately Pines. That land had already been filed for, but Ole knew that nothing had been done on the land in the way of improvements and thought that it could easily be acquired by contest. William decided to take it and now we were ready to return to the city. Again, we walked by compass due east where we knew we would hit the railroad grade. We were both tired and starved when we at last emerged through the swamp and saw an old shed called Camp 13. We cooked the last of our rice and were soon lost in a dreamless sleep.

Four o'clock the next morning, June 20th, we were on our way to Ashawa. We arrived there at seven and a gravel train was just pulling out for Virginia. We jumped on and rode about a mile when a brakeman came along the flatcars and demanded $1.00 from each of us. When we refused, he stopped the train and chased us off. So, we walked the track until we came to a little store (later called Angora) where we could buy something to eat. It was our first meal that day. We were now about twenty miles from Virginia. After resting a while, we resumed our walk. We reached Virginia and continued to Mountain Iron, where William and I arrived at 8 o'clock in the evening. We figured we had walked forty-four miles that day in sixteen hours. That was the longest hike I had ever done in one day!

The next morning, we took the train to Duluth to file on our claims. At the land office, I was informed that the land I had selected had been filed on while we were in the woods. So I did not take a homestead. However, I did not regret the trip. It was quite an adventure for me.

37
As a Brakeman on a Dinkey Engine

Returning from Duluth after my homestead claim was denied, I was again dead broke. I finally landed a job in Virginia for Richardson-Lundin Stripping Company. This was at the Higgins mine, about a mile out from town. I was sent to work on the dump with a crew of Finns, and even the boss was a Finlander. Consequently, I did not hear anything but that language and it became quite monotonous when I did not understand a word of it. It was hard work besides, and many times I cussed myself for not going back to Worthington where I was treated like a human and were among people whom I could understand. Here I felt like an outcast without friends and money. However, in my circumstances I had no choice. I had to work or starve, and this seemed to be the only way for me to eke out a living.

After the first two weeks, however, things did not look so bad. I was getting used to the work and I learned to know my fellow workers. In the camp I met several men of my own nationality and I made friends with them. Often, we walked into town after supper and we always found some amusement.

On the third of September, the foreman asked me to work as brakeman on a Dinkey engine. I told him that I did not know the first thing about that kind of work, but he insisted that I try it. He introduced me to the engineer, or "Dinkey Skinner" as they were usually called, whose name was Charley Greenberg, and who was a Swede like myself. He taught me the various signals, told me to be careful in getting on and off the train and assured me that we would get along fine. I took a liking to this work, and Charley and I got along good. When I had been with him a few weeks, he often let me run the dinkey when we returned from the dumps, and I learned fast. The best of it was that I had somebody that I could talk to and who understood me. We always used the American language, but if there was anything which I didn't understand, he told me in Swedish.

One dark night I had an accident. In spotting the cars at the steam shovel, I stood too close to the car, and a large rock fell from the dipper and grazed my right leg. The shock knocked me down and out. I came to when they carried me to the camp, and I could feel the blood running down into my shoe. There was no bone broke, however, and next morning I was able to walk into town to the doctor's office. I was under his care for two weeks and during that time I worked as switch tender. As soon as I was able to, Charley insisted that I should come back as brakeman, but I was limping all that fall.

The 9th of October that year I become of age. When I told the boys about it, they insisted on a celebration. That meant that I had to set up the drinks for all my friends in the camp. There was no way out of it, I had to accompany the bunch to town. Including the extra bottle that I had to buy for the boys in the camp, the party cost me around four dollars. On account of my sore leg I was excused from drinking myself. Thus, for the first, last and only time in my life, my birthday was celebrated in a drinking party. If I had refused, I would have lost all my reputation according to established camp ethics or customs.

The work was closed down on November 29th, and I had about 150 dollars to my name when I had cashed the last check. I wrote a long letter home to my father and sent him a Christmas present of 100 crowns ($27.00), but I didn't tell him of my hardships during that summer. I imagine that when he received that letter, he thought that I was just scooping gold out of the mines in America.

1909 - Engine #39. John Ostlund 3rd from left.

John Ostlund collection

38
New Year's Night in the Woods

In company with my cousin Alfred Stevenson, I celebrated Christmas 1904 in the city of Virginia. My cousin had recently arrived from Worthington, and we decided to hire out as lumberjacks for the winter months. We were told about a camp being operated by the Cloquet Logging Company about four miles north of Mountain Iron and we decided to go there after the holidays were over.

However, we had money to spend and many friends in Virginia and we did not leave the city until in the afternoon of the last day of the year. We were to follow their railroad spur until we saw the camp, so we were assured that we could not miss it. It was snowing quite heavy, and we trudged along the track and when we came to where the camp was, no trail was visible. We passed it and when darkness set in, we realized that we were lost. It had stopped snowing by that time and turned bitterly cold. We were looking for some shelter where we could spend the night, but no house was visible. Finally, we came to a small board shack where dynamite had been stored during the building of the railroad spur. There were no door or windows in the shack but it was somewhat of a shelter from the wind and we decided to stay. To return and look for the camp in the dark night was of no use when we were unable to see it in daylight.

The first thing was to look for dry wood and build a fire. This proved to be quite a problem as the snow was two feet deep. However, we managed to find a couple armfuls of dry limbs and succeeded to scrape away the snow in the doorway and build a fire. We were hungry, but we had not brought any food with us as we expected to eat our supper in the camp. Towards midnight we both fell asleep and woke up a while later finding the fire all burned down and all our wood gone. Almost frozen stiff, we had to get out in the darkness of the night and hunt for more wood. Tramping and wading through the deep snow and breaking off dry twigs where we could find any, soon brought circulation and warmth back into our bodies and we managed to get our fire going again. Now we stayed awake and took turns hunting for wood and feeding our fire to keep warm. It was a long and dreary night, but at last the dawn of a new year greeted us and we were glad that we were alive.

We now shouldered our packs and walked back several miles until we spied smoke rising from a chimney and there was the camp we had been looking for. We arrived just in time for breakfast and we greatly appreciated the warm coffee and hot pancakes heaped on our plates that New Years morning. The foreman told us that it was 32 below zero that morning, and he was surprised we survived the night in the open shack. We rested that day and caught up on our sleep and the next day we commenced work and stayed until the camp broke up in the last days of March.

However, if we live to be a hundred we will not forget our New Years night in the wilderness.

39
First Time Building a Log Cabin

In the spring of 1905, I met my old friend William Carlson, and he induced me to accompany him up to his homestead and help him build a cabin. This turned out to be another tough trip, but by this time we were both accustomed to hardships and we did not mind it much.

It took us almost three days to locate the claim, that is to find the respective corner post, and could determine just where his land was. Then the weather turned against us. It rained continually, then it turned into sleet, and finally it snowed about twelve inches on top of the ice. We had constructed a lean-to shelter beside a large boulder and had a continually burning fire in front of it. When the rain or snow let up a little, we worked on the cabin. It was our first experience in log building. Our only tools were a saw and two axes, and to make a good job in fitting in the ice-coated logs in the walls was almost impossible. When we at last had the four walls up and the rafters strung, our food supply was all gone and we had to leave.

The Willow River was overflowing. We felled a long Spruce across the river and came across, but had to wade knee deep in water across the meadows. When we reached the railroad grade, the corduroy was floating in two feet of water and we had the time of our life to get through. The bridge across Flint Creek had been washed away by the flood. We followed the creek until we found an Irish homesteader, who took us across on a raft. For this he had the nerve to charge us one dollar. When we at last reached Oshawa, we were hungry, tired and disgusted with the whole world. In the first house we came to, we went in and asked for something to eat. A redheaded girl met us at the door, telling us that we were just in time for dinner. A little woman was standing at the stove and when she noticed that we were wet, she told us to come to the stove and take off our shoes. She gave us dry socks to put on and invited us to the table, where we partook of a good, home cooked dinner which tasted like a banquet to us. When we had eaten our fill, rested up, and were dry and comfortable again, we asked her how much we owed her. "Keep your money boys", she said, "and good luck to you. I am glad that I could help you." I have always thought a lot of that woman ever since. She was Mrs. Ardine of Cook, the goodhearted pioneer woman of that town.

PART 4 -
"Getting Acclimatized"

The three first years in America, I've always considered to be the toughest years of my life. Unacquainted with the language, habits and customs in a new country, I had to take what was offered me and be satisfied. I was kicked, cussed and trampled upon. I was only a poor, ignorant immigrant from an unknown country, a foreigner, who was looked down upon as not much better than a dog. Through my troubles and tribulations, my hardships and my sufferings, I learned a good lesson in life; To take care of myself and to depend on nobody else.

Now, however, I experienced a change in the general attitude towards me. I had a fairly good knowledge of the language, had been broken in as to the habits of living and customs of the new country, and my previous longing to return to Sweden had disappeared. I was getting acclimatized.

The day I submitted my application as brakeman to the Master Mechanic, Mr. Ed Thomas at Mountain Iron, I consider as a turning point in my life. I was not satisfied with common labor anymore. I felt that I was qualified for a better paid job.

John Ostlund

40
My Experience as a Locomotive Engineer

It was one of the proudest moments in my life when I passed the examination as a Locomotive Engineer and was handed my license. It was only a third class license, but it was stamped and signed by the State Boiler Inspector, Louis Boe, and I valued it more than if he had given me a hundred dollar bill.

I had been firing a dinkey locomotive in the Iroquois Mine in Mountain Iron during the summer and had been allowed to run the machine occasionally when we returned with empty trains from the dumps, but I had never ever given a thought to the idea of being promoted. One evening I was called into the office and the Superintendent, H. C. Hanson, asked me if I thought I was capable to take over a dinkey engine used in assisting the trains up the grade to the dumps. I told him that I was willing to try. He said, "The State Inspector will be at the hotel in town tomorrow. Take the forenoon off and go down for examination. If you pass, you can report on No. 3 tomorrow night."

The next day I was at the hotel at the appointed time and was called in the office. Mr. Boe told me that I had been recommended for examination and he asked me a few simple questions on the care and maintenance of steam boilers. It took only a few minutes and he handed me the license already stamped and signed. I was the happiest boy on earth.

On October 16th 1905, I commenced running dinkey locomotive No. 3, a twelve ton engine. A few weeks later, however, the night shift was laid off and I became hostler, watching three dinkey's at night. This lasted until the middle of February 1906, when the stripping work was shut down and I was laid off until spring.

The Winston Dear Company, which I had been working for, had taken a large contract stripping the Burt mine in Hibbing, and I was sent there in the spring of 1906. On May 15th, I took out dinkey No. 6 which I operated all summer and everything went fine. A few days before Christmas the work shut down for repairs and I was offered the job to remain and work with the Master Mechanic on repairs of the locomotives. However, I had saved my money during the long summer and wanted a vacation, so I refused the offer to stay. I went to

Minneapolis for the winter and spent my savings. I was called back, however, a few days after New Year 1907, so had hardly more than two weeks' vacation. The temperature had dropped to below zero, but we were warm and comfortable in our cabs. In June that year a general strike broke out in the mines and we had a two weeks' vacation. Then we worked steady until December 22nd. I had saved about $800.00 and decided to take a trip back to Sweden.

I remained in Sweden for a year and did not return until spring of 1909. On May 15th, the stripping work commenced in the Burt mine, and I was assigned a new 20 ton dinkey No. 39. We worked steady all summer until November 15th. Then I worked in the roundhouse with repairs until after Christmas.

On March 18th, 1910, the work was resumed in the Burt mine. We were told that the company had just received a large contract to strip another mine site, the Buffalo Susquehanna, east of Hibbing and as this was a five-year job, they had decided to purchase standard locomotives and larger dump cars. This was great news to us engineers and we were wondering if we were to be entrusted to operate the big locomotives.

1909. John Ostlund (in the window), Engineer on Engine 39 of the Winston Dear Company at the Burt Mine in Hibbing, Minnesota.
John Ostlund collection

I was happy in being one of three dinkey engineers who were sent to the new location to do the preliminary excavation and grading of the new tracks. I took the second train out from that great mine. The new locomotives arrived and were steamed up. On September 7th, I was transferred to one of the new engines as fireman, and told to practice with the new E.T. brake valve which was operated by air. On the dinkeys we had steam operated brakes.

Three weeks later, on September 22nd 1910, I was placed in charge of No. 103, a new Pittsburg engine. Everything went fine that fall and we worked until January 18th 1911, when the work was shut down for repairs. A few weeks later, the company took a contract to excavate a new viaduct to the new Mesabi Depot. I was called back and put in charge of a Baldwin locomotive, No. 104. The work on the viaduct was completed in the middle of April and on April 17th, we resumed work in the Buffalo Susquehanna. I now received my old No. 103 back and everything went fine that summer. That is until the 13th of November when I suddenly was discharged. I had a new fireman who tricked me one day. The steam shovel took water from us, and when we were loaded and left the mining pit, I asked the fireman to see how our water supply was. He returned and told me that our tender tank was about half full. I then passed the water tower, as I thought we had plenty of water until we came back empty. Before we reached the dumps, the injectors refused to work. I ran back to look in the tank and found it empty. I did not usually swear, but that time I called that fireman all the bad words I remembered. I had to leave the train on the mainline and back the empty locomotive down to the water tower. No harm was done to the engine, but we were delayed in getting back to the shovel and I knew that hell was brewing. Of course, I was blamed as I was operating the engine and was responsible for my fireman. So, I was discharged and lost my seasons bonus amounting to about $150.00.

After spending the winter on my land in Gheen, where I built a little cabin, I went to Virginia in the spring to look for work. I met the Master Mechanic for Roberts-Kingston stripping company and took a job running dinkey in the Union mine just out of the city. On the 6th of May, I reported for work and was given an old 20 ton dinkey engine that had not seen repairs for many years, evidently. It was knocking and pounding and rattling, the fuses were leaking, and the cylinder valves had slipped out of place until it had lost all the power it ever had. The darn engine barely pulled itself on a level track and disgusted, I run it back to the roundhouse and told the mechanic that I wanted to quit. However, he induced me to stay on and helped me fix the trap up somewhat. Every spare moment I had, I worked on the old wreck, tightened up set screws and bearings, repacking cylinder rods and shimming up excentrics. After the first week, the old No. 28 and I got along fairly well.

1911. On the locomotive Engine #103 working in the Buffalo Susquehanna, east of Hibbing. Engineer, John Ostlund in the window.
John Ostlund collection

That summer, 1912, the Roberts-Kinston Company borrowed two standard locomotives from the Mesabi Railroad Company and I received one of them. It was one of the last days in July when I ran my old dinkey in on the sidetrack and exchanged it for No. 52, a Baldwin locomotive in fairly good shape, though it was not as new as the engine I had been running in Hibbing. We were now taking out iron ore from the Union mine and had a three mile run out to the railroad yard where the trains were made up for the ore docks in Duluth. It was easy work. I had good luck and a good standing with my superiors in the company. The general superintendent, Mr. Kingston, seemed to take a special liking to me and almost every day he came up on the engine and rode with us out to the yard, and every time he treated me with a good cigar. When the work shut down that fall, he offered me a job as pumpman for the winter, saying that he wanted me on hand when they opened up again in the spring. I declined, however, as I wanted to go up on my land where my father was staying alone. When I received my last check, I was surprised to receive full bonus of $20.00 per month from the day I started on the dinkey in the spring. It was the 3rd of December when I ran the 52 into the roundhouse.

I spent Christmas on my land and at New Year 1913, I went to Chisholm to visit relatives. There, one day, I met Fred Holliday, who now was superintendent for Winston Dear Company and was running a stripping operation at the Dunwoody mine, just outside of the city. When he learned that I was not working, he immediately offered me a job as an engineer. I could begin that same evening as he needed an engineer badly. His offer was too tempting to refuse, so I promised to be there at 7 o'clock that evening. I did not have time to go out there in daylight and see what it looked like, and when I reported at the office that evening, I was told that my engine was in the pit with a loaded train. The number of my engine was 104 and I found it without difficulty. But, to take the first train out over unknown tracks and grades in total darkness, on a cold winter night, was a ticklish undertaking. However, I was fortunate in having a dependable fireman, Ephraim Anderson, whom I knew from Hibbing, and he served as co-pilot on that first trip and everything went well.

Everything went fine that summer of 1913 and I was well liked by Mr. Holliday and the Master Mechanic, Charley Braden. If there were any difficult engine work to be done, moving steam shovels, etc., I was selected to do it. They depended on my alertness and skill and I appreciated their confidence and done my best. Just before Christmas the work was shut down for repairs on machinery. During that summer I had become married.

On March 20th, I steamed up No. 104 again and we commenced work. Now I could choose my own fireman and I selected my brother-in-law, Charley Hedberg. On a locomotive, the engineer and the fireman are close partners in the work and have to depend on each other in the work they have to do. So, having a dependable fireman is worth a lot. We were getting down quite deep in the mine. The grades we had to climb were getting steeper and many accidents happened. Olga and I decided to move to our homestead in Gheen when the stripping shut down. We crated our furniture and shipped it and on December 20th, 1914 we arrived at our future home here in Gheen.

41
I Worked in a Boiler Shop

In the spring of 1906, I visited my uncle P. E. Selander and his family in Warren, Pennsylvania and as it was quite early in the spring, I decided to look for a few weeks work while I was there. My uncle was working at the Hammonds Boiler Works, and on his recommendation, I was employed there. It was only a few blocks from our home so we could walk the distance to work in a few minutes.

I was given a metal disc with a number on it, and this disc was to be turned in every morning before 7 o'clock. If I was five minutes late, I was docked half an hours wages, if 10 minutes late, I lost an hour. The wages were $1.50 for ten hours work, or 15 cents per hour. We worked only half a day on Saturday but were paid for a full day and we received our paycheck for the week every Saturday. The infernal din and noise was hardest to get used to. I carried cotton plugs in my ears, everybody did, but still I was almost deaf every night when I came home. My work consisted of drilling holes in large sheets of steel plating. A pattern was marked on the plate with chalk and the holes had to be drilled exactly, or they would not fit in the boiler where they were to be placed. A mistake of ⅛ inch would make it difficult for the riveters, and when sometimes it happened, it was hell to pay.

After working for two weeks, I was laid off with a group of other men one night. The next morning I went to another boiler shop, the Struthers Wells Boiler Works, where I was employed at once. Here I joined a riveting gang in contract work. We were three men together and as the other two were experienced riveters. I worked under a handicap the first days getting a lot of abuse for my clumsiness and inexperience. However, I stood it and soon we became friends. We made boilers, bridge spans and large cooling tanks. Often we worked outside the shop and it was cool and not so noisy, but when we had to work inside a boiler or tank and drive hot rivets, it was "hotter than hell" as one of my companions used to say.

As we had contract work we were paid by the number of rivets we drove. On large rivets we received ½ cent a piece, or 50 cents per 100 rivets. But we had to heat the rivets ourselves and it was quite a trick to get them the right temperature when we needed them. To begin with, I was the one to heat the rivets and there was where I was mostly cussed. But I learned after a while. On cold rivets we were paid 20 cents per hundred, and it was no trick to drive 3,000 cold rivets in a 10 hour day. Often, if we had long seams, we had made our $2.00 each by 4 o'clock and then we took it easy the last two hours of the day. If we made more than $2.00 a day, we were docked at the office. That was considered maximum wage at that time.

Living was cheap also, at that time. Board and room could be had for a range of $12.00 to $15.00 per month. Rooms alone ran from $2.50 to $3.00 per month. As all of the factories and shops in the city of Warren closed at noon every Saturday, the streets in the city overflowed every Saturday afternoon with young people of both sexes and it was like a carnival. There were several textile factories where a lot of women and girls were employed, and when they all received their freedom on Saturday, they were celebrating. I never missed the excitement on the streets and in the park that afternoon.

But, I received a letter from the Master Mechanic in Mountain Iron, calling me back to work in Minnesota, and I left Warren just when I was enjoying everything, even a girlfriend.

42
An Enjoyable Christmas

During the summer of 1906 I had been working as dinkey engineer in the Burt mine stripping in Hibbing. The work was shut down just a few days before Christmas and with a friend, Fred Winberg, I decided to take a trip to Minneapolis over the holidays.

We stopped over in Cambridge for a couple days to visit friends and it was Christmas Eve when we arrived in Minneapolis at my friend William Glyer's home. I was just like a son to these friendly people and we were both invited to spend Christmas with them. However, my companion had relatives and friends in St. Paul and after breakfast with the Glyers, we took the streetcar to that city. We first located Charles Sandberg on Edgerton Street. He was the cook at the camp where we worked in Hibbing. Charles had recently been married to a Swedish girl and they were going to celebrate Christmas in Swedish style with "dopp i grytan" (dunking in the kettle). This was a real treat and we stayed and partook of it. It reminded us of the old Swedish custom and, in company with these friends, the afternoon passed before we knew it. They insisted that we stay for lutefisk supper and would not accept any excuses. We had promised Glyers to be back for supper at their home, but we had to eat here, and it was after eight before we finally reached Glyer's home. Now we had to sit down to a loaded Christmas Eve table again, and never in my life have I been so stuffed with good food as I was that evening.

During the following days we were royally entertained by our many mutual friends in the Twin Cities. Every evening we were invited to different places. One evening, Fred's aunt gave a party and we met a celebrated Swedish opera star, Madame De Veer, married to a Belgian Duke, who had been singing at several royal courts in Europe. She entertained us with several songs that evening, among them some Swedish selections.

One day we met an acquaintance of mine from Worthington, Minnesota, Jacob Selin, who had been a farmer, but now had sold his farm and was running a boarding house in Minneapolis. He invited us to make his hotel our home while in the city and we accepted because as we always came home late to our hosts, the Glyers, and often had to wake them when we came, we felt that it would be better to live at a hotel where we could come in any time of the night. We soon became friendly with two of Selins waitresses, who were members of a Good Templar lodge, and we accompanied them to the lodge meetings. Fred was engaged to a girl in St. Paul and had a date with her one evening. One of the Good Templar lodges had arranged a Christmas party that night and we were invited there. So Fred called his fiance and told her that we were called back to Hibbing and he could not meet her. On our way to the Good Templar festival, we rode a streetcar and suddenly at a street corner, Fred's girl stepped in and saw us. If eyes could have murdered, Fred would have been a dead man. It spoiled the evening for him and it was the end of his engagement.

New Year's Eve we received a message from Hibbing calling us back to work. It was with great reluctance we left Minneapolis that time just after we were getting on good terms with the pretty maidens at the hotel. But, considering everything we had a very pleasant Christmas vacation.

1909 Photo Op. Hans Paulson, Gotfred Stevenson and John Ostlund.
John Ostlund collection

43
I Became an American Citizen

I had now been in the United States for five years and was entitled to become a naturalized citizen. However, my first 18 months had been spent in Worthington, and I would have to get two witnesses who had known me during the entire five years. Corresponding with friends in Worthington, I learned that a former farmer from there, Nels Moberg, was now living in Duluth. I wrote to him, explaining the situation, and asked him to be my witness. He advised me by return mail to be in Duluth on a certain day and he would go with me to the Courthouse. As his sister, Mrs. Ole Nostrum, also from Worthington, happened to be visiting in Duluth, she would be my second witness.

I took the day off, went to Duluth, and submitted my application for citizenship. Three months later I was to come back for the final hearing in court.

It was on September 23rd, 1907 that I was called into court. Mrs. Nystrom had returned to Worthington and I anticipated that this would cause me trouble. However, Mrs. Moberg was permitted by the Judge to take Mrs. Nystrom's place as witness, and that worry was over. I expected a lot of questions and a severe test, but it was really very easy. I was only asked a few simple questions by the Emigration official, the Judge nodded and that was all. I took the oath, denouncing all allegiance to any foreign ruler, and especially to King Oscar II of Sweden. From that day I am an American.

44
In a Chinese Opium Den

I was on my way to Sweden in the early spring of 1908 and stopped over for a few days in Chicago. I did not know anybody in the city and took a room at a hotel on Clark Street. From my hotel I strolled around in different directions, seeing the sights of the large city. One afternoon I found myself in Chicago's Chinatown, near the river. On both sides of the street were stores and chop suey houses and most of the people I met on the sidewalk were Mongolians. I was alone and felt out of place there.

Suddenly, a white man passed me whom I thought I knew as he resembled one of my friends from Minnesota. He crossed the street and entered a large building. Curious to see and talk to him, I followed him and went inside. I entered a large room which was empty, but across the room another door led into another room. A heavy set chinaman bowed and asked me what I wanted. I told him that I was looking for a friend that just had entered the place. The man I had followed evidently knew the place and had walked into the next room. I passed the chinaman and walked across the floor and pushed open the door to the next room. A peculiar smell met me and in the room I saw several persons reclining, smoking from bowls standing on small tables. Now it dawned on me that this was an opium den and I quickly backed out and turned to leave the place.

Now I met two jabbering Chinese who grabbed me, one on each side. They wanted to know what business I had there. I told them the same as I had told the doorman, and added that I was going to wait for my friend outside. They pushed and dragged me towards the corner of the room where a door led to the basement. When one of them opened the door and I saw the stairway I jerked myself loose, stuck my hand in my overcoat pocket and pulled out my revolver, which fortunately I had put in my pocket when I left the hotel. When I pulled the gun, the men stepped back and I backed over to the door to the street. Trying to open it while still facing them, I found it locked. However, I felt along the edge of the door, found a bolt which locked it and soon got the door open. When I reached the street I ran as fast as I could, thinking that the chinamen were after me, and ran right into a policeman. He stopped me and inquired where "the fire was". I told him that I had been in a trap and escaped and he asked me if I had been robbed. When I assured him that my watch and pocketbook were still in my possession, he told me to stay away from Chinatown in the future.

If they had succeeded in robbing me, which evidently had been their intention, they would have found $800.00 in gold and currency which I carried in my inside waist pocket. Then perhaps they also would have disposed of me in the river and nobody would ever have heard of me again. It was one of the closest calls I have had in my life. I had a good scare and learned a valuable lesson that evening in Chicago's Chinatown.

PART 5 -
"A Trip to Sweden"

I was in New York and all prepared for a visit to my homeland, Sweden after almost six years in the United States. It was an odd day of the year, the 29th day of February, 1908. The Cunard Liner, S.S. Campania was steaming up ready to leave for the old world, and I had secured passage on her.

With my traveling companion, Fred Reitan, from Springfield, Illinois, I had spent nearly two days in the great metropolis sightseeing. Now our trunks were checked and transported aboard, and after buying a few things needed, we went aboard.

The liner left the pier at 11 o'clock sharp. She turned slowly and headed down the Hudson River. We passed the great Statue of Liberty, which seemed to salute us "farewell - and - come again"! At 12:30, we were out of sight of land.

I remained in Sweden a year and did not return until the spring of 1909, and in my company now were my sister Mae and brother Peter.

John Ostlund visiting in Sweden 1908.

45
Almost Shipwrecked

In the early spring of 1908 I decided to return for a visit to my homeland, Sweden. On February 29th, I embarked on the Cunard Liner "Campania" in New York. This boat was not as large as some of the other Cunard boats, but it was one of the speediest and it had just been equipped with the new Marconi invention, "the wireless telegraph".

We were barely halfway across the ocean when we had run into a storm. We received our first warning when a monstrous tidal wave broke over the ship in the forenoon of March 5th. A little later the hurricane hit the vessel. The ship rolled so it was almost impossible to walk. Everything loose was hurled from one side to the other in our cabins. I did not get seasick, as many of the other passengers did, but it was no longer a pleasure ride.

The storm continued all night and prevented any sleep, and in the morning of March 6th the engines ceased working. We were informed that both propellers were broken and later we were told that the rudder was gone. We were drifting helplessly with the monstrous waves washing over the deck. Lifebelts were distributed and we were ordered to put them on and wear them. Towards the northeast we could see the white breakers from the rugged Irish coast and that's where we were drifting. The lifeboats were readied and swung out from their davits, but if lowered in this storm, they would not have remained afloat for very long.

The passengers had been confined to their cabins under the deck, but that afternoon the canvases which had been covering the stairways were opened and some of us were let out on deck. Ropes were stretched along the deck which we held on to, but we soon were soaked to the skin. Below deck, hysterical passengers were cussing and crying. Some were praying and wringing their hands, while the stewards tried to console them and tell them they needed to be ready to leave the boat when the alarm sounded. In a few hours they expected that we would be among the rocks.

However, the wireless saved us and the ship. S.O.S. calls had been sent out intermittently, but no answer had been picked up by the wireless operator. Suddenly, we saw smoke pillars on the horizon and there were four tugboats coming towards us. When near enough, lines were shot across and the sailors grabbed them. All of us on deck helped to pull in the great hawsers attached to the ropes and fasten them. Soon the great Liner swung around when the howsers tightened and the powerful tugboats pulled us out into open water and away from the dangerous breakers. We were saved just in the nick of time.

The storm subsided somewhat and we slept soundly all night. The next morning we were approaching Liverpool, where we debarked that afternoon. Passengers for Ireland boarded another steamer which took them back across the Irish Sea to their home. Campania went into dry lock for the rest of the summer. I am sure that none of it's passengers will ever forget that crossing.

46
At the May Fires

There is an old custom in northern Sweden to burn large fires in the evening of the last day of April. These fires are called "May Fires" and signify the entrance of summer. They are generally built on high hills and are lit after sunset when they can be seen for long distances. In or near the village where I grew up, there was an old fortress built during the war with Norway about 1809. On the high hill where this fort was built we boys used to build our May fire. We dragged in brush and dry discarded logs or lumber until we had a great pile. Then we generally received an old wood barrel which had contained tar or some other inflammable substance which we placed on top of our brush pile. Everything was then ready for the event.

In the evening of April 30th, young and old gathered on the hill and at dusk the fire was lighted. This was the year 1908 and I had just returned home after spending six years in America. That evening I met many of my former schoolmates and friends around the fire and everybody welcomed me back home and wanted to know how things were in the U.S.

Suddenly, a young and very pretty girl came up extending her hand and asked if I remembered her. I did not and told her so. She told me her name was Selma Hedberg. Then it dawned on me who she was as we had grown up neighbors. But she was only 11 years old when I emigrated at the age of 18, and now she had grown up and developed into a very desirable woman of 17.

I could not help being very pleased by meeting Selma again and she seemed happy, too. We took a walk by ourselves away from the gathering, she took my arm and we seemed to have so much to talk about and I felt like I was in heaven, walking with this pretty girl that warm spring evening. After a while we went to a dance pavilion where a dance was going on and we danced with each other the whole evening. She refused other invitations to dance and I did not see anybody else that I would rather dance with than Selma. I evidently was in love with her already. When the dance ended at 2 a.m. I took her home, received a warm goodnight kiss and promised to meet her again soon.

So far, so good! However, the next day I had a visit from a young man, whom I had also known when he was a young lad. He was Alfred Andersson, and had also been a neighbor of ours before I emigrated to

America. He asked me if I intended to take his girl away from him. Told me that he and Selma were engaged and that they had planned to get married that summer. He told me that he had been at the dance pavilion the previous evening and seen that Selma and I danced every dance together. He did not want to stir up any trouble there, so went home and decided to have a talk with me before he broke up his engagement. Well, I did not have the slightest idea that Selma was engaged and she had not even made a hint of it during the evening we were together. Now I assured him that I had not come home to cause any trouble for anybody, and that I was not going to date Selma again. I congratulated him for winning such a pretty girl and wished them all happiness in the world. We parted as good friends, but I am pretty sure that I could have broken that engagement if I had dated Selma again.

47
Invitation Dance

It was a custom in Sweden in the beginning of the century to arrange invitation dances for a select number of friends. These dances were generally arranged by ladies, often married couples too, and it was an honor as well as a great pleasure to be invited and partake in these socials.

I had recently returned home from America when I was invited to a similar party at the Rödningsberg, about a mile from my home. The farm is one of the oldest farmsteads in the province and it has an ideal location situated on a high plateau with a view over the whole surrounding area and the little village of Järpen.

When I arrived at the farm I was met by the owner, Olov Nilsson, who took me out in front of the house and we sat down on a bench in the shade of the great birch trees surrounding the house. He told me that he had inherited this farm from his parents and that his forefathers had lived and farmed the place for at least 150 years before he was born. Nilsson was now past 50 and his oldest son Nils would inherit it after him.

It was his daughter, Olivia, who had invited me as it was her birthday. Her parents had promised her that she could invite her friends and have a dance in the large hall room adjoining the dining room. The women were doing the milking when I arrived early and the farmer himself entertained me. He asked me about conditions and even politics in America and after we had talked a while, he took me along for a walk down to the creek where he had a little flour mill. The creek was dammed up and provided power for a large water wheel which pulled the mill. There they milled their own flour and made ground feed for their stock. At that time they milked 30 cows on the farm.

When we returned from the millpond a dozen young people had arrived and were seated in the hall room. The carpets had been removed and chairs placed along the walls. Tufte was there with his accordion but we could not begin dancing before our hostess, Olivia, arrived and she was still occupied helping her mother with the evening chores. A guitar hung on the wall behind where I sat and I took it down and strummed a few chords. One of the girls commenced singing and I accompanied her on the guitar. Soon others joined in and we sang several old folk songs and lays until Olivia and her mother, Mrs. Nilsson, came in and treated us with raspberry juice and cookies.

Then the musician took over and we danced and danced until the sweat ran down on our faces. It was a warm evening and the dances were all fast polkas or schottisches. We were even couples and none of the girls wanted to sit over a dance, so we men were obliged to dance whether we wanted to or not.

Around midnight we were invited to the table set in the large kitchen for a wonderful meal of all the goodies produced in a well to do farm home. Then we were supposed to dance again but couple after couple disappeared and only a few of us were left. The last dance I had with Olivia's mother, and after that was over I said goodbye and thanked them all and walked home with Tufte, the accordion player. But it was an evening of fun just the same.

48
Planting Pine Seed

In the spring of 1908 I had been home in Sweden only a few weeks when I was approached by a Forest Ranger, Nels Grandberg, who asked me if I would take a job with him in planting pine seed in the nearby community of Mörsil. They were going to replant a tract of land that had been devastated by too close logging operations a few years earlier. The work would not take more than a month and that would give me plenty of time to spend loafing the rest of the summer.

We were six young men in the crew. Besides me, the others were students at the forestry college. We were going to board and room on a large farm about a mile from the village of Mörsil. We received a couple of rooms in a little house across the yard from the farmer's home, but received our meals with the family in their large dining room. Every morning the housewife had prepared dinner for us for the day as it was too far from where we were working to come home. It was a delicious menu with large sandwiches with goat cheese, sometimes ham or trout, coffee and "filbunke" etc. and we enjoyed every meal eaten out in the fragrant woods. We worked about three hours before dinner, took two hours rest after our meal, and worked again a couple hours before we went home around four in the afternoon. Then we had afternoon coffee and played cards until supper was served.

The farmer's wife had a hired girl 18 years old by the name of Gerda Nilsson. She was a good looking girl, always neat and clean and we all loved her. But she was shy as a bird and when we spoke to her she answered only "yes" or "no" to our questions. However, she seemed to trust me more than the others and when we had known her a week, she asked me to accompany her to her home in the village one evening. We became friends and after that I accompanied her home several times. On our way back we could sit down on a stump and talk and she always asked questions about America. She let me kiss her sometimes but that was all. There was a limit to our love and that made me more interested in Gerda. Perhaps if I had stayed there longer, I would have fallen in love in earnest with the pretty maiden. I believe that she would have married me if I had asked her.

After five weeks, we had completed the seeding and said goodbye to our hosts. I did not see Gerda that day, although I looked for her. And I never returned to the farm during the time I remained in Sweden. I sent her a postcard a few weeks later but never received a word back. And, soon I realized that there were many more nice girls in the world and I forgot her. I hope that she forgot me, too.

49
Midsommar on Island

My hometown in Sweden was located near a beautiful lake called Liten. In this lake was an island by the name of "Kringelholmen". It was an ideal place for picnics or outings for the people of the community and particularly for the younger generation. The center of the island was cleared and there was an open grassy meadow about one acre, where games could be played, races arranged and where even the young people could dance. Along the edges and near the trees, tables and benches were placed where people could enjoy their lunches and a fireplace where they could cook their coffee.

Midsommar Eve 1908, when I visited my hometown, I was invited to join a group of youngsters, many of them old schoolmates, to spend the night on Kringelholmen. We were about a dozen boys and about the same number of girls, all of the age of 18 to 25 and we had invited the community accordion player, Tofte Toreson, to furnish the music for dancing. The girls were the ones who had planned the outing and they all carried well filled baskets when we met at baker Schenk's boat landing. There, four sturdy boats were at our disposal for the night. Some of the boys had arranged for and rented the boats and we left for the island anticipating an enjoyable Midsommar celebration.

When we reached there and unloaded our baskets, games were arranged and led by Mathilda Uhlin, a good leader and singer. We played "Last Couple Out", "Change Partner" and other games for an hour, and worked up our appetite. The girls made coffee and set a table with all kinds of good things to eat. We were teasing the cooks and they teased us back, and everybody laughed at the jokes and had a good time. Two of the boys brought water from the lakeshore and washed the cups and dishes, and now we were going to dance.

Tofte uncovered his accordion and played a lively polka and we grabbed the nearest girl and joined in the dance. The polka was followed with waltzes and schottisches and we ended up with a grand march when everybody was warmed up and tired of the dances. Then our musician put his instrument away and some of the boys ran down to the shore and brought a case of soft drinks that had been left in the water to keep cool. Some of the girls remarked that we should have brought ice along to cool the drinks. However, it tasted wonderful in our dry throats.

It was midnight and the sun had disappeared behind the hills in the north while we were all stretched out on the soft grass. Somebody suggested a swim in the lake but nobody had brought swimming suits. We solved that problem easy enough. The boys should go to the south end of the island and the girls to the north end. The company broke up for a while. We undressed under the trees and jumped in the water stark naked.

In a half an hour we returned and the girls were already there and had the coffee kettle on the fire. Now it tasted good and we were all teasing each other and joking with the girls, telling them that we had spied on them when they were swimming.

After a while, we assembled at the boats and returned home, but we all agreed that we had had a swell time at our picnic on Kringelholmen.

50
The "Hoverberg" Mountain

In company with my sister Mae, we were visiting cousins in the parish of Berg, Sweden in the summer of 1908. Our cousins' home was at the foot of Hoverberg Mountain, a peculiar rock rising up on a narrow peninsula in Lake Storsjön. It is approximately 800 feet high and contains a very famous cave about which many stories are told. One of these tales concerns the giant "Hoverbergs-gubben" who by superstitious people is believed to be sleeping in the mountain. It is claimed that he can still be heard snoring.

We decided to climb the mountain and also visit the cave, and a neighbor kindly offered to be our guide. His name was Johannes Rödin and he claimed that he owned the entrance to the cave. The trail up the mountainside was quite steep and in several places we had to assist the girls. Near the top we reached a crevice or cleft in the rock several hundred feet deep. In some places it was not any wider than we could jump over it. Down in the bottom we could see snow and ice where the rays of the sun never reached. From the mountaintop we had a wonderful view over the entire Lake Storsjön, another lake by the name of "Näckten" and smaller adjoining little lakes. Around the land area we counted to eight church towers which we could see with the naked eye, representing that many parishes. This is very unusual in the province of Jämtland where many mountains and high ridges obscure the view.

We descended and followed a narrow trail to the entrance of the cave. The entrance itself was so narrow and low that we had to bow our heads and walk in single file, but well inside it widened out to great rooms a hundred feet or more in height and width. We were asked by our guide to stop and listen and we heard a noise sounding like heavy breathing and deep sighs which evidently emanated from air currents forced through the immense galleries in the cave. It explains the belief of ignorant and superstitious persons that the giant is still sleeping in the mountain. A peculiar feeling came over us all as we stood there listening. The lantern carried by our guide flickered and cast shadows that we could well imagine were sneaking ghouls trying to hide themselves in some corner.

One of the girls suggested that we sing. We all joined in singing the Swedish national anthem; "Du gamla, du fria, du fjällhöga Nord", etc. and after the singing we felt better and Johannes continued telling his stories, making us all laugh again. We walked from one room into another and still another, and admired the many various formations of the rocks, the stalagmites and stalactites that had formed during millions of years of lime rock droppings from the ceiling of the cavern. We must have remained in the cave well over an hour when Johannes told us that we had to find the entrance as his lantern was dry of oil and might go out leaving us in the dark. We hurried back and were soon out in the bright sunshine again.

I have heard that now this cavern is commercialized. The entrance has been blasted out and enlarged and protected by heavy portals. Electric wires have been strung through the entire cave and walks have been leveled out and sanded. A steady stream of tourists visit the cave every summer.

51
Birthday Party in "MO"

I was visiting in Sweden 1908 and one day I received an invitation to attend a party in the nearby hamlet of Mo, about three miles from my home. The party was arranged by two sisters, Anna and Martha Swärd, daughters of a farmer that I had known before I emigrated to America. I had recently met both sisters and they were both charming girls. The occasion of the party was that Anna celebrated her 18th birthday. Martha was a couple of years older.

I naturally was quite pleased in getting the invitation and I joined a group of about twenty gathered at Swärd's home on that beautiful summer evening. A long table had been placed on the lawn and was surrounded by birch trees tied together at the tops, forming a pleasant shady room. Chairs and benches were placed near the table and Mrs. Swärd and her daughters carried out all kinds of good "smörgåsbord" food, coffee and raspberry juice. The girls entertained us with songs with guitar and we all had a good time.

Old Anders Swärd did not come out and join us and we heard that he celebrated together with a young neighbor farmer by the name of Ante Nilsson. They had a bottle of whiskey between them and as the rest of us all were Good Templars, they stayed by themselves in the bedroom in the house. Ante was courting Anna and wanted her as his wife, but did not have much success with her. However, he evidently thought that if he could stay on the good side with her father, the girl would also accept him.

After our sumptuous lunch we played games on the green and roomy lawn. Then when the sun set, the girls announced that we would go to the granary and dance. We had an accordion player with us and we found a couple of lanterns and marched over to the granary. Naturally it was a race among us boys to dance with the two hostesses, Anna and Martha. Ante Nilsson had accompanied us to the granary but he was no dancer and he sulked in a corner, jealously watching when other men danced with his sweetheart. I imagine that every time he heard Anna's silvery laughter, he suffered the pains of a jilted lover. The drinks he had taken aboard together with Mr. Swärd also made him see red when somebody's arms encircled his girl in the dance.

I had a waltz with Anna and when it ended we stopped near the corner where Ante stood. I still had my arm around the girl when I suddenly received a slap with a rubber boot in my head and everything turned dark. I fell to the floor and did not wake up before someone poured cold water over my face. When I sat up I saw Tofte, the accordion player, standing in the middle of the floor while he slapped Ante until blood oozed out of his nose and mouth. Then I heard Anna telling him to never come back to their farm anymore. After this she would not have anything to do with him. Disgraced, he was kicked out through the door and disappeared. The dance continued, but my head was aching and I did not enjoy it anymore. Soon I was ready to leave for home, and both of the hostess girls accompanied me nearly half way there.

52
Among Tourists and Laplanders

In the little mountain village of Kolåsen, in the province of Jämtland, the Laplanders meet every fall for their "lapp-mässa" when they have their dead buried and their newborn children baptized and attend services in the old church built for them by the government. At that time, many tourists assemble in the village to see the people from the mountains and study their customs. The tourists are not the only ones. Salesmen of all kinds also make it their business to attend; trading and selling dry goods, watches or knick-knacks to the Lapps.

Together with a companion, Hans Paulson, I also went out there in the fall of 1908, when I visited my homeland. We were on a fishing trip up in the mountain area and visiting some of Paulson's relatives who lived near Kolåsen. It was my first visit in the village but Hans had been there several times before.

We crossed the little lake "Jeweln" by rowboat and when we landed below the village, we met a group of English tourists who were stranded there. None of them could speak or understand the Swedish language and their guide, who had brought them there, had disappeared. They were sure happy when they learned that I could talk English and I was glad to help them get lodging for the night and supper at the little hotel.

Leaving them there, Hans and I went to the assembly building from where we heard dance music. There were a lot of young people dancing to the music of two violins. There were also tourists, Laplanders and peasants from the village all enjoying themselves. We soon joined them too and before we realized it, it was after midnight and we had forgotten to arrange for lodging for the night. The hotel was overfilled and so were several homes where we inquired. Hans knew a family who lived about a mile from the village and we walked over there. The sun was just coming up when we reached the place and woke the people up. They had a bed in the attic and there we soon fell asleep. We did not sleep long however, as we were awakened by their young daughter who came with a tray of coffee and cookies. A little later we sat down at the breakfast table and were served pancakes and lingonberry sauce. As we had not had any supper the previous evening, it tasted very good.

We then went to a sightseeing tower from where we could see far into Norway to the west. There we again met the English tourists that I had helped the previous evening. They had now found their guide so they were happy again. We also met several of the girls that we had danced with and in pleasant company the time flies. Before we knew it, it was afternoon and we were getting hungry. On our way back to the place where we had stayed overnight, we met a boy who carried a string of brook trout he had caught. We bought the fish and our hostess cleaned and fried them for us.

Back at the assembly hall, we found a traveling minister preaching for a group of Laplanders and a few old women. In a corner behind him sat a group of Norwegians, native peasants and Laplanders at a long table playing cards. How the preacher could stand it, I do not know, but cuss words in several languages often interrupted him and made him wince. Finally, he closed his sermon and came around the floor to "collect money for the heathen" as he called it. I suspect that his collection was kept in his own pocket however.

The next morning we were so tired that the little girl could not get us awake. We slept until after dinner. When we left we gave our little waitress some silver coins which brought tears to her eyes.

53
Hiking Across Mountain "Åreskutan"

In the early fall of 1908, when I visited in Sweden, I and my companion Hans Paulsson decided to walk across the mountain Åreskutan, from the parish of Kall to another parish of Åre. We took a steamboat to the hamlet of Husån on the shore of lake "Kallsjön", where we stayed overnight with an old timer by the name of Jöns Fors. He was born and raised up there and had lived there all his life far from civilization. However, during his long life he had been in many adventures and had many various experiences of which he told us that evening and his tales were both historical and entertaining and we could have listened to him all night.

In the morning of September 7th we were up before daylight and left for the mountain. For a while the trail led through a tract of timber which had recently been logged over. Gradually the trail became more steep and we emerged through the timber belt and saw only brush and short rugged mountain spruce. After a while we reached a large open plateau where we sat down and rested. We had a wonderful view of the large lake to the north and the little farms and hamlets along it's shore. Back of us, the great mountain loomed bare and desolate with glistening snowdrifts here and there. The air became cooler and a penetrating wind swept the mountainside. We had been carrying our overcoats but now we were glad to put them on. Higher and higher we climbed while the temperature dropped lower and lower. Soon we passed large drifts of snow, which protected from the sun under great cliffs had perhaps been there for generations.

Four hours from the time we left Husån, we reached the top and found the little tourist cabin built by the Swedish Tourist Association. Every board and every plank, yes every piece in that cabin had been carried on the backs of husky men up the steep mountainside. When we stood there on the bleak mountain top, we marveled over the foresight of the Tourist Association in their efforts to accommodate the travelers in building this little haven. Snowstorms are common up there and a shelter may save lives many times.

It was clear on the summit, but we saw the mountainside towards Åre, where we were going, enveloped in dark clouds. It would not be very pleasant to be caught up there in a snowstorm and we did not linger very long at the summit. We hurried down the trail and soon met cold, sharp, biting snow, which blinded us and we lost the trail many times. My companions instinct, more than anything else, brought us back on the trail and after a couple hours of struggling descent we finally reached "Mörvikshummeln" another plateau where a tourist cabin had been built. By then the snow had turned into rain and before we reached the cabin, we were soaked to the skin. We found the cabin filled with other tourists which had been driven back by the storm, who were huddled around the stove trying to dry themselves out. We joined them and rested several hours before we finished the descent and reached the village of Åre, from where we took the train home to Järpen.

54
A Broken Engagement

Andrew Paulson was the son of a well to do timber superintendent at the sawmill company in my hometown in Sweden. He was also my former schoolmate, and when I returned home after six years in America, we became close chums and spent a lot of time together that summer of 1908.

He was engaged to Bertha Hallman, the only daughter of the well respected farmer Magnus Hallman, on the farm "Backen" which was situated about four miles from our home community. Bertha was a very intelligent girl, a member of the local Good Templar lodge, and many were surprised that she intended to marry Andrew, as he was often seen taking a drink too much when he associated with the class of men who thought that intoxicating liquor was indispensable in social company. He never touched liquor when him and I were together however.

It was a New Year festival at the local Good Templar hall and Andrew and I went there. He told me that Bertha had promised to meet him at the hall, and we soon found her in company with another girl, Martha Swärd, whose home was not far from Berthas. Andrew suggested that we should take the girls home and I willingly consented because I knew Martha and enjoyed her company. Andrew owned a young horse and asked me to go to his home and hitch him to the riding sleigh and bring the rig to the hall a little later that evening.

It was almost midnight before we left the hall with our lady companions. Andrew whispered to me that when we reached Backen, the home of Bertha, to leave him there and drive Martha home. And, he said, "Don't be in a hurry to come back." "When you come, knock on the bedroom window and I will come out."

Consequently, when we reached Berthas home, we left the engaged couple and drove to "Mo", the home of Martha. I told her what Andrew had whispered to me, and on her suggestion I unhitched the horse and put him in the stable while Martha went in and put the coffeepot on. There we sat for a couple of hours drinking coffee and talking and it was almost 3 o'clock in the morning when I hitched up and returned to Bertha's home. I tied the horse by the gate and went up to the house and knocked on the window where I had been told that Bertha slept. I did not hear anything and knocked again a little harder. Steps were heard and the door opened and there was Magnus Hallman himself and wondered what in the name of blazes I wanted at that time of the night. I felt pretty timid and did not answer, but then Bertha appeared behind her father and told me that Andrew had left long ago and walked home.

Quite humiliated, I excused myself for waking them up and returned to the horse. When I, a little while later, arrived at Andrew's home, he was waiting for me. He was in bad humor and I could smell whiskey from him. After calling me down for staying so long, he calmed down when I told him that I had put his horse in the stable, and I reminded him of his own words that I should not be in a hurry coming back. Then he told me that Bertha had broken their engagement and had given him his ring back. And she told him to stay away from her home for good. He said that it was all my fault that he lost her.

1908 - In Sweden. From left: Andrew Paulson, Bertha Hallman, John Ostlund, Martha Swärd.

John Ostlund collection

55
A Real Surprise Party

I had been visiting my hometown, Järpen, almost a year and I was getting ready to return to America. I had won many friends in the community and particularly in the local Good Templar lodge, in which I had taken active parts on their programs and entertainments during the year.

The lodge held their meetings every Sunday afternoon and I seldom missed any of the meetings. The last Sunday before I and my traveling companions were leaving the community, I came up to the lodge hall as usual and was rather surprised to see it filled with members, more than the usual attendance at meetings. However, I did not suspect anything unusual. I was talking to one of my old schoolmates when the Chief Templar called the lodge to order and we took our places.

Now something unusual happened. The Marshalls, instead of taking up the password, came to me and asked me to accompany them up on the platform. There we were met by the Chief Templar who seated me in a chair beside him. He then announced that this meeting had been arranged special as a farewell party for a Good Templar brother by the name of John Ostlund, who was leaving the community for his adopted country, America.

I was so surprised that if he had called on me to say something, I would have been quite unable to utter a word. But, he called on three girls for a song. That was the beginning of a long program consisting of songs, music, recitations and speeches that lasted for about two hours while I sat there spellbound and unable to realize that all this was for me, and me alone. At last the Chief Templar, A.J. Lallander, who by the way was also my former school teacher, took the floor and thanked me for what I had done in the lodge while I had been with them, wished me good luck in the future and sent the greetings of the lodge to the lodge I belonged to in Hibbing. He then presented me with a gold watch chain and a fob with the name and number of the lodge, Hjerpe Skans No. 813, I.O.G.T.

Now it was my turn to talk and I tried my best to tell them how much I appreciated the party, the program, the well wishes and the nice present given to me. It was a pleasant memory for the rest of my life and I told them so. I urged them all to be true to the principles and the program of our Order of I.O.G.T. as I assured them that I would. When I sat down I saw many that wiped their eyes, so perhaps they were a little bit impressed by my farewell speech.

Shortly after I returned to America I lost the present I had received from the lodge in Järpen. I believe it was stolen or I would have found it. But the memories are left of that meeting and the many friends in my home community.

1908 - Mock Wedding. Standing from left: Stina Edlund - Bridesmaid, Stina Larson - Groom's mother, Rudolf Kjärv - Groom's father, Beda Johnson - Minister's wife, Jack Erikson - Minister, Johan Dahlström - Bride's father, Stina Erikson - Bride's mother, Karl Howberg - Usher. Sitting: John Ostlund - Marshal or Best man, Erik Olson - Bridegroom, Olivia Viklund - Bride, Elin Gustavson - Matron of Honor. In front: Karl Johnson - Violinist.

John Ostlund collection

"Mock Wedding" - Given by a group of young Good Templars in Järpen, Sweden in the fall of 1908. The play was given every night at the annual bazaar held for a whole week at the Good Templar Hall in Järpen, and once in the nearby village of Mörsil, and once in the adjoining community of Underåker. It was well received and the cast were treated and their pictures taken several times. This is one of the pictures.

56
We Lost Our Boat

In the spring of 1909 I returned to America after spending a year in Sweden. In my company was my sister Mae, my brother Peter, my neighbor and friend Hans Paulson and two other girls from my home community. In the city of Tronhjem, Norway, we bought our tickets and boarded the tourist steamer "Haakon VII" for the journey along the coast of Norway and across the North Sea to New Castle, England.

The trip along the coast was very interesting. Our boat took passengers and freight at almost every little hamlet and village in the many fjords, and sometimes we laid in the harbors for hours while the crew was loading fishboxes, which was the general cargo. While the loading went on we passengers had the opportunity to step off the boat and visit a cafe, or take a walk around sightseeing a while.

We arrived in the little city of Aulesund one afternoon and I inquired from one of the officers on the boat, how long they would remain in the harbor. He said it would be at least for an hour. Hans, Peter and I left the boat and walked up the street in search for a store where they sold postcards, as we wanted to send some back to our hometown. About a block from the pier we stepped into a restaurant for a cup of coffee. The Norwegians were noted for their good coffee. We took a table by the window facing the harbor, where we could see our boat, Haakon VII. Suddenly we heard the boat signal for leave and we saw it back out from the pier and turn about. We ran out and down the street waving our hats and shouting at the top of our voices but nobody on the boat noticed us. We were left behind while all our belongings and our companions were on the way to England. I had all the girls tickets and passports. What would happen if they called for them? The girls would be put off at the first landing and left there.

There were no fast motor boats to hire at that time to overtake the Haakon. We inquired at the office of the harbor police, and were informed that another steamer, Salmo of the Wilson Line, was in the harbor and would leave for Bergen within two hours. The police also informed us that our boat, Haakon, was to land at Bergen and if we were lucky we might catch up with it there. We found the boat Salmo, purchased tickets and went aboard. Those two hours lengthened into three hours and we were still in Aulesund. I found the captain and told him my story, and asked him if he thought we would reach Bergen in time for us to resume our voyage on the Haakon VII. he told me laughing, that if we did not, we could remain on his boat and he would bring us to England, to the city of Hull. From there we could take the train to Liverpool and overtake our companions.

We did not sleep much that night. We went out on the deck at three o'clock that morning, too worried to remain in our cabin. We arrived in the harbor of Bergen at 9 o'clock and were happy indeed when we recognized the Haakon VII at the pier. Our girl companions had quite naturally been worried when they could not find us and had reported our absence to the chief steward. He had searched the boat for us and they had called Aulesund as soon as they reached Bergen and had been informed that we would be in Bergen on the Salmo that morning. I immediately reported our presence to the chief steward.

PART 6 -
"Back in America with Family"

When I arrived from Sweden, March 21st 1909, accompanied by my brother Peter, sister Mae and my good friend Hans Paulson, we decided to rest up good after the trip before we went north to Hibbing. We registered at the Sherman Hotel on Hennepin avenue, which was in the center of the city, and a clean and moderate priced hotel.

I took my sister to a large department store, where she purchased American clothes, hat and shoes, changing her from an emigrant girl to an up to date American lady.

For an entire week we remained in Minneapolis. I had many friends in the city and we were cordially welcome everywhere we went. From Minneapolis we went to Cambridge. I made arrangement with my friends, Anderson's, to leave sister there for a while or until I could find a good place for her in Hibbing. With these good people I knew that Mae would be well taken care of and at the same time she would have an opportunity to pick up some English through their daughter Clara.

1909 - Portrait of John Ostlund (left) with sister Mae and brother Peter.

John Ostlund collection

57
As Warehouseman in Store

When I returned from my visit to Sweden in the spring of 1909, I was down to my last 20 dollar bill. It was too early for any work in the mines and it seemed that I would have to go into debt for my board and room before I would be able to earn my living. However, in Hibbing I had many friends who I knew would be willing to loan me the money I would need until payday would come around again.

One day I was offered employment as a warehouseman for Carlson Mercantile Company in their store on Pine Street. I had never worked in a store before in my life, but I accepted it and did not have any trouble whatsoever adjusting myself to my duties.

I went to work at 7:30 every morning, half an hour before the store opened for business. I had a key to the back door to let myself in. Then I carefully folded the light canvas sheets which had been spread over the merchandise the previous evening, and took them out in the backyard and shook the dust off. With a dust cloth I went over the whole store, dusting off the desks and wiping off merchandise that had not been covered with the canvases. By that time the clerks had arrived and the store was open for business. By 8 o'clock the freight wagon generally arrived at the back door and I had to be there and assist in the unloading of merchandise boxes. These were carried into the warehouse and the different items had to be placed where they belonged and convenient for unpacking when needed. When the wagon was unloaded and left, I had to unpack goods needed for the shelves in the store and bring it in. I also took care of the furnace in the basement and if it was too warm or too cold in the store, I was the man who took the blame. If I had any leisure time after doing my regular chores, I helped to wait on customers in the store.

When the store closed in the evening, which was 8 o'clock every evening except Saturday, when it was kept open until 9, it was my duty to do the sweeping of the entire store. When I was through sweeping the canvasses were brought in and spread over the merchandise to be left overnight to catch the dust. It generally took me an hour to do that so it was always 9 or 10 every evening before I could lock the backdoor and go home. They were long days but my principal treated me like a son, and always defended me if any of the clerks complained about the temperature in the store. Often he took me along to his home for afternoon coffee, and then he asked me about conditions in Sweden, from where I had recently returned.

Gust Carlson, the owner of the store, had a daughter in her early twenties, and I believe that I could have married her if I had asked for her hand. But while she flirted with me, she was not the kind of woman I could love. When I resigned to resume my work at the mine, Carlson coaxed me to stay, telling me that I would have a better future as a businessman, and hinted that I could remain with him as long as I wanted. He even hinted that some day I could take over his business as his son in law. That was enough to make me shun the store afterwards.

John Ostlund collection

58
I Sang in the Church Choir

Before I left for Sweden, I sang in the choir at the Swedish Lutheran Church in Hibbing. In my youth I liked to sing and develop my voice, and that was my reason for joining. At that time they had a young sympathetic minister by the name of Ed Ljungberg who really knew how to attract people, and the church was almost filled every Sunday.

The choir was mixed and consisted of young singers, and was led by a talented woman, Mrs. S.W. Levin. During the summer we were about twenty of us in the choir and the majority of us also belonged to the Good Templar lodge. We practiced every Tuesday evening and sang Sunday forenoon at the service, and sometimes at funerals or special events.

When I returned from my trip in the spring of 1909, I again joined the choir. It was not as lively as it had been when I had left, but I assisted in getting it back to twenty members when I induced several girls from the Good Templar lodge to join. Everything went good that summer and the following winter, and we became quite efficient in harmony and were given credit for good assemblies in church.

Then Mr. Ljungberg left Hibbing and in his place came an older minister by the name of Idstrom. He was more conservative and held on to the old rules and regulations of the Lutheran Synod. Among these was the rule that nobody who belonged to a secret organization could belong to the church. One evening when we were rehearsing in church he came in and listened. After a while he asked how many of us were dues paying members in the church. Our leader informed him that we were members of the local temperance lodge, and as such we were not allowed membership in the church. He flew into a rage and demanded that we immediately dropped the lodge and joined the church as that was our duty. If we did not do that, we could not come back and sing anymore. Our leader tried her best to calm him down and explain things, but he was too enraged to listen to her. The Good Templars were a sinful group who distracted people from God's temple, and he would not tolerate having any of them singing in his church.

I was the first one to take my hat and leave, and the other Good Templars followed me. The next Sunday the choir consisted of only one soprano, one tenor and Mrs. Levin.

About a week later when I returned from work to my room, there was Reverend Idstrom and Mrs. Levin waiting for me. I at once realized the reason why they were there, but pretended that I was surprised. Idstrom told me how sorry he was that his temper had caused the outbreak in the church, told me that he had received information about the Good Templars that he did not know before and now realized that they were excellent citizens and were doing a lot of good in the community. He invited me and the other choir members to come back and sing, and we could remain members of our lodge.

I thanked him for changing his opinion about the I.O.G.T. but told him that my mind was made up to not go back. I would not take the chances to be driven out of church again. Finally, they left and the Reverend never saw me again, even when we met on the street in Hibbing. There were not choirs reorganized in that church for many years.

1910 - Sitting from left: Hans Paulson, William Winberg, John Ostlund. Standing: Andrew Anderson, Peter Ostlund, Oscar Englund.
1910 - "Six Jämts" all from Jämtland, Sweden.

John Ostlund collection

59
Our String Orchestra

In the fall of 1909, we were four young men in Hibbing who organized into a string band. It was beside me, Walfred Stenborg, who played first violin, Oscar Pearson with his guitar, Edward Flank with zither and I played second violin. None of us had any musical schooling and we were not very familiar with notes, we all played by ear, but we enjoyed music and got along good with each other. As we all were members of the temperance lodge, we often played on the programs and received much encouragement from our listeners.

We were asked one day to play at a wedding dance at Sampo Hall. The committee for the dance offered us $10.00 if we played three hours. That amounted to $2.50 for each of us, more than a days work at common wages at that time and we could not refuse. When we arrived, the hall was filled with wedding guests, many of them intoxicated, and when they saw us come in with our instruments they commenced to tease us. "Ooh, here comes the Good Templars, give them a drink and they will play a lot better!" they shouted. But that was before we had even begun playing.

We commenced with a lively Swedish waltz and the floor filled with dancing couples. Then we played a polka in a fast rhythm and everybody cheered. Nobody suggested drinks after that. We kept their spirits up without being intoxicated. When our time was up and we played the old "Home Sweet Home" the dancers would not let us leave the stage. So, we played a couple extra dances for them, and felt that we had given them their money's worth.

That dance was a great encouragement for us. If we could entertain fifty wedding guests for a whole evening, why could we not arrange dances ourselves? Ed and I went to the owner of Sampo Hall and rented the hall for a Saturday evening. The rent was only $4.00. We had posters printed and distributed and practiced almost every evening before that first dance. One of our girlfriends offered to sell tickets at the door and we asked two of our fellow workers to help keep order if it would be needed. The admission was 50 cents, or 75 cents for a couple. Everything turned out perfectly. The hall was filled and we played an hour later than usual at dances, to give everybody satisfaction. When it was over and we counted our receipts, we had made $28.00 clear.

We rented Sampo Hall every other Saturday that fall and early in the winter. Sometimes we made good, but sometimes the attendance was small and we were discouraged. One night during a blizzard we sold only six tickets and we returned their money as we did not play. We each had to chip in a dollar to pay the rent. Oscar was leaving the city and resigned from our orchestra. We disbanded and it was only Walfred and I that practiced with our violins together. But it was fun while it lasted and for me it is a pleasant memory.

John Ostlund collection

60
Running a Boarding House

When I returned to America in the spring of 1909, I was accompanied by my brother Peter and my sister Mae. I left her in Cambridge with some friends I knew when Peter and I continued to Hibbing. In my company was also a young man from my hometown in Sweden by the name of Hans Paulson. One of my old friends suggested that I should take my sister to Hibbing, where she could keep house for us, as he knew of a little house that was for rent very reasonable, and he thought that if I accepted his suggestion, we would find that we could save expenses and at the same time we would all three be together as a family.

I pondered his suggestion for several days and the result was that I wrote my sister and told her of the proposal. She answered immediately that it suited her as it was hard for a young girl to find a place in Cambridge when she was unable to speak the language. So in company with my friend, Hans Olson, I went to the owner of the house for rent and leased the house for six months.

I spent about $200.00 for second hand furniture, household goods and dishes, and Peter, Paulsson and I batched a few days until sister Mae arrived. Several of my friends came and wanted to board with us but we only had three bedrooms and limited space in our dining room, so I could not accept all of them. Our star boarders were brother Peter, Hans Paulson, Hans Olson, my cousin Gotfred Stevenson and Oscar Englund. It was a nice, jolly bunch and we had a lot of fun together. We were all members of the local Good Templar lodge and our little home became the place for committee meetings and it was hardly an evening that we did not have visitors.

There was a lot of responsibility for me in the beginning when I had to make up all orders for groceries and other necessities for the house, but soon Mae was able to take over. She was a good cook and well liked by everybody as she not only served good meals, but she also kept the house clean and in good order

In October, I rented a larger house on North Street and we moved there. I had to purchase more furniture to fill all the rooms but now we could accommodate more roomers and still not be so crowded. Among our boarders we now accepted a shovel engineer, Carl Johnson, and his cranesman, Axel Linder. In all we had ten boarders.

1910 - Sister Mae scrubbing the floor.

John Ostlund collection

Our home was also the headquarters for the Good Templars in Hibbing. There they met for committee meetings, for practicing plays, dialogues and songs and for social gatherings. Almost every night we had company, and how Mae alone was able to keep the house in order, feed the ten boarders we had, and entertain the many visitors was more than I could understand. However, she had been accustomed to hard work from her early youth and she never complained.

During the winter of 1909-10 she had it somewhat easier as many of our boarders left when the stripping shut down in November. I worked a few weeks in Nashwauk during the winter and Mae just looked after the house and rested up after the summer's hard work. Then spring came and the boarders came back. Then in July my friend Fred Backstrom had just built a new house in Brooklyn addition and offered me to rent it cheap, provided we let him board with us. So we moved again July 25th. However, sister was engaged and resigned as my housekeeper and I sold everything to Backstrom on September 25th. The deal amounted to $125.00 and while this was only a fraction of what it had cost me, it was a relief to be free again of all responsibilities connected with running a boarding house.

In the play "Olles-Olle" in Chisholm, Minnesota 1910. Seated: G.V. Dahlner, Gust Anderson, Jenny Gunderson. Standing: Mary Larson, John Ostlund, Peter Forsmark, Oscar Englund.

John Ostlund collection

61
I Became a Land Owner

Ever since I grew up in Sweden, and after I emigrated to the U.S. it had been my ambition to be an owner of a piece of land. While I did not plan on being a farmer, I wanted a tract of land that I could call my own and where I could go during poor times in the city.

When I failed in 1904 to get a homestead I gave up my dream idea for a while. Then in January 1910, I spent a couple of weeks with my old friend William Carlson at Gheen and listened to the stories of his carefree life in the woods. Here he was his own boss, could work when he felt for it and rest when he wanted. Living was cheap as the woods were full of game and it was not far to lakes where fish could be caught any time, winter or summer. One day we went to visit an old Civil War veteran by the name of Seth Nichols, who had homesteaded a quarter section of land near Williams place. He was getting too old to clear land and farm it, and told us that if he could find a buyer he would sell reasonably.

The next day William and I scouted over Mr. Nichols land. It was partly spruce swamp and meadow and partly high land. The Willow River ran through the land and along the river were several large meadows which could be cleared very easily. I saw Mr. Nichols again and asked him about price and terms, and he wanted $1,000.00 for the 160 acre tract. If I could pay him all cash, he would give me the mineral rights to it, which otherwise usually was reserved. I returned to Hibbing with my mind almost made up to buy the land.

I had saved up $600.00 that spring of 1910 when I received a letter from William that he had talked to Mr. Nichols and he had promised to reduce his price 10% if he could get it all cash or within 30 days from the date of sale. William had also talked with a neighbor, Gust Johnson, who had some money saved up, which I could borrow at 4% interest if I needed it. At the time I was running a boarding house and I figured that it would not take me long to save the additional $300.00 that I needed to buy the land. So I wrote Mr. Nichols to come to Hibbing and we would have the deal made.

It was on March 18th that I met Mr. Nichols, withdrew my savings from the bank, and became the owner of the W. ½ of S.W. ¼ Sec. 12, and the N. ½ of N.W. ¼ Sec. 13 in Twp. 63 Range 20. I paid $600.00 down and promised to have the balance paid within 30 days. At the first opportunity I visited Gust Johnson at Gheen and asked him if he would accept my note for $300.00. He opened a trap door in the kitchen floor and climbed down into his cellar from where he returned with a tin can containing gold coins. I drew a primitive note on a piece of stationary and signed it and he counted out the gold coins, $300.00. I exchanged the coins for a quit claim deed that Mr. Nichols held and the quarter section of land was mine and all paid for. My old dream had come through.

In 1911, I planned to build a log house 14 x 21 feet on the south eighty. I had already purchased a stove and some second hand furniture and shipped it to Gheen. In a few days I had the logs cut and hauled together. I was all alone building. It was sometimes very difficult to place the logs the way they should be, besides it was an exceedingly slow job.

When I reached above breast height, I was unable to do anything alone and William took a few days off from his own work and helped me. Now it did not take long before we had all the logs placed and the house ready for roof.

1911 - John Ostlund with his homestead, built by
his own hands from tree to structure.

John Ostlund collection

On Christmas Day I dug the cellar under the kitchen floor. I was all alone during Christmas. It was lonesome, but as I was quite busy from morning to night, I did not mind it much. During the summer I had become engaged to Olga Flank, and the thought that I was planning and building a future home for her and me made the work light and pleasant. In January my brother Peter came. When the weather was moderate, we worked on the house, and when it was too cold, we cut ties, as it was never too cold for that work. When we had the door and windows in, we put up an airtight heater, and after that we could work in any kind of weather. We put in the ceiling and rough floor upstairs, and we laid the floor downstairs, with a trapdoor to the cellar. Then we bought blue building paper and covered the walls and ceiling. Late in February I made up an order to Sears Roebuck and Company for needed household goods and some groceries. When this arrived the first days of March, Peter and I moved home. We were just like a couple young kids. Everything was fun and we cooked, fried, baked and cleaned house and we were neither master, nor slave at anything. If the soup burnt dry, we threw it away and made new soup. We always had a large supply of fresh meat on hand, in fact more than we could use. It felt good to be at home, and we had the swellest home in the world.

1911 - A successful rabbit hunt. John Ostlund, Peter Ostlund, William Carlson.
John Ostlund collection

On this land I have spent the largest part of my life. Here I have raised my family, here I have made my living and here I have taken part in the development of a pioneer community. Here I hope to lay after life is over, near my friends and neighbors gone before me.

John the rabbit hunter - 1911.

John Ostlund collection

1911 - Peter Ostlund, William Carlson, John Ostlund, Walfred Stenborg.
John Ostlund collection

At the homestead. William Carlson, Peter Ostlund, John Ostlund.
John Ostlund collection

62
Humiliated and Promoted

It was the last week of June 1910 and I was running a dinkey locomotive in the "Buffalo-Susquehanna" mine in Hibbing. The Winston Dear Company for which I was employed had just opened this great iron mine that spring and were removing the overburden (sand and clay) from the iron ore body. Dinkey engines and dump cars were used in the beginning to build the grades and fill the trestles along the three mile route out to where the overburden was to be deposited.

The company had purchased new standard locomotives and air operated dump cars and standard gauge tracks were built beside the narrow gauge dinkey track. The locomotives and cars had arrived and were standing on the siding ready for use. Some of us dinkey engineers, among which I was one, had been promised by the master mechanic, Mr. Ed Thomas, that we were in line to be promoted to operate the new equipment as soon as we could handle the E-T-Air brake system. The dinkeys were equipped with steam brakes.

One day I was sent in with my train to the new roundhouse where they filled with gravel. The general superintendent, Mr. H.C. Hanson was there himself and led the work. When my last train was dumped he came up and told me that they had enough gravel and I should tell the man at the switch to go back to the track laying crew, where he had worked before, and I should proceed to the dumps with my next load. So the next time I passed that switch, I never looked towards the roundhouse, but drove straight ahead on the mainline to the dumps. The superintendent had been standing at the roundhouse and signaled to me to come in there again, but neither myself or my brakeman noticed his signals.

Returning from the dumps with the empty train, we saw the super coming up the track and from the way he walked, I remarked to my brakeman that something must be wrong. When we met, he flagged us down and climbed up on the dinkey. His face was red as a roosters comb and he commenced bawling us out. "We were a couple of nincompoops who were not worth the salt on our bread even. We were sleeping on our job and it was a miracle that we had not run our train over the head block on the dump and into the woods! We should have been fired and sent to hell out of there long ago! Etc. etc." for me to get a word in was impossible. When I stopped at the water tower to fill up our water tank, he stepped off and now I told him that he was the one who ordered us out to the dumps with that train. I further told him that we are watching the tracks ahead of us when we are running our train and were not looking at the scenery on the sides. But I also told him that if our work was not satisfactory, we were ready to go home any time. If he heard me or not, I don't know. Gone were now our hopes for promotion. That he would let us work any longer was unthinkable.

At noon we saw the master mechanic come, followed by two other men. I told my brakeman, Elmer Westman, "Here comes our replacement". I almost fell over when our foreman told us that he had orders from the super to replace us on the dinkey and tell us to report that evening as fireman and brakeman on the new locomotive No. 102. As the fireman on the standard locomotive, I would earn more than I had running dinkey. Three weeks later I was promoted as engineer on No. 103 and Elmer followed me as fireman.

John Ostlund (on the left), Engineer of Locomotive Engine #103.

John Ostlund collection

63
4th of July Picnic Party

Sweethearts, Olga Flank and John Ostlund July 4, 1912 in
Gheen, Minnesota.

John Ostlund collection

For the 4th of July in 1912, we arranged quite a picnic party. We
met in Virginia, a large group of close friends from Hibbing, Chisholm
and Virginia, and we took the evening train to Gheen. In the party
was besides myself; sister Ester and brother Peter, Olga Flank, Walfred
Stenborg, Oscar England, Ida Greiff, Vendla Norgard and others. We
arrived at Green just at midnight, but were met by William Carlson
and taken to his home. We filled his cabin to capacity, but there was not
much sleep that night. The girls finally arranged to sleep crosswise on his
bed downstairs, and we boys were driven upstairs, where we were locked
in, and we slept wherever we could.

The recently organized Farmers Club held their first picnic at the
England Grove, where we all had a great, good old time. In the evening
we danced in Gust Johnson's barn, a genuine barn dance if there ever was
one, in the presence of calfs and chickens and the genuine barn smell all
about us. However, we were all young, gay and happy, a healthy group of
youngsters on their vacation.

1912 - 4th of July celebration. From left: William Carlson, Olga Flank, Walfred Stenborg, John Ostlund, sister Ester (Ostlund) Stenborg, brother Peter Ostlund.

John Ostlund collection

1912 - 4th of July celebration. From left: Walfred Stenborg, John's sister Ester (Ostlund) Stenborg, Olga Ostlund, John Ostlund.

John Ostlund collection

64
A Lonesome Christmas

I was staying with my friend William Carlson in December 1911 and was building a house on my land. William was engaged to a girl, Martha Berg, in Duluth and she had promised to become his wife at Christmas. He had been writing letters to her every week but very seldom were his letters answered. One evening he asked me if I would stay and look after his place, milk his cow and care for his young stock while he went to Duluth to get married. I had planned to go to Hibbing for Christmas, but could not turn him down, so I promised to stay. My father, who also had been staying with William, had been offered to spend the winter with John Olson in Cook and had left, so we were all alone.

During that summer I had also been engaged to Olga, my future wife, and I wrote to her that I would be unable to see her until after Christmas. William left home a few days before Christmas and now I was all alone. I did not mind it much to begin with as I was quite busy. On Christmas day I dug a cellar under the kitchen floor in my house. I worked until after dark and when I walked back to William's place in the dark evening, I thought the timber wolves were going to attack me. Several of them were howling on both sides of the trail and it sure was a relief when I reached the clearing and could leave them behind me. It was unusually cold and the beasts were hungry. The next morning I saw their tracks right by the house, so they must have followed me even across the clearing.

In the mornings I fed the stock and milked the cow. She did not give me much milk as she was drying up, but I think the main reason was that I was not used to milking and was unable to milk her dry. Then I had to carry water from the well for the cow and two yearling calves, which consisted of all William's stock. As soon as I was through with the chores I went over to my place and worked on my house. It was a pleasure to prepare for a home for myself and the girl I loved. Some day I would bring her here and we would live happily together.

However, as the days went one after another, I became quite lonesome and every night I hoped that William and his bride would show up the next day. Finally on New Years Eve William returned, but alone. He told me that Martha had broken her promise and he had found her keeping company with a young minister. She had returned his ring and told him that she could not go with him up in the wilderness. He was pretty downhearted and cussed the man who had won his sweetheart, and I didn't blame him. He needed a woman and had depended so much on her.

Now it was my turn to go and visit and I left the next morning, New Years Day 1912, for Hibbing. Nobody had run away with Olga and she seemed so happy to see me again. Forgotten were the lonely days of Christmas. We renewed our pledges and were happy!

Portrait of John and Olga.

John Ostlund collection

65
We Were Married

usband and Wife

John Ostlund.
(HUSBAND'S NAME)

Date of Birth *October 9th 1883.*

Place of Birth *Trångsviken, Sweden.*

Olga Maria Flank
(WIFE'S NAME)

Date of Birth *March 16th 1892.*

Place of Birth *Sörsjön, Sweden*

THE WEDDING

Place *Virginia, Minnesota*

at *Swedish Mission Parsonage*
(CITY)   (STATE)

Date *June 24th 1913.*

Reception *None.*
(PLACE AND TIME)

Wedding trip to *Minneapolis, Minn.*

Marriage Performed by *Sw. Mission Minister*

Attendants *Esther Ostlund*

Walfred Stenborg.

Marriage record of John Ostlund and Olga Flank 1913.

John Ostlund collection

The most important episode of my life is of course my marriage. When a man is married he takes on a lot of responsibility that he had not had before. I had realized that for many years and while I had met many girls during my early manhood who gladly would have accepted a proposal of marriage, I had hesitated when I thought of the responsibility.

I met Olga shortly after she arrived in America from Sweden in the spring of 1911. She was the sister of one of my best friends, Edward Flank, and when we met, it was love at first sight from my side. She was somewhat shy, however, and it took some time before I had the nerve and opportunity to become friendly with her. One afternoon I invited her for a buggy ride. We drove to Chisholm where we attended a meeting of the Good Templar lodge. On the way home I asked Olga to become my wife and she consented. What a wonderful feeling!

Olga wanted to be a June bride and we resolved to get married on Midsommar Day 1913. We had then been engaged for more than a year and knew each other pretty well. We did not announce our wedding day to anybody but our closest friends, my sister Mae and her husband and sister Ester and her fiance, Walfred Stenborg, who I wanted to be the witness at our wedding.

I was working in Chisholm at that time and lived at the home of my sister Mae and Charley Hedberg. June 24th I met Olga and Walfred, who both lived in Hibbing, and we took the street car to Virginia where my sister Ester then was living. She met us and together we went to the home of the minister of the Swedish Mission Church and I produced our marriage license and we were duly married. We then went to one of the best restaurants in the city and ordered our wedding dinner, just the four of us. Then to a photographer where we had our wedding picture taken just on postcards. In the late afternoon we said goodbye to Ester and returned to Chisholm where my sister Mae had arranged a nice supper for us and where we stayed over night.

We had just gone to bed that night when we were roused by an infernal noise across the street. It was a chivaree - but it was not for us. It was for a neighborhood couple who also had been married that day.

The next morning we were up early and took the morning train for Minneapolis. It was our honeymoon trip and served two purposes. I was a delegate to the Grand Lodge convention of I.O.G.T. which that year was held in Minneapolis. When we arrived there my cousin Nels Holmer met us at the depot and had made all arrangements for lodging and board for us at the place where he lived. He had also planned the program for our entertainment while we were there and took time from his work to take us around and show us the beautiful parks and lakes of the city. So we divided our time between the convention and sightseeing the three days we had at our disposal. It was a short but sweet honeymoon trip and when it was over we returned to Chisholm and set up housekeeping and I resumed my work at the Dunwoody mine.

John Ostlund and Olga Flank married June 24, 1913.
John Ostlund collection

Wedding photo of John and Olga with attendants Walfred
Stenborg and Ester Ostlund, June 24, 1913.

John Ostlund collection

66
Smoked Out

When we were first married we rented a small house on 4th Avenue in Chisholm, for which we paid $10.00 per month, and started housekeeping. While I realized that my responsibilities had mounted, I felt that now I had something to live and work for. Our many friends soon found out where we lived and hardly a day passed but that somebody dropped in for a friendly visit. In the fall, in order to have a warmer and more comfortable living quarters for the winter, we moved to an upstairs apartment on Lake Street where we rented four good size rooms, all up to date with bathroom, water and electric lights, and for which we paid only $17.00 per month. Our apartment was located over a dry goods store and one bedroom and the front room were facing the main street.

My aunt, Mrs. P.E. Selander, from Warren, PA was visiting us and we had hired a maid, Vendla Norgard from Hibbing. One night in late November we were awakened by smoke which filled our bedroom, almost suffocating us. I jumped into my pants and rushed into the other bedroom where our visitors slept and woke them up. Olga followed me and together we all groped our way to the stairway leading down to the main street, choking with the thick smoke. We finally reached the bottom of the stairs and unlocked the door and came out where we could breathe fresh air.

Across the street was a drugstore which was lighted up and open and I assisted the women over there. They only had their night clothes on and were barefoot and were shivering in the cold night air. There I left them and ran back across the street to try to salvage some clothing. The fire department just arrived and were breaking up the front door to the store where the fire was blazing. I groped my way up the stairs again and into my bedroom where I gathered up some valuable papers and some money that we had in a dresser drawer. The smoke was now so dense that I had to lay almost flat on the floor and crawl like a snake in order to not suffocate. Every breath burned in my throat and for a minute I was lost and could not find the door. My head was spinning and I felt like fainting when a fireman grabbed my arm and told me to get out. I wanted to find my clothes as all I wore was my nightshirt and my pants. However, I got out on the street only carrying the handbag with our money and papers and I remember how cold the sidewalk and the street were for my bare feet.

The fire in the store was soon quenched by the firemen and after a while I was again able to enter our rooms and find our clothes and a blanket which I brought over to the drugstore to the ladies. It was impossible to go back and sleep in our apartment that night so we walked three blocks to the home of my sister Mae and woke them up. Mrs. Selander and Vendla were taken upstairs to their spare bedroom and Olga and I were bedded down on a couch in their front room. But sleep was out of the question for both of us. We were still coughing from the smoke and too excited from our adventure to go to sleep.

The fire never reached upstairs but the smoke penetrated the floorboards and our clothes and furniture smelled from smoke all that winter. Nothing was spoiled however and we were fortunate that none of us caught pneumonia after being exposed to all the smoke and after being chilled on the cold street.

67
I Became "Daddy"

It is a great event in any man's life when he becomes a father. I will never forget how proud I felt when I first saw my first born son, Alvin. A week before his birth we had been smoked out from our apartment on a cold November night and it was a miracle that my wife did not get pneumonia from exposure and smoke that night.

We had prepared for the coming of the baby a long time. We hired a good girl, Vendla Norgard, several weeks earlier as I did not want to leave my wife alone at any time, and as I was working nights at the Dunwoody mine, two miles outside of the city of Chisholm, it would be difficult to call me on short notice.

In the evening on December 4th when I left home for work, Olga felt as good as usual. Later in the evening, however, she became ill and Vendla called the doctor, E.S. Nelson, and also asked a neighbor lady Mrs. Twah, to come to our apartment. Everything went naturally and just before midnight our 9 pound baby was born. The doctor did not think it was necessary to send for me as everything went perfectly at the birth.

I was on my way home the next morning when I met a neighbor, Claus Johnson, who was coming to work. When we met he grasped my hand and congratulated me for being a "daddy". I hurried home and met Vendla on the stairway. She shouted, "We have a baby boy, John!" She evidently thought she was breaking the news for me, but I told her that I already knew it. Olga met me with a great smile and I am sure she was just as proud as I was, if not more so. She was a mother for the first time and we were both so happy that everything had turned out so well. I sat by her bed for a long time holding her hand and we both looked at our first born baby, who slept beside her.

I did not sleep much that day. I guess I was too happy to sleep. In the afternoon I went out and bought a box of cigars and distributed them among my friends and fellow workers at the mine. "How lucky can a guy be?" shouted my fellow worker Billy Johnson. "I have five girls and I would give my right arm for a baby boy. But I am going to have a boy yet", he said. I also met a doctor Gautcher from Hibbing, whom I knew when we both took violin lessons there. When he received his cigar he said, "How in the hell did you do it, John? I have been married twelve years and we have no baby yet." This was just a couple of the compliments given to me from envious friends in Hibbing and Chisholm.

Alvin grew up robust and healthy and has always been a pride for Olga and I. We managed to give him a high school education even though we lived forty miles from the nearest high school at the time he finished grade school. After he became old enough to support himself, he has helped his parents in many ways, and has proved to be a son that we have always been proud of.

1914 - On the farm with son Alvin, sister Ester and father Per.
John Ostlund collection

68
Mining Life Ends with a Close Call

Olga and I had been planning all summer to leave town and the dangerous work in the mines and move out on our homestead. Accordingly, when the job shut down, we packed and crated our furniture and shipped everything to Gheen. A few days were spent saying goodbye to our many friends in Chisholm and Hibbing, and on December 20th, a few days before Christmas, we arrived in Gheen with the intention to make our future home there on the farm.

The community was just growing out of the brush those days. The Willow River road was just built westward from the depot at Gheen. A small depot had replaced the old boxcar that for several years had served as a combination depot and freight room. The settlers were few and far between. Their means of transportation and power were oxen. Nearly every settler had an ox, those that were better situated owned two. The principal activities in the community were logging in the winter, land clearing and haying on the wild meadows in the summer.

This was pioneer life, and it seems peculiar now that it could appeal to me like it did. I enjoyed the break of every day and I rejoiced to be my own boss and hew my home out of the wilderness. The fresh, crisp air made me feel strong and vigorous as never before. And here I had everything that I loved in life. Here was my dear wife, little Alvin and my old father, and we were free and together.

A new road was under construction, which would pass along the west side of three of my forties. It had been partly graded in the fall. On Christmas Eve, William and I drove down to Gheen after my furniture, which had just arrived. We hauled it out along the new road, and it was the first load ever taken over that road.

Christmas Day found me and Olga busy unpacking everything and putting our house to order. It was the third Christmas Day I had spent in succession at Gheen, but the last two I had been all alone.

William was taking out considerable pulpwood that winter and had several men working for him. We made an agreement that Olga should do the cooking for the crew in exchange for our board and room, and we stayed there all winter. I was cutting some spruce on my land and besides I built a small barn and other outbuildings on my place.

I had bought a cow from a neighbor, A.W. Erikson, for which I paid $50.00 and which we kept in William's barn while living with him. Around March 15th, we moved home. However, by this time I realized that I had to go back for another seasons work on the range. I had paid for my land, but there were so many things that I needed to get a start in farming, and those things had to be bought. Leaving my family, and my brother-in-law, Ed Flank, there to help them, I left the first week in April and resumed my work in the Dunwoody mine.

I roomed with my sister Mae on Walnut Street, but boarded at Swan Anderson's boardinghouse that spring of 1915. Later, when Olga had planted the garden, she left the cow in care of William Carlson and came to Chisholm. We rented a couple of furnished rooms on Birch Street and set up light housekeeping.

We were getting down pretty deep in the Dunwoody pit by that time, and the inclines were steep and crooked. Several bad accidents happened that summer, and though I was lucky enough to avoid any serious mishap, I had a couple close calls and I resolved that if I could stick it out until we were through, it would be my last season in the mines. The company was finishing their contract and expected to get done early.

One dark night a car broke loose in the yard and came down the incline with a furious speed. I was with my train, loading at a steam shovel in the bottom of the pit, when I heard continuous warning signals from a locomotive a quarter of a mile away in the yard. Realizing that something was wrong someplace, I looked around and found that my engine was just over the switch to the mainline. I did not see any danger, but I felt that if something was loose on the mainline and coming down, I ought to be in the clear. I rung the bell and moved ahead. I had barely cleared the switch when a terrible crash behind me occurred. The runaway car had hit my tender, derailed and crashed against the bank, showering us with a cloud of dust. Fortunately, the car glanced sideways and did not do so much damage, but if I had been only half a minute slower in getting out of the way, it would have struck the cab and would no doubt have killed me instantly.

Later in the fall, one night I came into the pit with an empty train and went on a sidetrack to wait for the loading train to pull out. When my train came to a stop, I saw that the other train was loaded and the brakeman was giving the engineer the "high ball" or signal to go. The engineer answered the signal and opened her up. I saw the brakeman make an attempt to catch the first car, when he slipped and lost his handholds. He fell down between the wheels of the moving cars. I immediately reached for my whistle and hung on. But, before the engineer of the loaded train was able to stop, the entire train had passed over the brakeman, and when we pulled out the body it was mangled beyond description. The engineer, Paul Braden, a brother to the Master Mechanic, lost his nerve and quit his job right there, even though nobody could blame him for the accident. Another engineer had to be called to take the death train out. The memory of that mangled body disturbed my dreams for a long time afterwards.

Incidents like the ones related above strengthened my desire to quit the mining life. Perhaps that next time it would be my body that would be carried out. On the third of October the last trainload was taken to the dumps and the contract was finished. I was the last locomotive engineer on the job, as I was retained to pull the steam shovels out. It was the 5th of October when I was through and left Dunwoody. Over the Duluth, Mesabi and Northern's tracks, I took the 104 to Hibbing, and when I had her safely tucked in the roundhouse, and turned over to the roundhouse crew, I heaved a great sigh of relief. My railroading days were over.

In a few days Olga, Alvin and I were on our way home again to where our cow and our garden were waiting for us.

Olga and John Ostlund with Walfred and (sister) Ester Stenborg.
John Ostlund collection

Part 7 -
"As Pioneer Settler"

It was the 8th of October 1915 when we returned to our little farmstead home in Gheen. The frost had bleached the leaves of the poplars, the maples were glowing red, and the forest looked more beautiful than I ever seen it before.

Our friend and neighbor, William Carlson, had left for a trip to Sweden, and would be gone all winter. Sister Ester had also returned to Sweden for a visit.

Fortunately, the frost had not done much damage to our garden crops. For several days we were busy digging potatoes, carrots, rutabagas and beets, and storing them away for winter in our cellar. Then I grubbed out a row of stumps and borrowed a team of horses and a plow. From early morning until dark we worked the ground, preparing for next years crop.

On January 1st 1916, my account book shows that I had $150.00 in cash, and while this would last no time in the city where we would have to buy everything, here it would go a long way. We had the cow to supply us with fresh milk and butter, we had a few chickens which furnished all the eggs we needed, and we had all the potatoes, vegetables and meat we needed for the winter. During the previous summer I had hired some of the neighbors to put up the hay on my meadows and there was enough winter feed for our cow.

With a neighbor, John Floodstrom, I took a contract to cut the pulpwood and logs on two forties owned by C.P. Keinmann of Minneapolis. This occupied me for about six weeks. Then I cut some of my own pulpwood and A.P. Olson hauled it out for me. In the spring I cut and sold one hundred cedar telephone poles for the new long distance telephone line, which was built that spring. These poles were 20 feet long with 6 inch top and I received $1.00 per pole delivered along the highway.

69
My First Deer

It was during the hunting season of 1915 that I shot my first deer. I had been hunting before several times with my neighbor Will Carlson, but he had always been the lucky hunter and my part of the hunt had been to help him carry home and butcher the game.

Olga and I had recently returned from Chisholm where we had spent the summer. William Carlson had left for a trip to Sweden, and we were busy getting ready for winter on our little farm. I had borrowed a team from Leopold Berg and was plowing a recently cleared patch for a garden, when my brother Peter and my friend Carl J. Nordmark arrived. They were going to hunt deer. I wanted to finish plowing and did not accompany them during the first days of the season. The game was scarce and they came home disgusted every evening.

One morning a light snow covered the ground and I decided to go out hunting with the boys. We parted near Carlson's clearing and I walked east towards the highway. For almost two miles I did not see a deer track and I was just ready to return home when I came across a fresh track in the snow. A deer had been there just a few minutes ago. I followed the track as fast as I could without making much noise and I saw where the deer had stopped several times and looked back. Evidently it knew that somebody was following it. The animal was heading towards home and I was hoping that one of my companions would meet it. In a thick cedar grove I suddenly saw the head of a deer looking at me. I cautiously raised my rifle and shot and the head disappeared. When I reached the place where it had been standing, I saw blood stains on the snow and I knew that my bullet had hit it. Further on, it's track was sprayed with blood and soon I came up to where my deer was laying dead. My bullet had passed through the neck and cut the jugular vein. It had already been bled.

From the place where the deer was laying I could see a glimpse of William's clearing and I dragged it there. I had Berg's team in Carlson's barn so went over and hitched it up to a dray and before dinner I had it home and butchered. It was a large doe. I sure had the laugh on my brother Pete and Nordmark when they came for dinner and saw my butchered deer.

A few days later Pete was lucky and shot a young deer buck on the hill north of the river. Nordmark then gave up hope and returned to his home in Chisholm. We had plenty of venison that winter as we kept it frozen until we needed it. It was my first deer but many have fallen from my bullets since.

70
On a Moose Hunt

It was a bright Sunday morning in November 1915. I had just recently returned to my home in Gheen after spending the summer working, running a locomotive for the Winston Dear Stripping Company in the Dunwoody Mine in Chisholm.

We were just sitting down for dinner when our neighbor Gust Johnson appeared at the door. He was almost out of breath from running, but told me to get my rifle and follow him at once. He said we were going to try and head off a family of four moose which were coming through the swamp west of Carlson's land.

We were soon on our way, traveling as fast as we could, to Carlson's and then cut out towards the peat bog. While we were on our way, Gust told me that he, in company with John Floodstrom and Leopold Berg, had found the tracks of the moose near the old log dam, about a mile west of my place. The animals had just passed and the other hunters were following the tracks while Gust had run ahead to get me and we would try to intercept the moose. At the place where he expected us to meet up with our game, the swamp is narrowing between two hills and there is a little island of high ground in the center of the bog. This constitutes an ideal place to hide and watch the open swamp in all directions.

We reached the island and no fresh tracks were visible in the new snow covering the ground. Gust stopped and told me to run to the other side and stay behind some cover while watching. I had stood there behind a bushy balsam tree for perhaps 10 minutes when I heard Gust fire six shots in succession. Thinking the moose had come across where he was standing, I left my hiding place and ran out in the swamp where I thought that perhaps I would get a glimpse of the fleeing animals. Nothing moved and coming back to where I had left Gust, I saw him standing there looking at his gun. He told me that a large deer buck had come up within 20 rods from him and he had emptied his gun at the deer without hitting him.

While we were talking we suddenly heard four shots from farther up the swamp where the deer had disappeared and from where we expected the moose to come. We walked over and soon met Floodstrom and Berg, both looking just as confused as Gust had looked when I reached him. They had met the same deer on the trail and each of them had shot two shots at it while the deer was standing still and looking at them. Then he had walked off and not a drop of blood was visible in his tracks. No less than ten bullets had been aimed at that deer and none drew blood even.

We returned to the swamp and followed the moose tracks. The four animals, one bull, one cow and two calves, had walked only a short distance from where I had stood on the west side of the island. If I had remained there I would have had a fine opportunity to drop at least one of them.

We all felt rather dejected when we returned home. Nobody said anything for a long time. Finally, Gust spoke, "Believe me boys, that was no real deer. That must have been the devil himself."

71
Farming with Oxen

Family of three at home in Gheen - 1914.

John Ostlund collection

We had recently moved up on our land in the spring of 1916 when I joined my neighbor William Carlson in the purchase of a team of draft oxen. We bought them from Peter Leander who lived south of Cook, and I drove them home, a distance of 20 miles. It took us almost a full day as those animals are very slow walkers. We named them Bill and Tom and by a drawing lot, I got Tom while William got Bill. Whenever we had any heavy loads we put the team together, but light work was done with one ox.

Many stories could be related about those animals' stubbornness and mischief and I am sure that I learned to use more cuss words in driving the oxen those years than I have used since. Also, I think that many of my grey hairs appeared at that time.

We were harvesting hay on the meadows by the river and I had been mowing with my new mower and the oxen all forenoon. The heat from the sun and the myriads of flies made the oxen almost impossible to handle. Suddenly they took the bits between their teeth and plunged into the river with me sitting on the mower. To hold them back was impossible and they did not stop before the water reached over their backs. I tried to turn them around but they ignored my shouts or the stout whip. So I had to get down and unhitch the togs and lead the oxen out one at a time and tie them to some trees. Then I had to walk home to get a long chain and an evener so I was able to pull the mower out of the river. If I had been as hot tempered as some men I have known, I might have killed the stubborn beasts.

A few days later my wife was driving one of the oxen hitched to the rake and was raking the dry hay into windrows, while I was busy shucking it. The other ox was tied to a tree in the shade. Suddenly the ox laid down and I heard my wife shout. I went over there and we tried every trick we could think of to get the ox up but it was impossible. In spite of whippings and kicks he just laid there chewing his cuds. I unhitched the rake and went to get the other ox to finish the raking. When I reached the place where I had tied him, he was gone and only a piece of rope was left. I searched the surrounding area but did not find the ox, so had to return to the meadow. A neighbor by the name of Alex Martin happened to come by and I told him of our predicament. He went into the woods and gathered a handful of birchbark which he placed under the tail of the resting animal and...lit it. The ox jumped up in a hurry. We hitched him up to the rake and finished the work.

I did not find the other ox until the next day. His harness was all torn to pieces and only the hames were left.

The oxen were economical as they did not require any grain in their feed, like horses do, but it was a happy day when I was able to buy a team of horses to do my farm work with. The oxen were butchered and I sold the beef to the logging camps.

72
A Great Fish Story

The suckers were spawning in Elbow River, east of Gheen and my neighbor William Carlson suggested that we go out there and see if we could catch some of the fish. This was in the spring of 1917. The road east from the townsite of Gheen was just an old tote road and our only means of transportation were our oxen.

It took us fully three hours to drive the five miles from my home to the falls in the river. When we finally reached there, an impressive sight met us. The river below the falls was practically alive with fish, glistening like silver in the sunshine in their efforts to climb the surging water. More and more fish constantly arrived and here they were literally packed like sardines between the rocks in the river.

We unhitched our oxen and fed them beside a large cedar tree and ate some sandwiches before we attempted to catch any fish. With a gunny sack each we went out on some rocks. Reaching down into the water we could grab a fish with our hands and toss it into the sack. When we had each caught a number of them, we realized that we could improve on our fishing method by putting a small stone in the bottom of the burlap sack and sink it down some deep hole. In a few minutes the fish crowded into the sack and we could lift it out with all the fish we could carry. Thus we carried fish between the river and our wagon where we emptied one sack after another.

After a while, we built a fire, cleaned and fried some fish and cooked coffee. We rested and smoked our pipes and gloated over our fish in the wagon box. Never had any of us seen and caught so many fish before in our lives. We wondered what our wives would say when we returned home with our catch. We resumed our fishing and soon the wagon was full of suckers with some pickerels here and there among them. Then we hitched up our oxen to the wagon and started for home. The load was so heavy that it was all our strong oxen could pull and the wheel rims cut deep furrows in the soft roadbed. When we came to a settler's cabin beside the road, we stopped and gave them a dishpan full of fish. This was repeated at several places and it lightened our load somewhat.

When we arrived home and our wives saw the fish, they were two very surprised women! They had never seen anything like it, but were of course as happy as Bill and I were over our success.

For two days we cleaned and salted down fish in tubs, in boxes and in barrels. We ate fish three times a day at first, then once a day until we became so sick and tired of fish that we could not even stand the smell of it. Most of it spoiled and we had to bury it. We realized that we had been too hoggish in catching more fish than we needed, and it was the last time we ever attempted any similar stunt. But, it was an experience and great fun while it lasted.

73
Smuggling Venison

It was October 3rd 1917 that our son Victor was born. Olga was in Hibbing and I was alone at home as little Alvin was staying with our neighbors William Carlson's. It had snowed during the night and tracking was good, so I took my rifle and went out to look for game.

I crossed the river and looking up the road I saw a deer who stood in the road about a half a mile away. I realized that it would be an impossible shot, but decided to try it. I laid down and aimed a little above the animal as it did not look larger than a fly in my sight. I shot and it disappeared. I took my time walking up the road, as I did not expect that my bullet would have hit it. When I reached the place, I was surprised to see it laying by the side of the road. My bullet had pierced the deer's heart and he was dead. This was the luckiest shot I have fired in my life. It was a young deer buck.

A few days later I went to Hibbing to bring my wife and our baby boy home and I took a chunk of venison along for my sister and brother-in-law, Walfred Stenborg, where Olga was staying. I took the morning train from Gheen to Virginia. When I stepped off the train in Virginia I noticed a stranger on the platform who looked hard at me and my pack. When I walked up the street he followed me. After walking a couple of blocks, I met an old friend and stopped and talked with him. The stranger passed us and stopped half a block away and stood watching us. My friend remarked, "There is George Woods, the sharpest game warden in Minnesota. If you have venison in your packsack, he has smelled it." I ducked down the alley and ran around the block where I saw a garbage can. It was empty and I deposited my packsack in it and ran another block and back to the main street. I did not see the game warden and went into a restaurant across the street where I sat down at a table and ordered coffee. From where I sat I had a good view of the street and soon I saw the warden come out from the side street where I had left my pack. He stood on the corner looking around and after a while he walked up to the bus station and entered it.

When I had finished my lunch, I walked back to the garbage can, retrieved my packsack and walked about ten blocks to the north side of the city, from where I took the bus to Hibbing. If he had caught me with the venison in my pack, I am sure I would have paid a stiff fine as I had shot the deer out of season. I was scared all the way to Hibbing and it was quite a relief when I reached my sister's place without being held up by any game warden.

74
Building My Home

Every young man and woman, when they reach maturity, are I am sure dreaming about a home of their own. I was no exception. When I first saw the place where my home is now, it was wilderness, but I loved it. It was in the summer of 1904 when on a casual trip through the territory that I happened to walk by the little log cabin which then was the home of Seth Nichols, a civil war veteran.

Six years later I bought the 160 acres with the log cabin on it. I paid $900.00 for the land which also included the mineral rights.

In 1911, I built another log cabin on my land on the south eighty. I now owned my own home, but it was not going to be permanent. In the fall of 1914 my wife and I, with our little son, Alvin, moved into the two small rooms. For my old father who also stayed with us, we built a little room upstairs.

Then in the fall of 1916 I sold the south eighty with our home to Hans Paulson for the amount of $2,000.00. With this money we were going to build a substantial home on the north eighty acres. The place was already selected.

John's father by Civil War Veteran, Seth Nichol's old log cabin.

John Ostlund collection

It should be built where the first log cabin still stood, but Mr. Nichols had been unable to find water there, and my first concern was good water. William indicated where a strong vein of water crossed the hill, and I dug down eight feet, drove a point down another ten feet, and I struck plenty of water. The next morning the water stood five feet high in the pipe. This was a great load off my mind. I drew plans for a living house, barn and outbuildings and cleared the land where the buildings were to be built.

In the spring of 1918 I had all the lumber needed ready on the place, all grown on my land and all cut by myself but sawed at the local sawmill owned by August Grund. I laid the foundation myself, 24 x 28 feet. I planned the rooms and made the blueprints myself. I hired a good carpenter, Charles Martinson from Bear River. He came, looked over the foundation and studied my blueprints and approved everything.

After haying we commenced building and I worked every day as his helper. In less than a month we had the roof on, the chimney finished, and we were ready for plastering the walls. My brother-in-law, Walfred Stenborg, was a plasterer and he came up and did the work. The carpenter did not like that Stenborg did the plastering, and refused to come back and finish the inside work so I was able to find another carpenter, Peter Guzman.

The new residence of John and Olga Ostlund and their growing family - 1922.
John Ostlund collection

A few days before Thanksgiving we moved into our new home. What a wonderful feeling to move into a new building, made substantially by myself according to my own plans, and best of all, there were no incumbrances against it. It was all paid for, and all mine.

The original foundation was heavy cedar posts, but I built a concrete basement under the house in 1929.

These remarks would not be complete unless I mention the cost of our home. Doors, windows, nails, shingles, plaster, cement, lime, brick and other supplies purchased amounted to $382.00. If I figure the lumber at $20.00 per thousand feet, it would add $450.00, planing $125.00, carpenters wages $220.00, paint and miscellaneous items $175.00. This made the total cost of the house at that time $1,352.00 beside my own labor. As I worked with the carpenters a total of 68 days at approximately $3.00 per day, it would add another $200.00.

The cost of the concrete basement later was $150.00 of which $82.60 was for supplies purchased.

1922 - The new house.

John Ostlund collection

214

75
Farmers Logging Company

Logging in northern Minnesota.

John Ostlund collection

The war in Europe 1917 boosted the price on forest products and there was a steady demand for railroad ties and pulpwood. Near my home, several timber tracts were for sale but the owners did not live on their land. They had homesteaded, proved up and left long ago. My neighbor, William Carlson, had received a letter from one of those landowners, Fred Schultz, who lived in Hutchinson, Minnesota and he had offered his land consisting of 160 acres for sale, as he was in need of money. William came to my home and asked me if I would join him in buying the land. We walked over it estimating the amount of timber on it, and it was considerably more than we had expected. Talking it over, we decided to take our neighbor, August Grund, and a friend, William Brown, with us in the logging enterprise and they joined us.

William Carlson took the train to Hutchinson and bought the 160 acre tract for $500.00. We did not buy the land itself, just the timber that was on it, and we had two years time to take the timber off, after which the land would revert back to the owner. We organized ourselves as "Farmers Logging Company" with Carlson as president, and I as secretary and treasurer. We hired several men to cut pulpwood and I made a trip to Bear River where I hired two teams with drivers to do the hauling. Besides, we also worked ourselves. On one corner of the land was a grove of Jack Pine which was made into railroad ties.

During the two years we made a net profit of $2,976.92 on our logging operations, besides what we had earned ourselves by our own work. This amounted to $744.23 for each of us, which was a lot of money in those early days, and a good investment on our start fund. We dissolved the company when Brown left the community and Grund did not care for logging anymore as he was getting up in age.

Carlson and I bought three forties in Section 3, originally owned by a Mrs. Mary Baker. Here we had to buy the land in order to get the timber on it, and we paid $1,200.00 for it. We hired four cutters and two teams, beside ourselves. When we had logged off the land we advertised it for sale in a Minneapolis paper and were fortunate to find two buyers almost immediately. We sold one forty to Gust R. Parson and two forties to John Newman, both from Minneapolis. This was in October 1920 and when we summed up our books we had cleared a net profit on this deal of $2,000.00, or $1,00.00 each. The prices on forest products had declined and while we could have purchased other timber tracts farther away from our homes, we decided to concentrate on improving our farms with the money we had made in logging. Farmers Logging Company of Gheen, Minnesota was dissolved for good.

John Ostlund plowing with horses.
John Ostlund photo collection

I purchased my first team of horses in June of 1921. I bought them from a neighbor, Magnus Peterson, and I paid $150.00 for them, or $75.00 each. I was getting quite disgusted with my oxen and felt that it would be a relief to drive horses instead. A few weeks later I bought a light buggy from F.H. Hill, near Cook, for which I paid $20.00. Now I could ride to town like a gentleman.

76
A Fishing Experience

My brother Peter came to our home for a visit in the summer of 1922, and one day we decided to go on a fishing trip to Pelican Lake. We hitched the horse to the buggy and drove to Alfred Gabrielson's farm where we left the horse and walked down to Sanders Bay on the lake. There we found a boat, but the oars were hidden in the woods and we were unable to find them. However, we found an old canoe paddle and from a piece of board, we hewed out something resembling an oar, and it had to serve as such in the emergency.

Getting out on the lake we got our spoon hooks out and soon we pulled in a nice pickerel. The fish were biting good, and for an hour we were quite busy pulling them in. It was great fun and we did not notice that the sky had clouded up and big raindrops began to fall. Suddenly a strong wind burst hit us and almost upset our boat. Peter was rowing and in his efforts to turn the boat against the wind, he broke the paddle. We were quite far from land and the storm was carrying us out towards the open lake. We had to get to the nearest land and our only means to propel the boat was our makeshift oar.

The waves were building up and they splashed into our boat, so I was kept busy bailing the water out with my hat while Peter wrestled with the storm, trying desperately to paddle to land. We lost our fishing gear and all of the fish. For fully an hour we battled the waves and the wind until we finally got behind an island where the wind could not hit us so strong. We reached the shore, almost totally exhausted and dragged the boat up where the waves could not reach it, then sat down for a long rest under a tree. We were both soaked to the skin and we soon were chilled, so we had to move to keep warm. I heard Peter shout and whistle. I answered and walked over to where he was and found him standing in the doorway of a snug little cabin built in a little opening in the center of the island. It sure was a welcome sight as now the rain was coming down in earnest. We found matches and dry kindling and built a roaring fire, dried our wet clothes and ate some sandwiches we had left. The wind was whistling outside and the rain pattered on our roof but we were quite comfortable. We were certainly fortunate to find this little shelter.

Our only concern was that they probably were worried for us at home and at Gabrielson's. While we had told them that we would probably stay overnight, the sudden outburst of weather might scare them. However, we would not risk our lives trying to cross to the mainland during this storm and without oars for our boat. Here we were quite comfortable and we slept undisturbed until daybreak. We found a board in the cabin and were able to hew out another oar and when the wind calmed down we rowed back to where we had found the boat. At Gabrielson's they were planning to send some men out to search for us.

We did not bring home any fish this time, but we were glad that we were alive after this adventure.

77
I Killed a Brown Bear

Early one morning in June 1923 on my way to the barn, I saw a large brown animal with my calves in their enclosure behind the barn. It was the first time that I saw a wild bear. He had his attention set on the calves and did not notice me. I returned immediately to the house for my rifle and loaded it. When I came in sight of the bear again he was just getting ready to attack one of my calves. When I shot and the bullet struck him, he leaped over the fence and made for the nearest woods. Just as he reached the timberline I shot again and this time I hit the bear in the head. He stood up on his hind legs, made a sweep with his forelegs and fell over backward dead.

My first bullet had hit him in the neck and the second struck him behind the ear. He was a big brute, a male fully six feet long and weighed about 400 pounds. As it was the first bear I had seen wild and was able to kill, I felt pretty proud over my feat. I called up my neighbors and told them about it, and they came over to see it. Usually, the bears in northern Minnesota are the black bears and none of my neighbors had seen a brown bear before in this part of the country. In fact, this bear resembled a grizzly bear, even to the size of it.

With the help of my neighbor, William Carlson, we butchered the bear and I distributed the meat among several of the neighbors. It was very dark and did not taste as good as we had expected. It had a strong taste and nobody in my family cared for the steaks. We buried most of it in the ground.

I did not know at the time that the bears were protected by law in Minnesota. The news that I had killed a bear on my farm leaked out and finally reached the game warden, James Beatty, in Cook. One day I met Mr. Beatty on the street in Cook. He called me aside and told me that it had been reported to him that I had killed a bear. When I readily admitted it, he asked me if I knew that I had been breaking the law. I told him that I thought I had a perfect right to protect my property, as if I had not killed the marauder, he would have killed one of my calves. He was very nice about it and said that he would have done the same under my circumstances. He told me to go home and clean up around my place in case he would be forced to come up for an investigation. So, I buried the hide in the woods. The game warden never came around in search for bear and I never heard any more from Mr. Beatty. He was a very kind and reasonable game warden and never prosecuted any settlers unless he was forced to do it.

1919 - The new barn, the cattle, sons Victor and Al.

John Ostlund collection

78
Driving School Bus

There were no prospects for logging during the winter of 1923 and I put in a bid for transporting the children to school. This was the first year the County School Board called for bids for transportation. The previous winter, Mrs. Nels Holmer had asked for it and she had been awarded some compensation for transporting her own children to school, but all other children had to walk.

My bid for $2.40 per day had been accepted and I received a contract specified at $48.00 per month for the nine months school term. A few weeks before school was to commence, I purchased a second hand Ford Touring car from Mr. Louis Sullivan in Hibbing. The car was only slightly used, but he was leaving the city and advertised his car for sale. I had never operated a motor car before, but after a little instruction from Sullivan, I drove it home. I now drove the car a little every day and soon became used to the controls.

When school started I had seven children to transport, but they were all young and had plenty of room in the Ford. There were two girls and five boys. They were Jack and Robert Parson, a girl whose name I have forgotten, who stayed at Parson's that winter, Evelyn and Reinhold Holmer and my two boys, Alvin and Victor. Robert and Victor were beginners in school that year of 1923.

After Christmas the snow became so deep that we could not use the car. No snow plows were in use and often the roads were impassable. Now I rigged up a large sled, building a canvas covered top on it and transported the children with this sled pulled by one horse. When it turned real cold, we heated bricks and wrapped them in a blanket, and the children could keep their feet warm on the hot bricks in my canvas enclosed vehicle. We got along fine and I never missed a day during the entire winter. When the snow melted or when the snowplow opened the road, I used the car. When school ended in the spring, I had earned over $400.00, which was a lot of money in those years.

In my spare time, I also trapped beavers that winter. I had applied for and received a special trapping permit for trapping in Willow river. The beavers were condemned because every spring their dams flooded the road and the meadows on which we were harvesting our hay. We had sent petitions to the State Game and Fish department and when the game warden investigated, he offered me the first chance to do the trapping. I did not know the first thing about beaver trapping, but I learned by several mistakes, and before spring I had trapped nine animals, and for their pelts I received $120.00.

It was not a bad winter for us when I could be home all winter and be my own boss. We had four cows and shipped a can of cream every week to a Duluth Creamery. We were all healthy and enjoyed life on our little farm in the woods.

School at Gheen, Minnesota - 1922

John Ostlund collection

PART 8 -
"Life on the Farm"

1923 - Olga and her prize canning.

John Ostlund collection

As pioneer settlers in a new, unbroken timber district, our principal means of livelihood had been the logging operations. Now in the year of 1924, the timber was getting scarcer, especially the pine and the spruce, which at the time was considered the only valuable forest products. There was still a lot of poplar and balsam, but this was generally considered worthless for commercial purposes, and was cut only for firewood or for building purposes on the farm.

Our next chapter would be farm life and we tried to wrest a living out of the new soil. During this period, the world wide depression set in and for several years we could not sell our products to any advantage. But, we lived through it and we never went without a square meal.

Victor and his prize calf.

John Ostlund collection

Alvin and his prize heifer, "Linda".

John Ostlund collection

79
Friends in Need are Friends Indeed

We made good on the farm during the year 1925 with good returns from our cows, and cream was the highest that I can remember. A 5 gallon can averaged $8.00 during the late summer and fall. We sold forty bushels of potatoes to Mr. Fogelberg of Tower and received $1.20 per bushel.

However, we had a little bad luck in November 1925. I had been butchering a hog one afternoon and had heated the scalding water on the big box stove in the poultry house. When we went to the barn to do the milking, the chicken house was on fire. Sparks must have penetrated the chimney and ignited the back wall, and when we noticed the fire, it was too late to save anything. Our chickens were all suffocated from smoke and within a few minutes from the time we saw the fire the whole building was ablaze. The only thing we could do was to try and save the barn only thirty feet away. The wind was from the northwest and whipped the flames right over the barn. Fortunately, several inches of snow had fallen the day before and that helped to save it.

While mother, Alvin and I were fighting the flames, Victor summoned help over the phone. He was only eight years old at that time. Soon the neighbors arrived and helped us keep the barn walls wet. We soon had the fire under control and the only thing we could do was to watch it burn itself out. I had stored 1,200 feet of dry, planed lumber in the loft of the coop, and this made a very hot fire. However, we considered ourselves very lucky that we were able to save the stable and the cow barn as well as our winter supply of hay. We did not have any insurance protection on any of our buildings and this fire taught us the lesson to always have our property insured for fire.

A few days after the fire we were pleasantly surprised to receive about twenty chickens from our neighbors. They were of all colors, breeds and sizes, but they were a welcome gift to us at that time. "Friends in need are friends indeed."

1923 - The first poultry house. It burnt in 1924.

John Ostlund collection

80
Taking the Farm Census

In the fall of 1924 I was approached by the District Manager of the government census department, and offered the job of census taker in the north end of St. Louis County which comprised no less than 58 townships. He left a long questionnaire, similar to a civil service questionnaire, with me to fill out and send in to him. His office was in Bemidji, Minnesota. When the questionnaire was approved, I received further instructions and the supplies.

I was to begin on November 10th. I was to use my own car and visit all inhabitable farms and also secure information from neighbors of farms who were uninhabitable and left idle. For every blank filled I was to receive 50 cents but I had to furnish my own transportation and pay for my own meals wherever I was. Every weekend I was instructed to send in my report of the week's work to the District Manager.

I commenced in Township 63-19, which was the south east corner of my territory, and covered the farms around Haley, then the farms east of Gheen. Then I covered my own town of Willow Valley and the unorganized towns of 63-21, 64-21 and 65-21. Then the town of Leiding which comprised four townships. From Orr I worked north through Cusson, Kinmont, Ash Lake and to Kabetogama Lake. The first two weeks I managed to drive home every evening, but from Kabetogama it was too far and the first night I was away from home I lodged at the home of William Fors on the western end of Lake Kabetogama.

When I had finished and visited every farm to the Koochiching County line, I came home and with the Census Manager's permission I took a couple weeks off for Christmas at home. I had some butchering to do at home, and had the bad luck to lose my chicken house from fire and also lose all of our chickens.

After Christmas I left my Ford home and rode with the mailman to Buyck where I made arrangements to stay and board at the home of Mrs. Hanson, who lived on a farm about a mile north of Buyck. She had three sons who were grown up and I made arrangements with them that they should take me out in the morning with their car, and I would walk back while taking census of the farms along the route. Thus, one day they took me to Vermillion Dam, the south edge of my territory and during the day I covered the territory back to their home. The next day I covered the farms west of Vermillion river and then the next day the territory north. Then I rode with the mailman to Crane Lake. The mailman was John Handberg and he offered me to stay at his new home, which I gladly accepted. So, for three days I walked on the ice covered lake, visiting settlers living around the big lake. They were not really farmers, but my instruction was to list every piece of cultivated land that comprised one acre or more, and even if it lacked in a whole acre, I put it in as it meant another half dollar to me.

In all it took me nine weeks to complete my job, and it was interesting because I met many people and all sorts of people. In the town of Portage, around Myrtle Lake, I wished that I could have talked the Finnish language, as often I came to a place where only the woman was home and she seemed to have difficulty in understanding me and I in understanding her. But it generally worked out when I was able to obtain information from a neighbor.

I earned about $300.00 from my job as Census taker.

1923 - The Farmer's Club Hall in Gheen, Minnesota.
John Ostlund Collection

1926 - Olga and John with their children (left to right) Alvin, Victor, Elsie and Mabel.

John Ostlund collection

81
Mingling with Society

In 1926 I served as a Director in the St. Louis County Club and
Farm Bureau Association, a county wide organization which comprised
Commercial clubs, Farmer's organizations and Civic and Women's Clubs.
The Board of Directors consisted of nine persons of which three were
elected by Civic or Commercial Clubs, three were farmers and three were
women. These nine members then elected and hired a secretary who
at that time received a salary of $50.00 per month for his services. The
members of the Board donated their services and received only traveling
expenses to and from the monthly meetings generally held at different
places in the county of St. Louis.

The June meeting that year was held at Tower, and an invitation
was extended to wives or husbands of Board members to attend and
to partake of an outing on Lake Vermillion. The following Directors
and their mates met at noon at the railroad depot where director G.C.
Carlson was agent: Mr. and Mrs. Al Dyer and son of Hibbing, Mr. and
Mrs. Willard Spring of Duluth, Mr. and Mrs. M.C. Fransisco of Saginaw,
Mr. and Mrs. Louis Christenson of Duluth, Mr. and Mrs. B.C. Erikson
of Duluth, Mr. James Moonan of Ely, Mr. and Mrs M.B. Elson of
Gilbert, our secretary and myself, my wife and daughter Elsie.

After dinner at the hotel we all boarded a large gasoline launch for a trip
up the lake to the Grand View Lodge where accommodations had been
reserved over night for the entire party and where our regular meeting
was to be held. It was a beautiful afternoon and everyone felt happy and
gay. Mr. Spring was a born clown and entertainer and with his jokes
and stunts he kept us all laughing and in good spirits throughout the
afternoon. For a nature lover, nothing can be more inspiring than such
a boat ride as we had. The lake, with its 365 islands and its rugged shore
land and rocky points, is one of the most beautiful lakes in Minnesota.
We beached at several resorts during the afternoon and mingled with
wealthy tourists and resort owners. Towards evening we reached our
destination, where our launch was tied up for the night.

The tables were set and we immediately sat down to a delicious pike fish
supper, or dinner as they called it. After supper the directors met in the
adjoining ballroom. The meeting was brief and we had an opportunity to
admire a beautiful and wonderful sunset on the lake. It was late before we

retired for the night and Olga and Elsie and I received a nice private room in a cabin by the shore.

The next morning we were up early and I had a dip in the lake before the others of our party were awake. When they finally came out and had their swim we assembled for breakfast. At 11 o'clock we again boarded our launch and were taken to Birchpoint Inn, across the lake, an elaborate and exclusive summer resort. There we remained for dinner, or lunch. At the table next to ours a millionaire from Alabama was dining. In the afternoon we returned to Tower where we bid goodbye to the others, found our old Ford and returned home. The old farm looked good to us after two days spent in recreation and pleasure and mingling with society people.

On the family farm 1927.

John Ostlund collection

1927 - Taking a ride in the 1926 Model T Ford. Pictured from
left: Victor, Olga (mom), Mabel, Elsie and John (dad).
John Ostlund collection

John, Kenneth, and Oliver on the farm.
John Ostlund collection

82
The Farm Bureau Picnic

During my term as Director of the St. Louis County Club and Farm Bureau Association, I suggested at one meeting that we should follow the example of other Farm Bureaus in the state and arrange for a county wide picnic. My suggestion was accepted by the directors and I was appointed to head a committee of five to arrange for a picnic during the summer of 1927, somewhere in the north end of St. Louis County.

Beside me were appointed August Neubauer of Virginia, James Butchart of Chisholm, L.F. Luther of Cook and Joseph Bauers of Wilpin. Our first committee meeting was held in Mr. Luthey's office in Cook where I was appointed Chairman, James Butchart Vice Chairman, August Neubauer Secretary and Joe Bauers Treasurer. We held several meetings, considered invitations from several communities in regard to the place of the picnic, and finally decided that it would be held at Side Lake, north of Chisholm and the date was to be June 20th.

There were many things to consider in planning for a gathering of this kind, and as I was heading the committee, the responsibilities felt pretty heavy. I assigned the duties of the other committee members in order to divide the responsibilities. Butchart was in charge of the picnic grounds, to see that everything was in order and provide for ample parking area for automobiles. Luthey was placed in charge of the orchestra and the dance following the days picnic. Neubauer was ordered to send out invitations to all organizations affiliated with the County Club and Farm Bureau and Bauers was to supervise games and contests. Everything was well planned and the only thing worrying us was - the weather.

June 20th dawned with the most ideal weather we could wish for and hundreds of cars brought people from all parts of the county to the picnic grounds. An orchestra from Hibbing furnished music during the afternoon and also played for a well attended dance in the evening. Games and stunts were arranged and led by B.G. Leighton, recreational director of Hibbing schools. Several amateur baseball teams competed for the championship of northern St. Louis County and it was won by the Indians of Net Lake. A stage had been built and I had the privilege to introduce the speakers and participants in a two hour long program. Our principal speaker was J.H. Hays, Assistant Commissioner of Agriculture of the State of Minnesota, who came all the way from St. Paul. Beside him I called on the County Club Chairman, Al Dyer from Hibbing and the County Agricultural Agents.

Eleven farmers clubs and six commercial clubs were officially represented. The officers and directors of the County Club were all there and the crowd was estimated to be well over 500 persons. This was more than anybody had expected, as this was the first picnic of its kind in St. Louis County.

A few days after the picnic, I received a letter of congratulations from M.B. Elson, Secretary of the County Club and Farm Bureau. He asked me to send him a bill for all my expenses in connection of the picnic. This was rather a surprise to me as I had not expected any remuneration. To me it was remuneration enough that the picnic I had fostered and lead turned out such a decided success.

AWARD BUREAU PICNIC PRIZES

County Farm Bureau Gives Out List of Winners at Side Lake.

Virginia, Minn., July 4.—(Special to The Herald.)—The complete official list of winners of events at the county farm bureau picnic at Side lake has been given out by County Agent August Neubauer as follows:

Diamond ball, won by Brown School Community club from Lakeland Community club by score of 6 to 4.

Baseball game won by Cook from Pelican Lake by score of 11 to 1.

Horseshoe, men's — First, Mike Terska and Alex Watt, Linden Grove Community club; second, W. B. Thurman, M. A. Nichols, Buhl Civic association.

Tug-of-war, Lynwood Farmers' club from All Stars.

Rolling contest — First, Bobbie Parsons, Willow Valley Farmers' club; second, Norman Larson, Brooklyn; third, Jack Parsons, Willow Valley Farmers' club.

Zig-zag contest — First, Walter Beasy, Hibbing; second, Howard Nicholson, Hibbing; third, James McHardy, Hibbing.

Wheelbarrow race—First, Gus Parsons and John Gorenc, Willow Valley Farmers' club; second, Iver Erickson, Nonte Jarvi, Brown School Community club; third, Mike Terska and Toiva Annala, Linden Grove Community club.

Girls' race, 25 yards—First, Helen McKinnon, Brown School Community club; second, Ella Setter, Linden Grove Community club; third, Lillie Terska, Linden Grove Community club.

Girls' race, 50 yards—First, Ellen Grekela, North Hibbing; second, Anna Mattassich, Hibbing; third, Ellen Setter, Linden Grove Community club.

Boys' race, 25 yards—First, Bernard Dulong, Brown School Community club; second, Jack Parsons, Willow Valley Farmers' club; third, Donald Brown, Brown School Community club.

Boys' race, 50 yards—First, David Summers, Brown School Community club; second, Bernard Dulong, Brown School Community club; third, Herbert Lundberg, Willow Valley Farmers' club.

Fat man's race—First, George Pauley, Hibbing; second, H. W. Reik, Cook; third, Frank Wardas, Pelican Lake Farmers' club.

Married woman's race, fifty yards—First, Mrs. Bert Smith, Lynwood Farmers' club; second, Mrs. J. P. Clune, Bear River Farmers' club; third, Mrs. J. A. Withers, Willow Valley Farmers' club.

Newspaper race for women—First, Chloris McHardy, Hibbing; second, Mrs. A. Marvin, Lynwood Farmers' club; third, Ella Setter, Linden Grove Community club.

Horseshoe contest for women—First, Florence Lang, Virginia, and Mrs. Carl Munyer, Brown school; second, Mrs. Bert Smith, Lynwood Farmers' club, and Mrs. A. Marvin, Lynwood Farmers' club.

1927 Newspaper clipping of prizes awarded at the St. Louis County Farm Bureau Picnic.

Financial Statement of North End

Farm Bureau Picnic

Side Lake, June 25, 1927.

Receipts

Receipts from County Club & Farm Bureau.......$200.00

Expenses

Prizes for sports program.........$92.00

Playground equipment............... 4.75

Road signs to picnic.............. 10.00

Police duty....................... 15.00

Meals for speakers and orchestra... 3.00

Rental of dance hall.............. 8.00

Orchestra......................... 30.00

                    Total expenses..............$162.75

                    Balance......................$37.25

            Balance in bank.............$39.25

            Unpaid checks...............$ 2.00

            Net balance.................$37.25...$37.25

Committee on Picnic

John Ostlund, Gheen
L. F. Luthey, Cook
Harold Aase, Virginia
August Neubauer, Virginia
J. Butchart, Hibbing

1927 Expense sheet for the St. Louis County Farm Bureau Picnic
John Ostlund collection

83
Traveling as Organizer for I.O.G.T. Lodge

John Ostlund

G. C. T. SPEC. DEP.
SCANDINAVIAN GRAND LODGE OF MINN.
I. O. G. T.

TRAVELING REPRESENTATIVE
OF THE GRAND LODGE   GHEEN, MINN.

During my long life I have had many experiences and tried many trades and while it has been interesting, I have not become rich in any of the various jobs I have undertaken. When I, in the fall of 1927, received a letter from my old friend, August Brodin of Minneapolis, who then was Grand Chief Templar of the Minnesota Grand Lodge of I.O.G.T. requesting me to visit the Good Templar lodges in the northern part of the state and if possible, organize new lodges, I hesitated to accept, but after thinking it over and consulting with my wife, I decided to go out for a few weeks at least and see what I could do. As remuneration he offered me $3.00 per day and free expenses from the day I left home until I returned.

I left home on October 24th for Eveleth, where I knew many of the older members of the lodge. I first contacted the Lodge Deputy, Oscar Wirsen, and received a list of delinquent members who it was my mission to visit and try to encourage them to renewed efforts in the cause of temperance. I spent two days in Eveleth, attended their meeting and felt well satisfied with my work in its beginning.

From there I left for Virginia, where I spent a day with less success. The lodge was dying as most of its younger members had left the city. So I took the streetcar to Chisholm where 12 years earlier I had been a member of the lodge. That lodge had already sent in its charted and did not exist anymore and I soon found out that there was no hope for reorganization.

From there I went to Bemidji, where I spent three days and succeeded in signing up enough candidates for organizing, but we were unable to rent a hall for meetings. So I called some of the candidates to my room in the hotel and they promised to do what they could for a future organization. I returned to Hibbing to the lodge where I had been a member for many years, and where I knew nearly all of the members. Scouting around for two days I received several applications for membership. I attended their regular meeting, installed new officers and encouraged them the best I could. I visited the lodge in Meadowlands but did not stay for the meeting as I was told by the L.D. that they were doing as good as could be expected.

From Meadowlands I visited Alborn where prospects were good for a lodge. Then to Munger where I organized a new lodge with 13 members, all young men and women. From there I was directed to Superior, Wisconsin and from there to Two Harbors, where I succeeded in getting several delinquent members back to the organization. In Blackhoof I attended their lodge meeting with every member present, which was very encouraging to me, and they seemed to appreciate my visit.

On November 19th I arrived in Minneapolis and was warmly welcomed by the Grand Lodge executives who congratulated me on my efforts when they had heard my report. I stayed there a week trying to revive a lodge in St. Paul, but without success. Accompanied the G. Secretary to Grandy, Braham and Rushpoint and we organized a new lodge in Stanchfield.

I returned home on December 5th after more than six weeks of traveling. It was interesting and a vacation for me and perhaps something good had been accomplished for the cause of temperance.

84
Motoring Across the State

In the spring of 1929 I traded automobiles and got a practically new Ford, a Model "T", but with several extra improvements such as a high compression cylinder head, new manifold, a special steering wheel, "Ruxtell" gearshift, etc., all of which added considerably to the use and the value of the car.

Now that we had a good car, Olga and I decided to take a vacation for a few days and visit her brother, Edward Flank and his wife who lived in the little town of Mizpah, about a hundred miles to the west. When I also at that time had an invitation to attend the Grand Lodge convention of the I.O.G.T., which that year was to be held at Fertile, we decided to combine the two visits and while Olga and the girls visited in Mizpah, I was to continue to Fertile.

On June 17th, we left my sister Ester and the boys, Victor and Alvin in charge of the farm and drove to Bear River where we took Olga's uncle, Peter B. Flank, with us. He had relatives in Fertile which he wanted to visit and he would accompany me over there. We motored west along a recently opened highway to Effie. It was a very poor road at that time and for many miles the roadbed consisted of loose quicksand, but we had a good car and plowed through. From Effie we continued west to State road No. 61 which led north a couple of miles where we reached the intersection of Park Avenue, (a poor road with a swell name) which we followed to Northome and Mizpah.

We spent the night in my brother-in-law's nice home and the next morning Flank and I left for Bemidji. From there we drove west through Bagley, Foston, McIntosh and Erskine. At Maple Lake we turned south and reached Fertile in the afternoon.

Flank had a brother-in-law living a couple of miles south of the city and we drove out there. We were invited to stay with them during the convention. This was to be held at the Polk County recreational building, a very large hall at the Fairgrounds in Fertile. The first evening a big reception and welcome to the Good Templars was held and more than 2,000 persons filled the hall. The city band furnished music and the Men's choir sang several numbers between the various speeches.

At the meeting the next day I was honored by being elected Grand Superintendent of Legislative Work, the first time I had an opportunity to serve as an officer in the Grand Lodge. After the convention adjourned the second day we were all invited to a lawn party at the home of August Stephenson in the city.

June 21st we said goodbye to our hosts and left for home. In Mizpah we picked up Olga and the girls, left Pete Flank at his home in Bear River and reached our home in Gheen at 9 p.m. that same day. And, we never even had a flat tire on the whole trip!

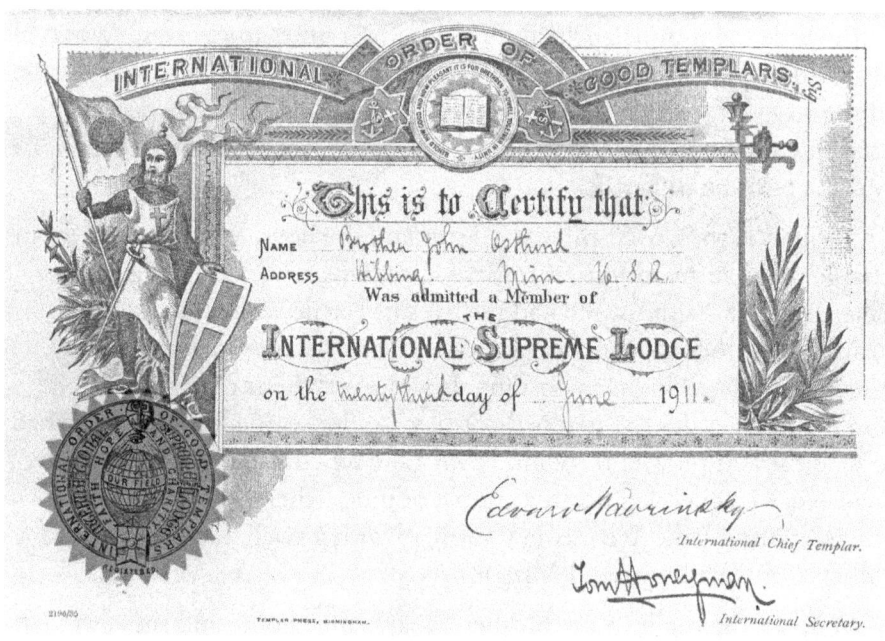

1911 - I.O.G.T. member certificate.

85
My First Plane Ride

In the summer of 1930 the city of Virginia had built an airport which was to be dedicated with many festivities to which owners of airplanes were invited from all over the state. My neighbor, Peter Olson, invited me to ride with him to Virginia and I accepted his offer.

We arrived in the city quite early and leaving our car at a parking place, we walked out to the airfield. Several planes had arrived and more were constantly arriving and landing. Outside the landing field were erected a long row of stands where hotdogs, coffee, balloons and other carnival equipment was sold, giving the impression of circus festivities and causing carnival spirit in the crowd.

At 11 o'clock all planes left the airport for an aerial parade over the city. There were more than thirty planes who flew in formation, circling the cities of Virginia, Eveleth and Mountain Iron and then returning to the airport. Then they had contests and various stunts in flying which was interesting to watch. There were several different kinds of planes, from the large enclosed Ford passenger plane to small cub planes.

After dinner it was announced that some of the planes would take passengers aloft and tickets were sold at the price of $5.00 for a 15 minute ride with any of the planes. When I saw Pete Olson buy a ticket, I decided to also take a ride. My old friend P.S. Engman advised me to go up in an open plane as I would enjoy the ride more than if I took an enclosed one. So, when a small monoplane landed near me, I walked over with my ticket and was seated in the only seat behind the flyer. Before he gunned the motor he asked me if I had flown before. He told me to tighten the safety belt and to take my hat off. And he said that if I felt that I would be airsick, there was a can under my seat.

We took off and the ground seemed to sink away from under us. Soon we were quite high and I saw the city and the surrounding lakes below us. The water had a dark blue color from up there, they looked almost like ink pools. The pilot was talking to me through a tube which opened as a mouthpiece at my right. When we were at 1500 feet over the ground he asked me if I cared to go higher. I told him that I thought we were high enough. He shut off the motor and we glided almost noiselessly through the air. All around us, other planes were circling at about the same altitude. It was the thrill of my life.

We descended and the earth came up to meet us. That was the way it seemed to me. Another plane was just landing and we were too close to land safely so the motor was speeded up again and up we soared for another big circle. When we approached the airport this time, we got the landing signal and soon we felt the ground. The landing was done so smoothly that I did not feel the least bump when the wheels struck the ground.

I enjoyed every minute of my first ride among the clouds above Virginia and I think I would enjoy a longer ride sometime.

86
A Foul of the Law

In the early days we were not so particular about the game laws. We were living off the land, and when we were out of meat, we felt that we were entitled to the game that grazed on our land. I have killed many deer out of season, not because I wanted to break the law, but because my pocketbook was empty and I did not want to see my family at starvation stage.

In the first part of October 1930 I shot a buck which was ravaging the garden of my neighbor, Peter Ohman, who then lived at my cousin Gotfred Stevenson's place. He had complained that the deer were there every night and ate their beets, carrots and cabbage. Ohman did not own a rifle, so one evening I took my gun and walked over there and laid for the deer. We divided the venison and my wife canned some of it. One front quarter I hung up in the icehouse.

A couple days later I was plowing in the field when Jake Gorence, driving the school bus, came by. He stopped and walked over to me and told me that the game warden was searching William Carlson's place for venison. As soon as the bus left I ran home and hid the quarter I had hanging in the icehouse under the floor in the well house. I did not think that any warden would look under the floor. Then I took the jars that my wife had canned and put them all into the water cistern in the basement. There I presumed they would be safe from any searchers. I went back and finished my plowing.

I had just returned home and unharnessed my team when the game wardens drove into the yard. There were two of them. One introduced himself as Munson, and told me what they were out for. He asked if he could look in my basement and of course I could not refuse him. Meanwhile, the other man went to the outhouses. I sat in the kitchen hoping they would soon leave when Munson came up with one of the jars from the cistern. He asked me what it contained and I said it was calf meat that we had put in for cooling it off. He opened it and tasted it and told me that he thought it was venison. A sharp whistle was heard from the well house and the other warden came carrying the venison I had hid under the floor. Now I could not deny it any longer. They fished out all the jars from the cistern and loaded it all into their car. Munson told me to appear before Justice of the Peace in Orr the next day, and they left.

I was not alone on the prisoners bench in Orr the next day. William Carlson and Peter Ohman were also there with me. When my turn came I pleaded guilty, but I told the Judge our circumstances, how we were trying to make our living off our land, and how the deer often ruined our gardens. The Judge was reasonable enough. He told us that he did not blame us for protecting our gardens, but as we had been caught having venison out of season in our possession, we were guilty to a legal offense, and he fined us $30.00 and cost a total of $35.00.

John with his horses.

John Ostlund collection

Olga got a new permanent.
The lilacs froze that year, so had no blooms.

John Ostlund collection

87
On a Manhunt

In the year of 1931 I served as Town Constable and my duties generally consisted in serving papers on delinquent persons who did not pay their bills. One morning in June, deputy sheriff Adolph Johnson came here and wanted me to accompany him to Ash Lake on law business. He did not reveal what it was, but told me to take my gun and star badge and ride along.

We were well on our way when he pulled a letter from his pocket which he asked me to read. It informed us that a parked automobile near Ash Lake had been broken into and robbed a week earlier, and the following morning a man was seen carrying a heavy pack along the road four miles west of there. Attempts had been made by local residents and those who were robbed to find the man, but wilderness had him hidden.

Now a week later, he had appeared at the home of a lone settler, Louis Lilienthal, after midnight and demanded food and matches. When his demands were refused, he threatened the farmer. The next night he returned again but Lilienthal was ready for him, and facing a loaded shotgun and a barking watchdog, he had disappeared into the night.

This was the story told in the letter and the sheriff was requested to order out a posse and apprehend the man, as Mr. Lilienthal was scared for his life. The letter told us that we would find a note pinned to a tree at a certain place, giving us further directions. The letter was written and signed by a neighbor to Mr. Lilienthal, a Mr. Jones.

We did not find any note however, but after inquiry in Ash Lake we found Jones who accompanied us to Lilienthal's cabin. The man was nearly sick with fright and told us that he had not slept for several nights as he momentarily expected a visit from the outlaw. He put us on the trail and with Jones as our guide, we set out for an old logging camp two miles into the wilderness, where the men thought the outlaw lived. Arriving there, we saw fresh tracks beside a spring where he evidently had taken water. Now we parted and approached the camp from different directions and ready for anything that might happen. We found the camp deserted, but the ashes were still warm in the fireplace. He had evidently heard our voices and was hiding in the woods. The only thing we found was a new blanket which was taken from the robbed car. We scouted around, but were unable to find any tracks. We visited another logging camp nearby, but nobody had been there, so we had to return to Lilienthal's place.

The fugitive was never seen or heard of anymore after our visit. Johnson figured that he had walked across to Nett Lake from where he probably escaped into Canada. It was late in the afternoon when we returned to Orr. As we had not had a bite to eat since early that morning, a good beef steak dinner at the cafe tasted wonderful. It was a fruitless manhunt, though it perhaps scared the hunted man and accomplished some good for the lonely settlers at Ash Lake.

88
I Served on the Jury

In April 1932 I was summoned to serve on the District Jury in Virginia. This was a new experience for me and a new episode in my life. At the courthouse the first morning, I was informed that I was one of 59 Jurors called, as no less than three courts were going into session that morning of April 18, 1932. The judges were Edward Freeman of Virginia, Martin Hughes of Hibbing and Bert Fessler of Duluth.

I was offered room and board with my friends, Mr. and Mrs. Carl Johnson on 9th Street South, during my stay in the city, which saved me the expenses of hiring a room in a hotel. The jurors compensation at that time was only $3.00 per day.

The second day I was drafted on one of the most important criminal cases ever held in the city of Virginia, State of Minnesota vs Carl Westling and Joseph Trudell. The charges were kidnapping and robbing an old recluse, Knute Nelson. The case lasted three days and was very interesting. The court room was packed every day by interested spectators. The culprits were found guilty and we returned a verdict of guilty to robbery in the first degree. They were sent to Stillwater prison.

I served as juror on six different trials during the four weeks. Number two was a "Breach of Promise" case where a woman sued a man for $15,000.00 claiming that he had promised to marry her after living with her for six years. She collected only $100.00 as it was proved that she was a prostitute.

Number three which I served on was a charge of illegal sale of intoxicating liquor, which drew a verdict of "guilty" and he paid a penalty of $100.00 fine and served 40 days on the Work Farm.

The fourth case I served on was for careless driving and damage to a car. Damage was assessed at $450.00 when the case was disposed of.

Number five was another civil suit in which two large men were accused of bodily assault on a small man. One of the assailants was Municipal Judge of Gilbert, but we penalized him just the same and he was ordered to pay the little man $100.00 and court costs.

The sixth and last case was another civil suit by a farmer from Alango suing the County of St. Louis for flooding his land with a drain ditch from a road. This case was quite lengthy as it took two whole weeks. The entire Jury was brought out to the farm to view the damages and the farmer was awarded the amount of $450.00. Later, I heard the County had offered the farmer $500.00 damages which he refused and sued for $6,500.00. As I was the only farmer on the Jury panel, I think that my opinion influenced this case considerably. There was not much damage done by the drain ditch as this land was only a swamp before and not fit for farming.

89
Peak of the Depression

The year of 1931 was a memorable year in the history of our country. The Republican administration under the leadership of Herbert Hoover, had brought America to the verge of starvation. Work was hard to find anywhere and thousands of people suffered all over the United States. No work was done on the county roads and the logging operations had ceased almost entirely. We farmers managed to live off our farms, but prices on farm products had dropped to the bottom. For a five gallon can of sweet cream we were glad to get $3.00, hay sold at $8.00 a ton. Butterfat dropped from 22 cents to 10 cents per pound and eggs from 19 to only 5 cents per dozen.

I had eight cords of peeled pulpwood, but I could not sell it. I then hauled it home, intending to cut it up for firewood. Before I had time to saw it up, Gust Johnson offered me $7.25 a cord if I hauled it in to Gheen and loaded it on a car myself. I did, but when the returns came, the freight on those eight single cords amounted to $31.58, leaving me only $26.42. However, it was better than burning it and I valued those twenty six dollars more than I would have valued ten times that amount a few years back.

Our credit had always been good at the Cooperative store, but that summer the Directors were forced to limit all credit, and ours was cut short like the other customers. We had to squeeze our pennies and be very careful that we did not spend more than we had in our pocketbook. In short, we had to make both ends meet.

The only outside work I could obtain that summer was that I agreed to cut the hay on A.P. Olson's place on half share. We cut and baled a total of 28 tons which we managed to sell to General Logging Company at $6.00 a ton, but when we had paid the baler and other expenses we had only made $90.00 clear, or $45.00 each.

The summer of 1932, I also undertook to do the haying for Pete Olson. We cut and baled 26 ton, but we had no market for it. This was a great disappointment for me as I had figured on this revenue to pay the last half of my real estate tax. For the first time, my taxes were delinquent that year, but it was a consolation that I was not the only farmer unable to pay my taxes. The worldwide depression was still very evident.

The winter of 1932-33 was an unusually cold one and with a lot of snow. On January 16th, the thermometer registered 65 below zero at the Orr Ranger Station. This was one of the coldest days that I can remember, and I appreciated the inside of our fairly warm home.

The American Red Cross was distributing flour and clothing through the Town Clerk's office, and we received 350 pounds of flour and some sweaters and overalls for the children. This idea of receiving something which we had not earned was new to us and we hesitated at first to accept it, but it was hard to refuse when the purse was empty and our income had dwindled to almost nothing.

On March 4th 1933, Franklin D. Roosevelt took office, and the new administration, with the help of Congress, immediately took steps to relieve the nationwide situation. Hoarded money was ordered released and put into circulation immediately. The banks were put under strict examinations, and they were opened only if they were on a sound and solid financial basis. The State Bank in Cook was closed for some time, and before they could open it, the depositors had to agree to leave 50% of their deposited money in a so called "trust fund" for the bank to rely on until it was financially able to repay it. The administration tried in every way possible to put the millions of unemployed back to work. The Civilian Conservation Corps was created which put 250,000 young men into conservation camps around the whole country. One of these camps was established at Cusson and Alvin enlisted there. He received $30.00 per month of which $25.00 was assigned to his family. This was a great help to keep the wolf from our doorstep.

Under the Work Progress Act (or as it usually was called, W.P.A.) older men who were in dire need of work, were employed. I did not apply for it as I knew many in our community were harder up than we were.

The Regional Credit Corporation, (RCC) had been established and when I lost one of my horses I applied for a loan of $200.00 to tide us over and pay for a horse. There was a lot of red tape or complications connected with that loan, however, and it took more than seven months before I actually received it. Meanwhile, and until I finally was able to repay this loan from the government, our cattle belonged to the government for several years.

The summer of 1933 was unusually dry. From the 1st of May until the 10th of August, we did not have any rain to mention. Everything dried out. The grain headed out too early, wilted and died. The garden had to be watered every day and still it did not grow as it should. The only vegetables that thrived and grew were the tomatoes. We never had so many large, ripe tomatoes any previous year. Another thing that thrived that summer was the grasshoppers. When we cut the hayfields, the hoppers infested the garden, where in one day they finished off all of the onion tops. Carrots and rutabagas were finished next. Fortunately, I received a sack of poison bran from the Ag teacher, Mr. Lindholm in Cook, and that helped to check the grasshoppers somewhat.

On September 12th we voted on the 21st Amendment to United States Constitution, repealing the 18th Amendment, ending national Prohibition. Our township voted 46 to 10 in favor of the repeal. As usual, I voted with the minority, but still I felt that I had voted right. Time alone will tell whether our country will benefit from the return of the saloon.

On October 8th I received the greatest surprise of my life. We had just had our Sunday dinner, and I was contentedly settled in the rocking chair with my pipe and a paper, when the dog commenced barking. Looking out I saw the school bus, followed by several cars, drive into the yard. Now it dawned on me that the next day was my 50th birthday and somebody had arranged for a party on me. The house was soon filled with friends and neighbors. Some of my friends had come all the way from Hibbing, nearly fifty miles away.

When everybody had found a seat and the greetings were over, a program commenced. William Carlson acted as toastmaster and called on several of the old friends, who told incidents from the years gone by. I tried hard to conceal my feelings, but when my daughters sang one of my favorite songs, I nearly wept. A lump lodged in my throat which stayed there and when I was presented with a beautiful and expensive writing set and a purse of cash, I was quite unable to express my feelings and gratitude.

Now that I am 50 years old, the best part of my life is behind me. What happens after this will not matter much. I have tried to live a life that I would not feel ashamed over. How I have succeeded in this is for others to decide.

PART 9 -
"My Declining Years"

"Now that I am 50 years old, the best part of my life is behind me. What happens after this will not matter much. I have tried to live a life that I would not feel ashamed over. How I have succeeded in this, is for others to decide." John Ostlund.

This was my diary entry shortly after my 50th birthday. At that time I felt that nothing further would happen which would be worth relating and that my autobiography was closed. However, now, 15 years later I am resuming it. Many interesting events have happened since. Looking through my diaries during these years I'll summarize these events to the best of my ability. Perhaps some day in the future it may make interesting reading for someone.

Family on the farm 1957

EXPERIMENTS WITH VARIETIES OF SPUDS

Gheen, Minn., Aug. 14.—(Special to The Herald.)—John Ostlund, president of the Willow Valley Farmers' club, is experimenting this year with four varieties of potatoes.

He has planted Rural Russets, Rural New Yorkers, Green Mountains and Early Ohios side by side under conditions exactly similar. At digging time he plans to weigh the product from each variety. Heretofore, he has raised only Green Mountains. Mr. Ostlund has this year five acres of the new Anthony variety of oats, originated by the plant breeders at the university of Minnesota.

He bought the seed from Austin Lind of Cook, who procured it last year from the Northeast experiment station at Duluth. It promises a high yield.

Newspaper clipping from the Duluth Herald.

I served as a member of the Cook Fair Board during 1934 and at the fair that fall I received first prize on my two potato entries: "Rural Russets" and "Rural New Yorkers". The only other two first prizes on potatoes went to William Carlson for "Cobblers" and "Green Mountains". All potato first prizes went to Gheen that year which was quite a disappointment for Cook and Little Fork Valley farmers.

90
A Tussle with a Bull

In the year 1936 I kept the club bull at my place. The members of the bull association took turns keeping the bull and then it was my turn. I built a heavy fence behind my barn with five foot woven wire and on top of that, several strands of barb wire so I had a safe corral for the bull. I let him out every evening for exercise and he remained outside during the nights. Then in the morning I took him in and fed him, as he had to be fed inside at all times.

One morning, it was on September 9th, I went out as usual and opened the door for the bull to come into the barn. He always had a halter on, but that night he had slipped it off rubbing his head against one of the fence posts. So I went out in his pen and found the halter and walked up beside him in the stall to replace it. It is generally presumed that a bull is a slow animal, but this time he was not slow. Like a flash of lightning he caught me and threw me down in front of the stall, next to the manger. I saw his large head over me and it was coming down on my chest. It was a matter of life and death. It would only take a couple of seconds to crush my chest and it would have been all over. Fortunately, I was able to reach the ring in the bull's nose and I twisted it with all my might. This made him raise his head so I was able to get to my knees, still holding on to the ring. When he backed up I was able to get to my feet and, letting go of the ring, I clambered over the manger into the feed alley. There I found a pitchfork and, limping to the door, I managed to escape outside where I collapsed and fainted.

Victor found me a while later laying on the ground. It probably was the scare and the shock more than injuries that made me faint and collapse, but I received a wrenched back and was unable to do any work for several weeks afterwards. Victor stayed home and did my work until I again was able to take over.

Nobody dared replace the halter on that bull, so he went out and in the barn as he pleased. It was decided that we should butcher it and sell the beef. One day, two of the neighbors came to my place and we roped the bull, hooked the staff in the nose ring and led him out to the slaughtering scaffold. I knocked him down with a bullet and I felt a lot better when I saw that animal dead. My tussle with that bull was about the closest shave I have had with death.

1936 - From left: John, Mabel, Olga, Elsie, Victor. Little
Kenny in front. (Missing oldest son Alvin)

John Ostlund collection

1936 - Back: John, Olga, Victor. Front: Kenneth, Mabel, Elsie.

John Ostlund collection

John on the farm in Gheen, Minnesota.

John Ostlund collection

The hottest day in my memory was the 11th of July, 1936, when the thermometer climbed to 105 in the shade. We had several loads of hay cured and thinking that it might end up with heavy rain, we worked through the torturing heat and took in three big loads.

91
A Trip to Michigan

In 1938 I served as chairman of the County Land Clearing committee and one day I received an invitation from the County Agent, Mr. Neubauer, to accompany him to a land clearing demonstration near Ironwood, Michigan. We were going to witness a demonstration of a new way to clear land by bulldozer.

I drove my car to Virginia in the early morning of September 16th and parked it behind the courthouse. Mr. and Mrs. Neubauer were there, and I joined them in their car. We left Virginia at 7 o'clock a.m. It was a nice day with clear skies, just ideal for a long auto ride. In Eveleth we picked up John Kneebone, who also was a member of my committee.

We reached Duluth at 8:30 where three more cars joined us for the trip across the State of Wisconsin. Among our fellow travelers were the South End County Agent, D.T. Grusendorf; Fred Ward, manager of the Work Farm; and Henry Ronningen, supervisor of the Federal Farm Security Administration.

We drove through Superior and took highway No. 2 eastward through the little towns of Poplar, Maple, Iron River, and Ashland. We rode along slowly viewing the scenery and soon lost the other three cars who evidently were more familiar with the road and traveled fast. It was just 12 o'clock noon when we crossed the state line and entered Michigan. A few minutes later we were in the city of Ironwood.

We had dinner at the Lincoln hotel and there we met our companions from Duluth. We were introduced to other land clearing enthusiasts from many parts of Michigan and Wisconsin. After dinner we assembled at the Courthouse and were instructed to follow the leader out about eight miles from the city, where the demonstration was to take place. When we reached the place we saw a large diesel Caterpillar with a wide steel blade in front, breaking out large stumps that already were decayed. The cat went from one end of the field to the other, making an eight foot sweep, rolling the stumps and large rocks to the side in windrows. It carried enough dirt with it to fill the holes and worked like a road grader leaving the cleared area smooth and ready for the plow. The soil here was a reddy sandy loam. We were told that the farmers paid $5.00 per hour for the Caterpillar and operator, which was a very reasonable price.

We raised the question if the same efficient work could be done in a field of green stumps, and after a while the machine went to an adjoining farm where a field had been cleared of timber just two years ago. The stumps were from three to four feet in height and I asked the farmer why he had cut the trees so high from the ground. He replied that the snow had been so deep that he could not get closer to the ground. I was glad that I lived where we did not have that deep snow. And I would not like to farm there where the soil is 25% rocks and boulders. In almost every field could be seen large piles of rocks and stone fences had been built three to four feet high in many places along the roads.

We left the place of demonstration at 2:30 p.m. and reached Duluth at 6 o'clock. It had commenced raining and was so dark that Neubauer turned on headlights. It took him two hours to drive the 65 miles to Virginia from Duluth. There I found my car and I reached home at 9, after a most enjoyable tour through three states.

92
Delegate to State Convention

When I was sent from the local Farmer-Labor Club to the District Convention in Duluth in the fall of 1938, there I was elected to serve as delegate to the State Farmer-Labor Convention to be held in St. Paul on January 27th and 28th, 1939.

When we assembled at the St. Paul Auditorium on the morning of January 27th, we found ourselves among about one thousand delegates from all parts of the State, of which about fifty were from St. Louis County alone. However, when we came to the registration tables, we were informed that no delegates from St. Louis County could be seated until action had been taken from the floor. When we asked the reason we were told that we had several communists among our delegation and they had to be weeded out before the rest were accepted and admitted. We were calmly wondering who had the authority to do the weeding. All our delegates had been duly elected from their respective organizations to represent them at the State meeting, and who was here to decide on anybody's eligibility as representative.

We waited around the lobby all forenoon while the chosen ones inside debated whether to let us in or not. Finally at 12:30 we received word that all, except four of our delegation would be admitted. Those that were refused were Herman Griffith from Duluth, John T. Bernard and Morris Greenberg from Eveleth and Mrs. Martin Mackie from Virginia.

Paul Harris from Thief River Falls had served as temporary chairman during the forenoon debate, but after we were seated we nominated George Lommen from Eveleth and he was elected chairman. He handled the gavel very well and I doubt if anybody could have done it better under the circumstances. All speeches were limited to three minutes and when that time was up, the gavel fell without discrimination.

It was a constant struggle between the conservative and the liberal factions of the party. Both were about equally divided on the convention floor, however, there was a lot of haggling and disorder when the chairman recognized only members of the conservative group, while the liberals were refused the floor on almost every instance.

In the forenoon of the second day, Elmer Benson, former governor, addressed the convention. It was a masterly speech in which he told us that this was no time for a split in the Farmer-Labor Party. We should instead make efforts to more solidly unite the liberal forces in the state and try to meet each other halfway and respect each other's opinions, even if they did not agree with our own opinions. However, after he stepped down, his good premonitions were disregarded. As soon as a liberal suggestion was made, the conservatives were on the floor shouting that it was "communistic". It was really disgusting to listen to it and I felt like leaving. But again, I thought that it was my duty to remain and at least vote for the liberal motions.

In the afternoon the Constitution Committee reported and recommended that all persons belonging to or supporting communist, fascist or Nazist organizations be excluded from membership in the Farmer-Labor party. I voted against this and remarked to the chairman that we are supposed to live in a free country, but the motion carried in spite of an overwhelming vote against it.

Well, this event was an interesting political experience for me and I learned a lot

Call to Colors.

It is now nearing the time when we again will be called upon to do our duty as American citizens and by the ballot signify who is our choice for the county, state and national positions to be filled next fall.

Even if our order is nonpartisan and non-political in its constitution, we as wide awake goodtemplars should take interest in politics, and very carefully select the candidates for the various offices whom we know are standing on a strictly temperate platform.

Furthermore, let us not only cast our ballot for the dry candidates, but let us each and everyone in our respective communities, boost for the men we want. The state and the entire nation is being flooded by a tremendous and influential wet propaganda for the purpose to discredit and nullify the 18th amendment and prohibition as a whole, and in order to, as much as possible, offset this propaganda of lies and intrigues, we as honest goodtemplars must turn politicians if we never did it before.

Especially do I wish to call the attention of our Lodge Supt.'s of Legislative Work to their part in this work. Get in touch with the candidates for the various legislative positions, and ascertain their stand on the temperance and prohibition issues. Then report your investigation and findings at your lodge and urge every member who is a citizen to vote.

I have written the candidates for the United States Senate and Congress from the State of Minnesota, and will endeavor to send a circular out to every lodge in Minnesota later.

Let us show our colors at the coming primary and general election not only in Minnesota, but in every city and hamlet where goodtemplars live, throughout the entire nation.

With fraternal greetings,
JOHN OSTLUND,
G. S. L. W. Minn. Jr.
Gheen, Minn.

Newspaper clipping, "Call to Colors" letter by John Ostlund - 1939.

93
Swindled by Fake Eye Specialist

Father and son (Kenneth) - 1939.

John Ostlund collection

A rather disgusting experience occurred January 11th 1940, when a fake eye specialist swindled me out of $13.00. I had never had an examination of my eyes and I needed glasses. This is how they worked it. They drove up in a nice car and one man came in the house and inquired about the road to a neighbor. I directed him and he was on his way out when he turned and asked me what was wrong with my eyes. When I told him that I had been reading a lot and my eyes were somewhat tired, he said, "I have an eye specialist out there in the car and he will be glad to examine your eyes without charge." So he opened the door and called his partner.

He came in carrying a bag and introduced himself. Told me that he was a practicing optician in Duluth and had been sent out to examine the eyes of some WPA workers and he was being paid by the Government. He was willing to look at my eyes and if I needed glasses he would advise me. He placed me in a chair and put up a chart on the wall. Now he placed some contraption over my eyes and asked me to read the chart. After several experiments he told me that one of my eyes was going bad and I had to have adjusted glasses if I wanted to retain my eyesight on the other eye. It sounded logical enough and never for an instant did I think that anything was wrong with the examination. He told me that he had different lenses with him and he would be glad to fit me out, but they were expensive lenses and the glasses would cost me $20.00. When I told him that I did not have twenty dollars in the house he told me that if I was willing to do some advertising for him here in my community, he would fix the glasses for me for $15.00. All I had in my billfold was $13.00 and I told him that I would send him the balance later. A while later he had my glasses ready and I paid him the $13.00.

After he had left I was trying out my new glasses, but I did not seem to get used to them. He had told me that one of my eyes was weaker than the other and required a different lens. When I turned the glasses upside down it did not make any difference and that was enough to make me suspicious. That evening I read a warning in the "Farmer" to look out for a couple of fake eye doctors and now I realized that I had been swindled. I took the glasses and drove up to Orr, found Deputy Sheriff Adolph Johnson and explained the case to him. He promised to look out for the pair around Orr the following day, but evidently they smelled danger and left for parts unknown.

John Ostlund collection

Our front room - 1939.

John Ostlund collection

Christmas Dinner 1941.

John Ostlund collection

In the summer of 1941, the government had purchased a lot of cotton from farmers in the south in order to help them out in stabilizing the price. This cotton was distributed to rural districts all over the nation and, through the agricultural extension service, mattress making centers were established in many communities. We were fortunate to get one of these centers placed here and I was appointed to supervise the work. On July 15th, we opened our center at the hall and kept it going for six days. Forty mattresses were made during these days. These mattresses, at a cost of $1.00 each, could well be compared with commercially made and sold mattresses at ten times the cost.

John Ostlund with son Kenneth - 1942.

John Ostlund collection

In 1942, Victor and Alvin had purchased a forty of land next to our farm and they told me to have it logged off, the profit to be used for building a new barn.

94
Fractured My Skull

On July 27, 1943 I had a serious accident which for the first time in my life landed me in a hospital. I was helping my cousin Ivar Ostlund with his haying. He had recently purchased the Grund farm. He had been helping me with my haying the previous two weeks and now I wanted to repay his work for me by assisting him with my team and labor.

We had unloaded a load of hay and were back in the field ready to load again. Ivar was pitching and I stood in the empty wagon. The reins I had just hung up and I was just catching a forkful of hay from Ivar. One of the horses stepped in a hornets nest in the ground, and jumped, scaring the other horse. Unprepared for the lunge, I fell and my head struck one of the iron uprights in the wagon bolster, which projected through the floor of the hay rack. It knocked me unconscious. The horses broke into a run heading for the barn and I fell off the wagon with my right arm caught in one of the braces of the hayrack. I was dragged for some distance before my arm came loose and left me lying in the field. I came to when Ivar's wife, Elida, was bathing my head with water. I was able to walk to the house with her help, but there I dozed off again. When I awoke, the doctor was injecting something into my arm. The ambulance was outside and they helped me into it. Alvin was there and he sat by my side during the ride to Cook. I was then conscious and was able to talk to Al, but he told me afterwards that he did not think I knew what I was talking about.

In the hospital I thought surely that I was dying. The room seemed to be rotating around and around and I held on to the sides of my bed as I thought it was turning over. I felt myself falling and I lost consciousness again. I do not know how long afterwards I awoke and saw Mrs. David Helstrom sitting by my bed. But, I felt better and everything looked normal again. My mind cleared up and I remember that I was glad to be alive. In the middle of the first night, Doc Heiam came in and examined me. He assured me that I would be well again.

The next day I was brought into the x-ray room and the picture showed that I had received a double fracture on my skull. My right arm had been pulled out of its socket at the axle and the doctor taped it to my body in order to hold it in place until it healed. Mrs. Helstrom sat by my bed for the two first nights and in the daytime the day nurse, Margret Savage, and the doctor were always near me.

After my sojourn in the hospital, I came home with strident orders from the doctor to not do any work for at least six months. It took a long time before I could use my right arm and I have never regained the strength in it. While my temple, where the skull bone was broken, still is sore when I press on it. It does not ache anymore. Bruises and cuts that I received healed up fast and I consider myself quite fortunate that I did not contact any complications from my serious accident.

On the hay wagon.

John Ostlund collection

Our home in Gheen.

John Ostlund collection

JOHN OSTLUND TELLS 'EM

JOHN OSTLUND, popular Gheen-Willow Valley farmer and club member, is discussing the program at the St. Louis County Club and Farm Bureau at Duluth Saturday, with J. J. McCann, agricultural agent of Hibbing, and August Neubauer, agricultural agent of Virginia.

Newspaper clipping of John Ostlund at an event
in Duluth, Minnesota.

John Ostlund collection

On August 29th 1943, the Farmers Club celebrated its 30th Anniversary and as a great surprise to me, I was presented with a gavel and a special gold pin from the St. Louis County Club and Farm Bureau as an award for community leadership. I did not feel that I had earned this recognition, but felt quite proud that others thought I had earned it. I had only done my duty as a citizen and a member of the organization, and I had found pleasure in the years of service.

95
War Time

On December 7th 1941 Japan had declared war with the United States and destroyed our country's large fleet at Pearl Harbor. It was a gloomy day for everybody. Victor was in the service and had received permission to come home for Christmas. This was of course cancelled and instead, his regiment was immediately sent out to the west coast. Nobody knew when Japan might try to invade our country.

During the first year of the war, Civilian Defense Councils were elected in almost every community. This community, including Gheen and Willow Valley Township, elected their council on April 19th 1942. I became Secretary. We met once every month and we sponsored a lot of activities in the precautional defense of our community as well as in encouragement to the servicemen from this area.

Mabel's husband George was also called in the service and was training in Fort Warren, Wyoming. In September Alvin, Aggie and Mabel went on a sightseeing trip to California and points west. They drove to Wyoming and visited with George on the way out. Then they drove south through Colorado, New Mexico, Arizona, California, Oregon and Washington. Victor was stationed at Fort Lewis, Washington and they stopped and visited with him. He was able to get a furlough at that time and came back with them through Idaho, Montana, North Dakota and home. They left on September 16th and returned October 7th. Victor had not been home since June the previous year and it was good to see him again.

Victor had been promoted fast and was serving as staff sergeant. The first days of January 1943, he was selected for officers training and came home January 9th on his way to Fort Sill, Oklahoma. On April 15th he graduated from the military training school at Fort Sill. He was now a Second Lieutenant in the Field Artillery. He came home on a 12 day leave and then left for Camp Roberts, California.

In the fall of 1943, Victor had been sent overseas and was stationed somewhere in the South Pacific. He wrote regularly every week and told us about the tropics and how pretty everything was over there. Never once did he hint that he was close to the fighting area. On April 14th, we received a letter from his commanding officer that Vic had had an accident and was hospitalized. At the end of the letter he mentioned that Vic had received the purple heart ribbon, and that revealed to us that he had been wounded in action against the Japanese. It had happened on Bougainville Island April 2nd. It is impossible to describe the feelings we tried to hide to each other. I tried to cheer Olga up, but when I saw her sad face I felt my tears coming. However, there was not a thing we could do. We had the opportunity to send him a couple cheering telegrams through the War Department.

On September 15th, he landed in San Francisco and was sent by plane to an army hospital in Indianapolis, Indiana. On October 3rd, we talked to him over the phone from Cook and it was a great relief to hear his voice again, cheerful as usual even after that frightful experience.

"PEACE IN THE WORLD" was proclaimed by President Harry Truman at 6 o'clock p.m. August 14th 1945. Germany and Japan had surrendered at last. Two atomic bombs had destroyed two Japanese cities and this was the last straw for greedy Japan. In Germany, the Russians and the Allied Powers had met in Berlin and crushed the Nazi armies besides demolishing nearly all the large cities in Germany and they had surrendered earlier.

I hope that the last war between nations is over. If there is another war, civilization is doomed and humanity will become cave men and women once again. The recently invented radioactive atomic bomb is the greatest destructive weapon ever used and it will either do away with armed conflict between nations or destroy civilization over the entire world.

For those of us who have been privileged to live during the last half century and follow the developments of civilization, it is indeed wonderful to say the least. Fifty years ago there were no automobiles, no submarines, no airplanes, the moving picture camera was not yet invented, neither was the radio or television. Science had not advanced very far in medicine or other technical problems that now is saving life and property. I am quite sure that more revolutionizing inventions have been made during the last fifty years than during five hundred years before this era. Consequently, I feel that we who have been living in this first half of the 20th century are fortunate indeed. I sincerely hope that we do not need to witness the downfall and the ruin of all this.

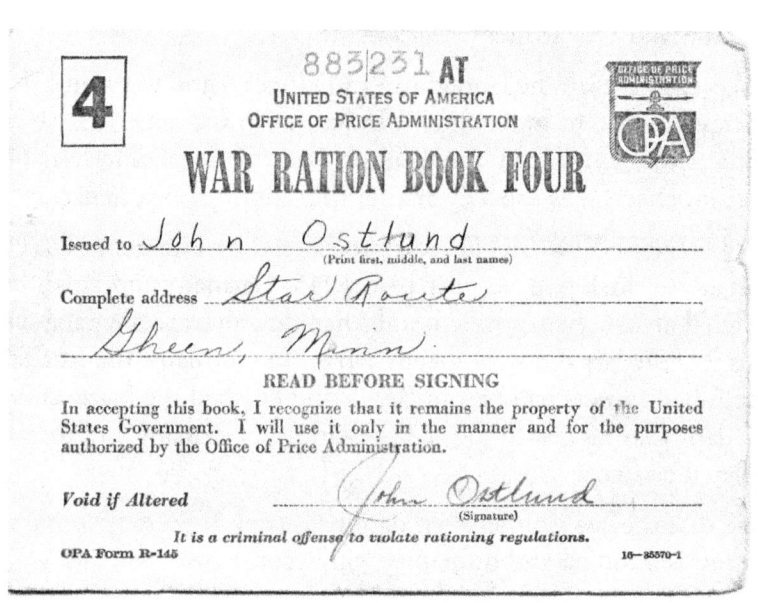

War Ration Book 1942.

John Ostlund collection

Quote on back of War Ration Book, "IMPORTANT: When you have used your ration, salvage the TIN CANS and WASTE FATS. They are needed to make munitions for our fighting men. Cooperate with your local Salvage Committee."

Form OPA R-1107

UNITED STATES OF AMERICA
OFFICE OF PRICE ADMINISTRATION

V - FUEL OIL RATION
Class 3 Consumer Coupons
(One-Gallon Coupons)

Copy this number in ink on each coupon in the space provided. After each 5 or 10 entries, check against original number for accuracy.

V 510593 C7

OFFICE
OF
PRICE ADM.

R-123
*U510593
C7*

Date
issued *11/25*, 1942
Date
expires *9/30*, 194*4*

These coupons
are issued to *John Ostlund* to be used at

Star Rt *Green*
(Number and street or R. F. D.)   (City or post office)

St Louis *Minn*
(County)   (State)

and consists of *100* coupons of 1 gallon each, a total
of *100* gallons.

Dealers in fuel oil or their representatives are hereby authorized to deliver fuel oil to the above person or his agent for use at the above address, and are required to detach from this sheet coupons having a gallonage value equal to the quantity of oil delivered, in accordance with the rules and regulations of the Office of Price Administration in effect at the time of such delivery. At the time of delivery, the dealer or his agent must fill in the delivery record below.

War Price and
Rationing Board No. *64694* at *Hibbing*
      (City)

St Louis *Minn*
(County)   (State)

By *E Lockhart*

Received by *John Ostlund*
(Signature of coupon holder)

COUPONS VOID
IF DETACHED

Permits Delivery of	Permits Delivery of	Permits Delivery of	Permits Delivery of
1 GALLON FUEL OIL OFFICE OF PRICE ADM.	**1** GALLON FUEL OIL OFFICE OF PRICE ADM.	**1** GALLON FUEL OIL OFFICE OF PRICE ADM.	**1** GALLON FUEL OIL OFFICE OF PRICE ADM.
No. *U510593 C7*	No. *U510593 C7*	No. *U510593 C7*	No. *U510593 C7*
Permits Delivery of	Permits Delivery of	Permits Delivery of	Permits Delivery of
1 GALLON FUEL OIL OFFICE OF PRICE ADM.	**1** GALLON FUEL OIL OFFICE OF PRICE ADM.	**1** GALLON FUEL OIL OFFICE OF PRICE ADM.	**1** GALLON FUEL OIL OFFICE OF PRICE ADM.
No. *U510593 C7*	No. *U510593 C7*	No. *U510593 C7*	No. *U510593 C7*

1942 Fuel Oil Ration coupons.

John Ostlund collection

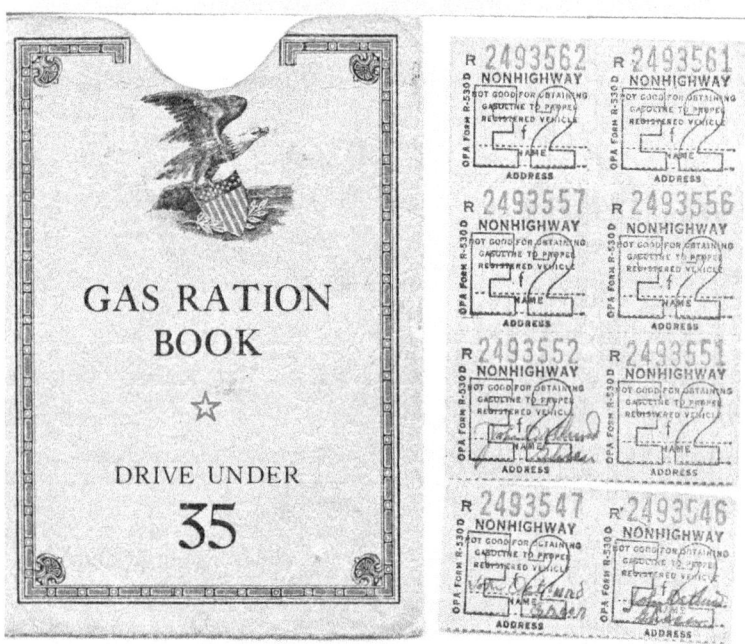

1945 Gas Ration Book.

John Ostlund collection

96
A Trip to California

January 10, 1946 I received a telegram from Sacramento, California that my brother Peter had passed away, and a request what to do with the remains. He did not have any relatives out there that could be depended on to see that he received a decent burial so I wired back that I would be there and to hold him until my arrival.

At first I intended to take a plane, but when I reached Duluth I was informed that all planes out west were booked full for two months in advance. So I took a bus from there to Minneapolis, where I bought a through ticket for Sacramento. We left Minneapolis at 8:15 p.m. January 11, 1946 and changed buses in Fairmont, Minnesota at midnight. Our bus reached Omaha, Nebraska at 9:30 the next morning, and without even having time for a cup of coffee, I boarded a bus for the west. At Sidney, Nebraska we were instructed by our bus driver to set our watches back one hour as we were entering the Mountain Time Zone. We were in the cowboy country and at every stop we saw men wearing broad-brimmed hats. In the late evening we reached Cheyenne, Wyoming where we stopped for supper. I changed a five dollar bill and received four silver dollars back in change. At daybreak the next morning we had crossed the Rockies and arrived at Evanston, Wyoming, where we had our breakfast, and at noon we came down the mountainside lined with fruit orchards, into Salt Lake City, Utah.

Our bus stopped for an hour in the city of the Mormons for dinner and I saw the great Mormon Temple across the street from the bus station. It was Sunday and I mingled with the people and walked around the temple. Our bus left at 1 o'clock p.m. and later we entered the Salt Flats of Utah. For 35 miles in all directions the desert is level as a floor and is composed of white, glistening sand. When we passed the desert, we entered Nevada and just over the state line we stopped for lunch. We climbed the mountain again to an altitude of 5,500 feet. When we again stopped, we were in Reno, Nevada, and it was 1:30 a.m. Monday morning. The gambling halls were lit up in all colors like a Christmas tree. We continued and arrived in Sacramento at 6:30 a.m. after three days and three nights of continuous travel by bus.

After a good breakfast, I located the hotel where my brother usually stayed, and found the proprietor, a Greek by the name of Tom Manthis. He acted very friendly and telephoned the hospital where Peter died. He was told that my brother's body had been turned over to an undertaker, and they directed us there. I checked through Peter's belongings at the hotel and found among his papers, War Bonds with my name and also his membership card in the "Veterans of Foreign Wars" organization. Now I was ready to visit the undertaker and arrange for the funeral. I met one of my brother's friends, Slim Ross, who had a car and offered to take me to the undertaker.

We reached Andrews & Grelich Funeral Parlors at 11:00 a.m. and found Mr. Grelich in. He was an Odd Fellow and when he saw my pin, he became real friendly. He advised me in the selection of dress and coffin and called the Veteran's Office and arranged for a military funeral. In the afternoon I visited the Public Administrator, John Garibaldi, at the Courthouse, where I found another perfect gentleman who gave me a lot of information on how to collect Social Security Death Benefits, etc. I took Slim Ross to a good restaurant where we had dinner at 3:30 in the afternoon. I had not had a bite to eat since early in the morning.

When we returned to the hotel after dinner, I met my cousin Otto Stevenson and his wife, Audrey, who were waiting for me. They lived in a little town by the name of Weimar in the hills of Sierra Nevada Mountain, 48 miles from Sacramento, and had heard that I had arrived. Now they insisted that I should accompany them home. Slim Ross promised to come out there the next morning and bring me back to the city, as I had a date with the undertaker the next forenoon. I had not seen my cousin for over 16 years and I had never met his wife, so I could not refuse the opportunity to visit with them.

Slim picked me up the next morning and brought me back to Sacramento and to the undertaker, where I was allowed to view my brother's body and visit with him for the last time. I sat with him for a long time and was thinking of the lonesome life that had ended for him after only 55 years. Now he was sleeping peacefully and had no worries any more.

That night I slept at the hotel and the following day was January 16th and my brother's funeral. Slim and I were at the cemetery and found the Veteran's burial plot where the grave had been dug. At 1:30 sharp, the hearse drove in followed by several cars with soldiers in uniform. Four of Peter's old friends carried the casket between a long row of soldiers to the grave and placed it on the slings. The Adjutant and the Chaplain stepped up and took over, reading the burial rites which they had learned by heart. The flag which had draped the casket, was folded and presented to me by the Adjutant. The Chaplain spoke again, dropped three roses on the coffin and bid goodbye to the departed comrade. The gun squad then stepped up and fired three volleys after which the bugler, hidden nearby, sounded taps while everyone stood with bared heads before the grave. This ended the ceremony which was simple, but very impressive. No minister was present at Peter's funeral.

Besides my wreath of flowers, a large spray of Chrysanthemums was presented from the Timberworkers Union of which Peter was a member. Many of the Union members were also present besides other friends who were in the city. Cousin Otto and his wife had been detained and did not reach the cemetery until everything was over, but they placed a wreath on the grave.

I accompanied them home to Weimar again and spent two days in their comfortable cottage in the hills. Then I took the bus for San Francisco, where I tried to recover some Bonds that Peter had there for safe keeping. Unsuccessful in this, as I could not identify myself, I went to the Bus station and purchased a ticket for Duluth, which cost me $42.60 and left San Francisco the same evening.

It was just getting daylight when we reached Reno, Nevada in the morning of January 19th. At 2 o'clock in the afternoon our bus climbed a peak in the Sierra Nevada mountain range and we passed through the Gila pass, which was 6,125 feet above sea level. At midnight we arrived in Salt Lake City where we had lunch. 14 hours later, at 2 p.m. Sunday, we arrived in the city of Chyenne, Wyoming. A bus marked Omaha was ready to leave and I and a couple of servicemen boarded it. The rest of our fellow passengers had to wait 4 hours for the next bus. At 4 o'clock Monday morning, we were in Omaha. Our bus for Minneapolis would not leave until 7:30, so we had three hours to wait. At 3 p.m. our bus passed the Iowa Minnesota line and at 8 o'clock that evening we arrived in Minneapolis. I called my brother-in-law, Victor Flank, and he picked me up at the depot and took me to his home. At 10:15 the next forenoon I boarded a bus for Duluth and at 6 p.m. we were in Virginia where my daughter and her husband met me and took me home for supper. Soon we were on our way home to Gheen. It was the longest and most eventful trip I had taken in almost 40 years.

"In remembrance"
1930 - John (on right) with brother Peter.

John Ostlund collection

The Farmall tractor - 1948.

John Ostlund collection

In the spring of 1948 we took over a contract to purchase a Cub Farmall tractor with plow and mower attachments. The tractor was delivered on March 22nd and we could now call ourselves tractor farmers. I was not so anxious for the purchase, but Kenneth wanted a tractor and I thought it might make him more interested in farming if he could work with a machine, rather than with horses. The tractor with mower, power take-off, plow and chains cost us $868.35.

Farming in Gheen.

John Ostlund collection

97
A Visit to Canada

It was a beautiful Sunday morning in September 1948 that we decided to drive to Fort Frances, Ontario. We had a new Chevrolet half ton truck and Kenneth had just received his driver's license. None of us had been north of the border before so we wanted to see some of our neighbor Canadians and their country.

Olga packed a basket containing a picnic dinner and I found my naturalization certificate and put it in my pocket in case it would be required. We left home at 9 a.m. and arrived in International Falls two hours later. From there we located the interstate bridge across the Rainy River and entered Canada. At the end of the bridge we were halted by the Customs officials, who asked about our nationality, residence, etc. and I had to show my citizen paper and the registration card on the truck. They peeked into our lunch basket and let us go.

We were now in the city of Fort Frances and soon noticed that we were in a foreign country. The number of bicycle riders on the streets was something very unusual for us Americans. It was not only boys and girls who were riding bikes. Many were old men and women. Only a few motor cars were visible along the streets. It was 11 o'clock and people were on their way to the churches. The church bells were ringing and we felt quite out of place in the religious gathering.

We drove through the city and reached a beautiful park on the bay of Rainy Lake, east of the city. In the parking court we parked our truck beside a car belonging to an elderly couple from Winnipeg. We took a walk through the park and admired the luxurant flowerbeds and the well kept lawns with tables and fireplaces here and there to accommodate the visitors and tourists. Very few people were there when we came, but soon other cars and people on foot arrived with lunch baskets planning to eat their dinner in the park. We too found a table and spread the contents of our picnic basket, and enjoyed eating without interference by flies, mosquitos or ants, who otherwise usually spoil a picnic. While we ate, we watched the speedboats in the bay and airplanes landing and departing from the water.

We spent a couple of hours in the park. Then we drove through some of the streets in the city before we returned to the Interstate bridge. At the customs office they had kept my registration card, and I had to go in and reclaim it. We were asked if we had bought anything in Fort Frances. If we had, we would have to declare for it. But we had not and they took our word for it and let us go.

We returned to International Falls, parked along the main street and went window shopping. At a log cabin restaurant we went in for coffee, and the front of the shop was a regular museum. Among the large assortment of mounted animals and birds was a large bull moose, a wolverine, an albino deer buck, heads of two deer bucks with their antlers locked together, the head of a large elk and many other animals only seen in the north woods country. It was very interesting and we lingered in the coffee shop for a long time.

We arrived home in time for milking after an enjoyable day.

98
Motoring Through the State

In the spring of 1949, my cousin Nels Holmer and I decided to take a trip back to the city of Worthington where we both worked on a farm the first year we were in America. More than 40 years had elapsed since we left there and most of the old people we had known were now dead, but I corresponded with Joe Wickstrom, one of the sons of the farmer I had worked for, and we were invited to visit him and his wife, who were now living in the city.

We left home in my Chevrolet truck and drove to Little Falls on May 31st. There we stayed overnight with my daughter Mabel and her family. The next day we drove through Willmar to Redwood Falls where we stopped for dinner. Then from there to Windom and southwest to Worthington where we arrived in the afternoon at the home of Wickstrom. Our speedometer indicated that we were 433 miles from Gheen.

We were cordially welcomed at the home of our friend, whom we had not seen since we left Worthington, and met his wife Olga whom we had never met before. We had much to talk about that evening and it was near midnight before we got to bed. We also met their daughter, Verna Schmith and her two sons, Glen and Dennis, who lived nearby.

The next morning we visited a retired farmer, Christ Salmonson, who recognized us both. He was 84 years of age, but unusually bright and quite talkative for his age. We then visited the home of my old girlfriend, Mary and Andrew J. Nystrom, also retired and living in the city. Mary was not as slim and pretty now in her sixties as I remembered her 47 years ago when we parted and I left the city.

In the afternoon we drove out in the country to the old farm where we had both been employed in our youth. The living house now stood empty with the windows boarded up and the farm was rented out to neighbors. We visited several places in the neighborhood and were invited for coffee at the home of Linden Moberg, whom we both knew as he once was on a hunting trip with his father Nels Moberg in Gheen. It was quite late before we returned to the city.

The next day we drove out in the country again visiting several old farms and found several old persons who remembered us. In the afternoon we visited Joe's brother, Peter Wickstrom and his wife Minnie and also Joe's sister, Emma Nystrom, who lived in the city. That evening we were invited to a party at the home of Joe's sister-in-law, Mrs. Lilly Wickstrom, and met her brother Ernest Nystrom, who was a young lad when I was there, but now owned and farmed the old Nystrom farmstead.

It was June 4th when we left for home after two days and three nights of pleasant visits in Worthington. We stopped for dinner in Willmar and drove from there to St. Cloud and back to Little Falls. We again stayed overnight and visited with Mabel and George. On june 5th we left and arrived in Gheen early in the afternoon after a trip covering a total of 890 miles. Nels and I had an agreement that he furnished the gas and oil while I furnished the ride. We had no trouble during the entire trip, not even a flat tire. As a companion, there was none better than Nels. He was always cheerful and happy, and in good companionship the time flies fast.

1949 - With our grand-babies.

John Ostlund collection

283

99
The Farm is Electrified

A great development was noted in our community in the fall of 1949 when the "Rural Electrical Administration" came into this area with the construction of the electric power and light project. Poles were erected at our place September 16th, but shortage of funds closed down the work for the winter. I hired an electrician, Matt Hannula of Angora to do the wiring work on our farm. He done a very good job and the total cost was $315.00 including all wire and fixtures.

Alvin bought a small electric light plant which he installed a few days before Christmas in 1949, and we had the entire house lighted by electricity for the first time, thus making it a more enjoyable Christmas than ever before. We had a beautiful Christmas tree also with electric lights.

In 1950 our farm was electrified by the Northern Electric Cooperative Association of Virginia, a branch of the Rural Electrification Administration, or R.E.A. of Washington, D.C. It was perhaps the greatest improvement in our rural farm life when we could discard our old Kerosene lamps and just press a button for light and electric power in all our farm buildings, except the poultry house. As to electric appliances we had a radio, a toaster and a flatiron and our children purchased an electric washing machine shortly afterwards.

Our Christmas tree in 1949 with electric lights.

John Ostlund collection

Olga, Kenneth and John in the kitchen.

John Ostlund collection

For several years we have been members of the North St. Louis County Dairy Breeders Association, selling most of our milk locally. But, the large creameries and milk producers were able to get a bill enacted in the state legislature to prohibit the sale of raw milk. All dealers in milk will be required to pasteurize their product before offering it for sale. This law will be in effect on July 1st, 1950 and that will be the end of our milk business as we will not be financially able to build a pasteurizing plant on our farm.

John (on the hay load) and Kenneth haying.

John Ostlund collection

Olga and John - 1950.

John Ostlund collection

We have heard a lot about "flying saucers", but for my part, I did not believe it to be anything but peoples imagination or falling meteorites. However, on the evening of March 22nd 1950, when Kenneth, Olga and I motored to Orr to see a class play, we were convinced that flying saucers really exist. We saw a green colored ball flying from the east in a westerly direction and it crossed the firmament with incredulous speed. If it had been of a different color we would have taken it for a meteor, judging from its speed, but it was quite large and of a bright green color. We all saw it clearly, but it is still a puzzle to me how it could travel so fast if it was a man-made object. From now on we do not doubt the existence of "flying saucers".

John's birthday - 1950.

John Ostlund collection

100
In a Highway Accident

My wife and I had been visiting and celebrating our wedding anniversary in Minneapolis during Midsommar 1951. On June 25th we left the home of Olga's brother, Victor Flank, planning to drive to Little Falls and visit our daughter Mabel and her family on our way home.

Well out of the big city we decided to turn in at a filling station to have our tires checked and fill up with gas. It was raining a steady drizzle and I had the windows of our pickup truck closed. Approaching the station I opened the window on my driver's side and stuck my arm out signaling that I was going to make a right turn. I did not see anything behind us and slowed down at the approach of the turnoff road when I felt a hard bump and everything went black.

Several minutes later I woke up laying on the grass with wet raindrops falling on my face and I saw people standing around me. When I sat up, every limb in my body seemed to ache. Finally my head cleared up and I got to my feet and looked around for my wife. She was laying behind me on the ground with her head between her legs, all doubled up. I thought first that she was dead, but when I lifted her up, she opened her eyes and smiled at me. Her scalp was badly sheared off and blood was running down her face. Somebody came with an umbrella and placed it over her head to protect her from the rain and a man asked me if he could call somebody I knew. He told me that the ambulance was on its way there. I told him to call my daughter Mabel Woods in Little Falls, but I could not remember her address. He ran back to the filling station to call and I walked over to the truck and picked up things that had fallen out when it turned over. The truck was standing on its wheels and I looked at the ignition key and saw that it had been turned off. I found my watch laying on the ground several feet from where I had been laying and then I found Olgas eyeglasses bent up a bit, but not broken, laying on the grass.

A large semi-trailer truck loaded with steel culverts was parked across the road and I presumed that was the one who had run into us. The man who offered to make the telephone call for me came back and I presumed he was the driver of the truck, but my mind was not clear enough to ask him his name or to take the license number on his truck.

Now the ambulance arrived and Olga was placed on a stretcher and taken in the ambulance. I told him to take her to the nearest doctor and he said, "You look like you need a doctor yourself, so you better come along." I climbed in beside Olga and we rode into Anoka, where he brought us to Doctor B.W. Bunker's office. His waiting room was full of patients, but he dismissed them all when we came. The time was now 10:15, so the accident would have happened about 10 o'clock a.m.

When the doctor saw Olgas lacerated scalp he said, "I thought the Indians had left this country!" with his kind and efficient assistant nurse, they clipped off her hair and sewed up the scalp, working over her for an hour. A while later a uniformed officer came in and wanted to question me about the accident. I showed him my drivers license and told him all I could remember and when he was through, he handed me the report and told me to read it. Now for the first time after the accident, I looked for my glasses, but could not find them. I told him that I could not read without my glasses and he promised to drive back and look for them. He asked me if I wanted the truck towed into Anoka and promised to attend to that matter as well. With that he left and we did not see him anymore.

It now dawned on me that I had not given the truck driver my daughter's address in Little Falls, and I thought that she perhaps never was called. I inquired from Doc about the nearest telephone office and he directed me to the next block. I walked there and found it without difficulty. I asked one of the girls to call Mrs. George Woods, 206 Third Avenue N.W. in Little Falls. She soon had the number and handed the receiver to me. I heard Mabel but when I tried to talk to her I was quite unable to say anything. I had to hand the transmitter back to the girl while I told her to talk to Mabel. She did and informed me that Mabel had been called and informed of the accident and that they would come to Anoka as soon as George could get away from his work.

They arrived in Anoka about 4 o'clock in the afternoon. The pickup truck had been towed to a garage and George and I went over there to see it. George stepped on the starter and the motor started immediately. He suggested that we should bring it to Little Falls and offered to drive it there while Mabel could drive their car with us. I paid the towing charges which were $6.50 and we took it out from the garage. All the windows were broken and the front wheels were somewhat out of line, but the tires held up and the motor worked perfectly. We reached Little Falls just as it was getting dark, about 8 o'clock in the evening. The distance between Anoka and Little Falls is 80 miles.

Neither Olga or I slept much that first night. Our harrowing experience combined with pains and shock kept us awake. The following morning Mabel called a doctor and he advised Olga to go to the hospital for care and penicillin shots. She remained in the hospital for six days and I stayed and rested up good. We brought the truck to a repair shop and total repairs and a new coat of paint cost us $272.50.

Olga was discharged from the hospital on July 2nd and the following day I took the bus home to Gheen. A few days later George and Mabel brought Olga home. We settled with the insurance company for $1,000.00 and were glad that we were alive. It was a close call for both of us.

John Ostlund collection

101
The Mayo Clinic

Our son Alvin had arranged for a medical checkup for his mother at the Mayo Clinic in Rochester, Minnesota in the fall of 1952. Olga had, for a number of years, been bothered with earache in one of her ears and defective hearing. As we had been invited to visit our son Victor and family in LaCrosse, Wisconsin, we decided to go there at the same time.

It was Sunday morning October 12th when we left home in Al's comfortable Buick car. Agnes was also with us this time as they had closed their resort at Crane Lake for the winter. We stopped in Spooner, Wisconsin for dinner and arrived in LaCrosse at 4:15 in the afternoon. LaCrosse is a city built between high bluffs on one side and the Mississippi river on the other. Victor took Monday off from his work and took us around and showed us the sights of the city and the surrounding countryside. He drove to the top of the highest hill and we were 1,195 feet above sea level, according to a sign. He also took us out to the project he was working on and we met some of his engineers.

On Tuesday morning we left for Rochester, where Olga had an appointment at 10 o'clock. In good time we reached the greatest clinic in America, the famous Mayo Clinic. The building dominates the whole city and is visible for miles as it is sixteen stories high. A continuous stream of people were seen entering the building. A doorman directed us to the admission counter where Olga received a card directing us to the sixth floor. Ahead of us were about fifty others suffering from head ailments only, who were to be examined that morning. Looking over the assemblage, we saw people from various countries in the world. Many were foreigners. Some were well dressed and looking prosperous, others like us of moderate means and a few even poorly dressed with patched clothes.

After Olga had been examined and told to come back at two in the afternoon, we drove to a motel or cabin court and arranged for lodging. We received a housekeeping apartment with two rooms and felt at home. The afternoon was spent at the clinic again and after another examination we were told to come again for x-rays the next morning.

The entire forenoon the next day was spent at the clinic, and Olga was told to come again the following day in the morning. We had the afternoon free and Alvin suggested that we should drive to Spring Valley, about 35 miles south from Rochester, and visit the Mystery Caves. An hour ride brought us there and we bought tickets for $1.10 for each person and a guide took us down to the caves. It was lit up with eclectic lights all along the paths. Ages ago a river had been running through the limestone mountain and had made the most wonderful formations on the rock. A large room was called "the Cathedral" and a hidden phonograph played hymns while we stood there. In another passage we came to a little underground lake with crystal clear water.

Thursday morning we were informed at the clinic that Olgas ear was healed up perfectly and she did not need any further treatment. She had been told by her doctor in Virginia that she would have to undergo an operation. The clinic charged only $35.00 for examinations and x-ray, which was very reasonable. So we sure appreciated that Alvin brought us there.

In the afternoon we left Rochester and were home by 9 o'clock that evening.

1953. John's 70th birthday celebration with his grown family. Standing from left: Alvin, Elsie, Kenneth, Mabel, Victor. Sitting: John and Olga.

John Ostlund collection

October 9, 1953. I have now reached the age of the proverbial "three score and ten" (70). There is not much to add to my autobiography. During the years, or days, I have left I am going to take it easy. I have nothing to worry about anymore. My children are all grown up and are able and willing to take care of their parents if need be. I am happy and contented and like to live as long as my health holds out. When I die, I hope that I do not need to suffer too much and be a burden to my folks. I hope death comes quick and I am ready for it. We all have to go the same way sooner or later and nobody can scare me by telling me there is a purgatory and hell after my death.

Grandpa and grandsons at the end of haying - 1953.

John Ostlund collection

We finished haying on July 24th 1953 after putting 40 good size loads in the hay barn. As we still had about 8 acre uncut, we decided to bale this and we built a drying shed adjoining the poultry house for this purpose. We later baled 290 round bales weighing approximately 9 1/2 ton. We also baled 105 bales of straw after threshing.

On the tractor.

John Ostlund collection

102
A Trip to Seattle, Washington

In November of 1954 I received a letter from my sister Ester, who then was confined in a hospital in Kirkland, Washington, asking me to come and visit her, as she did not expect to live. She had contracted cancer of her lungs. I left home on November 29th and took the bus to Virginia where I bought a ticket for Seattle. I left there at 10 a.m. by bus for Aitkin, where we arrived at 2 p.m. There I changed buses for Fargo, North Dakota, where I arrived at 7 o'clock that evening. 45 minutes later we left Fargo and I slept in my seat most of the night.

It was 5 in the morning when we arrived in Glendive, Montana and I had breakfast. We were now in the cowboy country. We reached Billings, Montana at 11:30 and stopped 45 minutes for dinner. At 3 in the afternoon we were in Livingston, Montana in the Rocky Mountain area and several big game hunters came onto the bus headed for Bozeman, Montana for elk hunting. We continued and arrived in Butte, Montana at 6:30 that evening.

In Butte we stopped for an hour and 30 minutes, the longest stop on the whole trip. We left at 8 p.m. and crossed the highest peak of the mountains and the continental divide, at an elevation of 6,548 feet, and at midnight we arrived in Missoula, Montana. When we left there, I fell asleep and slept until we reached Spokane, Washington at 4:40 in the morning. We had crossed the state of Idaho while I slept.

We reached the city of Ellensburg at 9:35 a.m. and from there we crossed the Cascades, where I saw some of the wildest scenery I have seen in my life. We drove through the Snoqualmie Pass and at 12:35 noon we arrived in Seattle.

A taxi took me out to the home of my friends, Dan Nylund's at 5026 California Avenue, but I did not find anybody home and waited all afternoon until 5:30 before Mrs. Nylund came home from work. They expected me and had paged me at the bus depot, but by then I had probably left there. However, I felt at once that I was welcome in their nice home.

After supper, Dan and Evelyn took me to Kirkland and I visited my sister. She was feeling pretty good that evening and was delighted to see me and I was well satisfied that I had made the trip. She had a private room at the hospital and a special nurse attended her. All expenses were assumed by her employer, Mrs. William Boeing, and she was given the best possible care and attention.

I remained in Seattle for about a week and visited my sister every day. Some days she did not feel so spry and the nurse asked me to not stay too long. Other days she felt better and we talked for hours at a time. The last day, when I came to bid her goodbye, I found her in an oxygen tent and she was pretty low. But she gave me one of her nice smiles and sent her love and greetings to my family at home.

It was December 8th when I boarded the bus for home at 10 a.m. At 12:50 noon we were in Ellensburg and reached Spokane at 6:40 in the evening. It had been snowing in the Rocky Mountains and the snowplows had been ahead of us so the roads were good. The third day after I left Seattle, we arrived in Fargo, North Dakota at 5:30 a.m. I changed buses at Aitkin and arrived in Virginia at 4 p.m. where the message reached me that my sister had died that morning, Friday December 10th.

At 7:30 p.m. I was back home after an interesting vacation trip to the west coast. The round trip ticket cost me $70.29 from Virginia to Seattle and back, but I felt it was well worth it.

John Ostlund 1950

John Ostlund collection

103
Visiting in Sweden 1956

John and Olga Ostlund took a trip to Sweden in 1956 to visit relatives and friends and tour the country. They traveled there and back on the ship Kungsholm of the Swedish American Line, sailing from New York on July 11, 1956 and returning October 30th. These are their travel letters and Ship Log for the trip.

105 Second Avenue South   Telephone No. 19

P. S. Engman Travel Bureau

Airline and Steamship Tickets

VIRGINIA, MINNESOTA

May 14, 1956

Mr. and Mrs. John Ostlund
Gheen, Minnesota

Dear Folks:

I am herewith enclosing a form which I would ask you to complete on the blanks I have left out and return it to me after signing it with the one exception on Item No. 6 and 7 and we will send this information to them after you receive your passport. I am also including information regarding the special train from Chicago which you will notice will leave at 11:00 A.M. July 10 so you will leave here the eveingin of July 9 per the enclosed notice from the Soo Line leaving at 7:30 P.M. from Duluth. I am also enclosing a penny post card regarding the type of transporation you want and would ask that you will fill this in also and you can return this card to me along with the Declaration form.

Al stopped in this morning and has taken care of your tickets and I think I also was going to stop and see you and tell you that I have now obtained a return W/B space for you on the Kungsholm leaving from Gothenberg, Sweden on October 30, but I am sorry to state at this time they could not give you a private room so it is still a split accomodation returning but they will continue to work on it and should someone cancel out with a private room they will give it to you so I hope we can get that before you leave and if not it might arrive while you are staying in Sweden.

                                                    Yours truly,

                                                    Paul Engman

PE'br
Enc.

Travel Bureau letter.

John Ostlund collection

P. S. Engman Travel Bureau

Airline and Steamship Tickets

VIRGINIA, MINNESOTA

May 17, 1956

Mr. John Ostlund
Gheen, Minnesota

Dear Mr. Ostlund:

    I received your letter with the declaration form which you filled out perfectly and the only additional information they need, is if you will drop me a line when your passport comes giving me the number of the passport and the date it was issued. I do not have to see the passport in your case just as long as you send me this information. I am also assuming that you and your wife will take care of your small pox vaccination with Dr. Hiem and be sure and take those cards that he fills out on your trip.

    As for these gifts to Sweden, you will have no trouble with such gifts as you mentioned in your letter as they know you are going home to visit relatives and frineds and will be bringing gifts. There are a few gifts of that type they do not declare customs on the only things they are strict on is such items as tobacco liquor, etc, which they are afraid of the black market. I know you will not be bringing these with you. As for the nylon stockings if she is going to bring a lot of them with her as gifts I have always suggested that you take them out of the boxes and just pack them in your suitcases between the tissue papers in which they come and should the custom man ask anything about them she can say they are her own and that she might need that many because she is going to be there for quite a long time and with nylon stockings you never know when they are going to run so be safe she is taking quite a few pairs, but I have never had anyone questioned about them, in fact they are so glad to see the American visitor that in most cases they do not even open the suitcases just ask you a few questions or they might open one bag, as they tell when you go through if you are trying to conceal something by your actions so the best thing to do is try and not conceal anything and I am sure you will have no trouble in paying for duties.

    As for your rail transporation generally speaking they buy that in Duluth when they depart, but if you want me to get the tickets in advance for you, I will do so as a service. I see you want coach seats. I might ask you if you want me to get in touch with Al on this too, if he is going to pay for same, I will give him the cost and get the check from him for that also, if you will let me know.

    It takes two nights between here and New York, which might be kind of hard on you sitting up so I would like to see you take at least a lower pullman for the two of you for one night, it might be crowded but at least you could lie down, but this you will have to decide.

                   Yours truly,

                   Paul Engman

Travel Bureau letter of trip details.

John Ostlund collection

JOHN A. BLATNIK
8TH DISTRICT, MINNESOTA
328 HOUSE OFFICE BUILDING

COMMITTEES:
PUBLIC WORKS
GOVERNMENT OPERATIONS

Congress of the United States
House of Representatives
Washington, D. C.
July 2, 1956

TO WHOM IT MAY CONCERN

This is to introduce my very dear friends,
Mr. and Mrs. John Ostlund of Gheen, Minnesota.

They are making a visit to Sweden, the land of
their birth, where they still have many relatives.

Any assistance which you may be able to give them
to expedite their travels and visiting during the limited
time of their stay, will be truly appreciated.

The Ostlunds are very well known people and highly
regarded in my area.

Thanking you kindly, I am,

Sincerely yours,

John A. Blatnik

John A. Blatnik, M. C.

Travel reference letter from United States
Congressman, John Blatnik.

John Ostlund collection

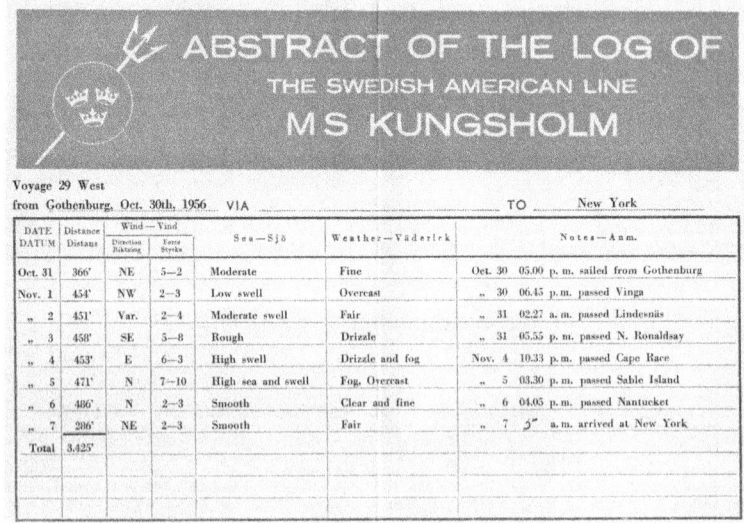

ABSTRACT OF THE LOG OF
THE SWEDISH AMERICAN LINE
M S KUNGSHOLM

Voyage 29 West
from Gothenburg, Oct. 30th, 1956 VIA _____ TO ____ New York ____

DATE DATUM	Distance Distans	Wind — Vind Direction Riktning	Wind — Vind Force Styrka	Sea — Sjö	Weather — Väderlek	Notes — Anm.
Oct. 31	366'	NE	5—2	Moderate	Fine	Oct. 30 05.00 p. m. sailed from Gothenburg
Nov. 1	454'	NW	2—3	Low swell	Overcast	„ 30 06.45 p. m. passed Vinga
„ 2	451'	Var.	2—4	Moderate swell	Fair	„ 31 02.27 a. m. passed Lindesnäs
„ 3	458'	SE	5—8	Rough	Drizzle	„ 31 05.55 p. m. passed N. Ronaldsay
„ 4	453'	E	6—3	High swell	Drizzle and fog	Nov. 4 10.33 p. m. passed Cape Race
„ 5	471'	N	7—10	High sea and swell	Fog, Overcast	„ 5 03.30 p. m. passed Sable Island
„ 6	486'	N	2—3	Smooth	Clear and fine	„ 6 04.05 p. m. passed Nantucket
„ 7	206'	NE	2—3	Smooth	Fair	„ 7 5ʳ a. m. arrived at New York
Total	3,425'					

ABSTRACT of the Log OF

MS KUNGSHOLM

Built 1953, De Schelde Shipyard, Flushing, Holland.

Displacement:	18,000 tons.	Engine power:	17,500 I.H.P.
Tons register:	21,140 tons.	Screws:	2.
Length:	600 feet.	Passenger capacity:	802.
Draft, Loaded:	26 ft. 4 in.	Crew:	355.

SWEDISH AMERICAN LINE

John Ostlund collection

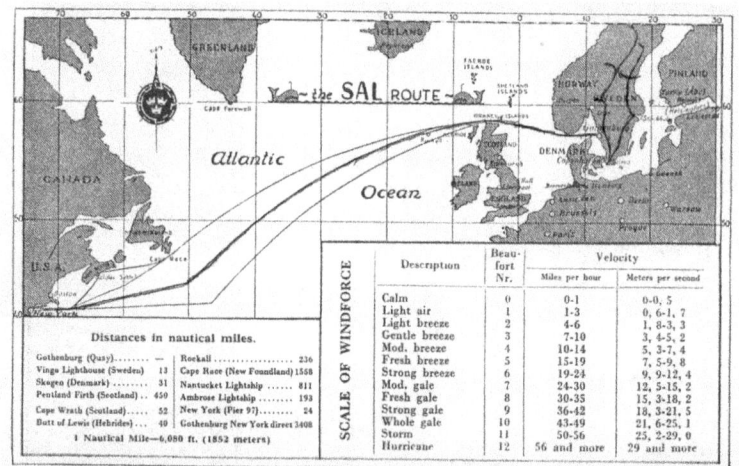

Travel route for the ship with John's marked route in Sweden added.

John and Olga 1956 on the ship.

104
Most Embarrassing Moment in Life

We were on our way to Sweden for a long vacation, my wife and I. We set sail from New York on the Swedish American Line's great motor ship "Kungsholm" on July 11, 1956 and would return on the same ship October 30th. It was July 19th when the "Kungsholm" arrived in the city of Gothenburg. We had our last meal aboard at 6 o'clock a.m. and were lined up for police inspection of our papers and passports.

The evening before we had been requested to pack our suitcases and bags and leave them outside the door of our staterooms so they could be brought on deck convenient for unloading after the ship was moored at the dock.

I had changed my suit and the suit of clothes that I had been wearing during the voyage was placed in our suit carrier and left with the rest of our baggage. When we debarked we found all of our baggage already stacked in large piles in the large rotunda where we were going through customs inspection. After some difficulty we found our suitcases and clothes hamper and I looked for the keys to open them for the custom official's inspection. I searched all of my pockets but could not find any keys. A customs official was waiting while I frantically searched my pockets. Finally I had to tell him that I must have lost the keys in our stateroom. He told me that he did not want to break the locks and advised me to go back aboard and look for my keys.

I left my wife by the baggage and walked over to the watchman by the landing bridge. When I told him that I wanted to go back on the boat, he asked for my passport and I had to produce it to show that I had been a passenger. So he let me return aboard. The door to our stateroom was locked and I had to find the room steward, Allen Jacobson, and he went with me to the room. We looked everywhere but did not find any keys. Finally, I had to return ashore and tell my wife. We had borrowed the suitcases and I thought that if they had to be broken, it would be just too bad.

Suddenly it dawned on my mind that I had changed suits the preceding evening and perhaps I had left the keys in the suit I had been wearing. I opened the suit carrier, which was not locked, and found the pants of my other suit. There I found the keys, and it sure was a great feeling of relief when I pulled them out.

After a while I found the same customs official that had waited on us and told him that the keys were found. I did not tell him that they had been in my pants pocket in the suit carrier, but let him believe that I had found them in our stateroom aboard the Liner. He was not very particular in searching our baggage. He just looked in one of the three suitcases and told me to lock them again and be sure to put the keys in my pocket.

It was a very embarrassing situation for me, and one that I'll never forget.

Fun in Älvdalen, Sweden - 1956.

105
A Great Good Templar Festival

While visiting in Sweden during the summer of 1956, Olga and I had the opportunity to attend the annual summer festival held by the Good Templars of the province of Dalarne and called "Siljanstinget". Many years ago a farmer on the island of Sollerön in Lake Siljan, willed his farm to the order of I.O.G.T. The farm is called "Gammalgården" and has a beautiful location in the center of the island surrounded by well to do farms. Nobody is at present operating this particular farm, but the buildings are kept up and preserved by the organization owning the farm.

We were in Älvdalen and on Sunday morning July 29th we rode with Olga's nephew Harry Olsson and family to Solleron. It was a warm sunny day, just perfect for an outing of this kind and when we reached the island, connected with the mainland by a long bridge, there was a good assembly gathered there ahead of us. We mingled with the crowd and Harry introduced us to several of the leading Good Templars of Dalarne. I carried my 50 year membership gold pin on my coat and that helped to assure them that I belonged and I soon realized that I was among good friends.

Two beautiful girls dressed in national costumes were selling raffle tickets on a great teddy bear. When they asked me to buy a ticket I told them that I would buy two tickets if I also could take their picture. They agreed and when I was ready to snap them, one of my friends from Älvdalen stepped up and offered to take the picture if I stood between the girls. So I did and received a nice memento of the occasion. One of the girls was the "May Queen" of the festival, Marianne Ekström of Falun.

When the afternoon program commenced there were more than 700 Good Templars assembled in front of the old cottage. There was no room inside, so the participants in the program used the old porch as a stage. We were welcomed by the District Templar, Mr. Erik Andersson and he served as program chairman during the afternoon. The program consisted of songs by Miss Ekström (she was a wonderful singer), of recitations and music by the Orsa music band, four violins and an accordion, and several numbers of folk dancing, etc. The main speaker was a congressman and Chief Templar, John Forsberg from Finland, who had traveled there specially for the festival. The program was concluded by folk games led by Mr. Bror Fredberg from Mora, who really was a wonderful leader of these games. While we did not partake of the games, we enjoyed watching them.

The ladies of the local Good Templar lodge served lunches in the backyard where tables and benches had been placed and where we sat and could enjoy the beautiful landscape with a view of Lake Siljan in the background. We took several pictures of ladies who were dressed in their pretty national costumes. Many of the young girls also wore them and it sure was a colorful gathering on the old farmyard lawn.

On our way home we stopped in the city of Mora where we entered a new hotel and ordered a chicken dinner with our hosts, Kerstin and Harry Olsson, before we returned to Älvdalen. It was a day that will linger in our memory.

Visiting in Älvdalen, Sweden 1956. John and Olga Ostlund,
Victor Flank (Olga's brother), Harry and Kerstin Olson
with their son, Lars.

John Ostlund collections

106
A Visit to Famous Salen

A very pleasant episode from our visit to Sweden in 1956, was an automobile trip to the community of Sälen, about 15 miles south of Sörsjön, Olga's home town. A relative, Karl Erik Bäckman, invited us to accompany him there one day. In the center of the village we saw the statue of King Gustav I, who in the beginning of the era of 1600 saved his country from the Danish invaders.

Olga had several cousins living in Sälen and we visited their homes and had lunch with them. Olga's mother was born and grew up there and her childhood home was now a museum and was called after Olga's grandfather "The Olnispa Homestead". The caretaker took us around in the roomy house and showed us the furniture, household goods and tools that had been saved and preserved since olden days. Some of the old relics were more than 300 years old. It was very interesting for me, but more so for Olga and her sister Victoria to visit the old home of their grandparents whom they both had visited when they were young girls.

From the village, Bäckman took us up on a large mountain called "Högfjället". A fairly good road had been built almost up to the top where a large tourist hotel had been erected. This hotel is visited every year by tourists from all parts of Europe and America. The hotel was said to cost over a million kronor ($200,000.00). It is 2,400 feet above the village of Sälen and we had a wonderful view of the surrounding landscape, the western Dala river and the beautiful valley which we could see for many miles. Only a few tourists were there when we arrived and as the day was cloudy and a light rain was falling, everybody stayed inside. We mingled with the crowd in the large lobby where we purchased a few souvenirs and mementos with pictures of the establishment.

We returned to the village where we visited other relatives of Olga and they all seemed happy to see and entertain us. They all spoke the provincial Dala Dialect and it was hard for me to understand everything they said. But I guess they are so used to their dialect that they did not realize that somebody unfamiliar with it was present. However, Bäckman and I pretended that we understood and when the natives laughed we laughed with them, even if we did not have an idea of what they were laughing at.

The villagers were busy harvesting their hay crop and we watched them hauling in hay from the racks where it had dried. The rain we had met on the mountain top had not harmed the hay here in the valley. The hay was just as green as when it was cut, but it was dry and smelled good. Some of the farmers used horses, but others had tractors or jokers built from old autos to pull the hay wagons with.

It was late in the evening when we returned to Sörsjön after a day well spent and enjoyed.

Olof Flank's home, where Olga was born. Sörsjön, Dalarne 1956.

Flank siblings Victor, Olga, Victoria and Oscar together after 50 years - 1956.
John Ostlund collection

107
Sightseeing Through Sweden

When Olga and I visited Sweden during the summer of 1956 we took advantage of an offer by the State Railroad Company, who then celebrated their 100th anniversary, to travel by trains around the entire country, an approximate distance of 3,000 miles or more for the amount of only $20.00.

We left Älvdalen, Dalarne, on August 17th by bus for Mora, where we boarded the train for Östersund. Arriving there in the afternoon, we took a taxi to the home of a former schoolmate, Stina Wågland, who had invited us to her home. The next day we went sightseeing on a bus through the city and around the island of Fröson. On August 19th we were invited to attend the "Swedish American Day" program in the city which was a memorable event for both of us.

On August 20th we left for my hometown, Järpen, about 50 miles to the west of the city, where we were welcomed by another former schoolmate, Fridolf Johansson, and where we stayed for four days looking over old landmarks and visiting old friends.

On August 25th we again boarded a train for Duved, further west in the province of Jämtland, where we met another former schoolmate, Thilda Uhlin, who invited us to her home and where we remained for three day of sightseeing. We visited the famous waterfall "Tännforsen" and the "Armfelt Monument" among other memorable events.

When we left Duved we took the train across the country from near the Norwegian border to the west, and to Sundsvall on the Baltic Sea, a long day's ride on the train. In Sundsvall we visited my cousin, Einar Falk, and we spent a whole week in his summer home on an island in the Baltic. Almost every day we took trips in his boat to other islands nearby.

It was September 4th when we again boarded a train for Erikslund, where another cousin of mine lived. She was Stina Staffansson and we spent three pleasant days in her home.

On September 7th we rode back to Östersund, and for the first time since we came to Sweden, we rented a room for the night at a pensionate there. We could have gone to Mrs. Wågland's, but arrived in the city late and did not want to bother her.

On September 8th we took the train at 8 a.m. heading north through the northern part of the province of Jämtland and into Lapland. In the evening we reached the village of Storuman, where we stayed overnight. The next morning we boarded the train again at 5:40 a.m. and during that day we saw the large electric power stations at Porjus and Harsprånget waterfalls. A very impressive sight. After 14 hours on the train we reached the city of Kiruna in the evening.

The following day, Sept. 10th, we took the train westward to the border and into Norway, and at noon we arrived in Narvik, on the shore of the North Atlantic ocean. We saw the greatest ore loading dock and it's giant crane that they recently built at a cost of 50 million kroner. In the afternoon we returned to Kiruna where we again stayed overnight at the same pensionate.

On September 11th we boarded a train going east and arrived in the city of Boden in the afternoon. We found a hotel near the depot and remained overnight.

Early in the morning of September 12th we left and rode the train all day and arrived in Forsmo late in the evening at the home of my cousin Mauritz Bergquist. He owned a new car and took us on sightseeing trips around the beautiful Ångermanland river.

After four well spent days in Forsmo we continued our trip. We left there on the evening of September 16th and took the night train to Stockholm. It was the first time during the trip that we traveled in the night. Our train was a fast express and that night we traveled through part of the province of Ångermanland, and the provinces of Medelpad, Jämtland, Helsingland, Gästrikland, Dalarne and Uppland and arrived in the capital city of Stockholm at 9 a.m. Here lived Olga's brother Oscar Flank, and he met us at the Central station and took us to his home. I also had a cousin, Ruth Ahlinder, living in the city, whom I was going to visit while there.

We spent six days in Stockholm visiting and sightseeing with Oscar as our guide. We saw the King's Palace and the old grand church "Storkyrkan" near the palace. We saw several of the parks, "Skansen", "Djurgården" and "Soliden" and many other places that we had heard and read about during our stay in the capital.

On September 23rd we said goodbye to our relatives and took the train to the city of Södertälje, where my cousin, Elin Åkerström, lived. There I also met another cousin, Nora Krook, who with her husband had come from Sollentuna, Uppland, to meet her American cousin. We visited with them all day and stayed overnight.

In Sweden with Oscar Flank, Olga's brother - 1956.

John Ostlund collection

On September 24th we continued our journey and at 8 o'clock that evening we arrived in Åseda, the province of Småland, where Olga had a niece who had invited us to visit her home. We were now in the southern part of Sweden and we noticed the change in the temperature. While we had seen snow in the northern mountains, here it was warm and the thermometer registered 80 above in the shade, and it was the last part of September.

It was September 27th when we left Åseda and that day we reached the city of Malmö in the province of Skane and on the shore of Öresund strait. On the other side of the strait was Denmark. Our ticket was good for a ride to the city of Ystad, still further southeast, but we decided now to return north along the west border of the country. In the evening we took a long walk through part of the large city. It is the third largest among Swedish cities. We stayed at a hotel overnight.

September 28th we took the fast express train north through the cities of Lund and Helsingborg and reached Gothenburg at noon. From there we continued north to the village of Kil, province of Värmland, where we arrived late that evening. We were tired and took a room at a hotel. The next morning we took a train to the city of Karlstad to visit one of Olga's cousins, Emmy Nyberg. We had to remain there five days and we saw many interesting places in and around the city.

It was not before October 3rd that we were allowed to leave our kind hosts in Karlstad and return to Dalarna. We took a railbus to Kil and from there took a train north. At 8:30 we arrived in Älvdalen, from where we commenced our journey around the entire country seven weeks earlier. We had visited and traveled through 20 of Sweden's 24 provinces, visited the three largest cities, Stockholm, Gothenburg and Malmö. We had received our money's worth many, many times during the trip. And we have met many of our relatives that we never met before. It was a memory for the rest of our life.

With hosts, the Johanson's, in John's hometown Jämtland - 1956.

John Ostlund collection

108
Svenskarnas Dag (The Swedes Day)

Midsommar day, June 24th is our wedding anniversary, and on that day in 1960 we celebrated our 47th anniversary with a trip to the city of Minneapolis. There, the Swedish organizations of St. Paul and Minneapolis had arranged their annual picnic in the Minnehaha Park which they call Svenskarnas Dag. It is always held on the Sunday closest to Midsommar Day, which this year was the 26th of June.

We stayed at the home of our son, Kenneth and wife Barbara, who met us at the bus station. We also had our granddaughter Katy Woods with us as she wanted to see the home of Kenneth and Barbara when she had been the flower girl at their wedding in Aberdeen, South Dakota in January.

Sunday noon they took us out to the park and we mingled with thousands of Swedes and their descendants, not only from the Twin Cities, but also from many parts of the state of Minnesota and nearby states of Wisconsin and the Dakotas. It was an ideal day for the celebration, warm and sunny and with a slight breeze to keep insects away. Barbara had packed a picnic lunch and we found a shady place on the lawn and enjoyed it.

Throughout the park under the trees were many stands erected by the various organizations who had arranged for the days program. There were "Stockholms Klubben", "Dalaförbundet", "Blekinge Gille", "Jämtamot", "Värmlandsföreningen", "Östgöta Klubb", "Smålands förening", "Dalslands föreningen", "Ångermandlänningarna", "Skånska Gillet", "Västgötaföbundet", "Hälsingarna", and "Good Templars Lodges of the Twin Cities". We visited the booths of Dalaföbundet, where my wife registered. From there we went to the booth of Jämtamot, representing my home province in Sweden, where I happened to meet a lady from my hometown, Järpen. We also visited the booth of the Good Templars where we met many old friends that we had not seen for years.

The afternoon's program had commenced and we found seats near the rostrum, or the speakers platform. It was a various program, consisting of speeches by many notable persons, among them were U.S. Senator Hubert Humphrey, the Mayors of St. Paul and Minneapolis, etc. The "Swede of the Year" Mr. Rudolph Bannow, President of American Manufacturers, was presented and gave an interesting talk. He told how

he had arrived in America as a poor emigrant, and how he had joined
the Good Templars and learned in the lodge how to express himself and
how to conduct meetings and be a leader. Another speaker was Assistant
County Attorney, Per Larson from Sörsjön, Dalarne, the hometown of
my wife. Then there were folk dances and singing by a large chorus of
men and women, and the crowning of the Queen of the Day. It was quite
late before the program ended and then dancing commenced around
the Maypole, with music by four fiddlers and an accordion, members of
Dalaförbundet.

It was the largest attendance in the history of "Svenskarnas Dag" as
they had sold ticket buttons and programs to 50,000 people. It was late
when we returned home that evening and we all decided we had spent an
enjoyable and memorable day in Minnehaha Park.

1911 in Duluth - Minnesota Sc. Grand Lodge.
John Ostlund in top right corner, third row from top, third
man in from right (next to woman with wide hat).

John Ostlund collection

109
Public Activities

I once heard a preacher ask one of his congregation, "Have you ever done anything for your neighbor or fellow man in your long life?" Evidently that minister knew that the man he was questioning had been concerned only by looking out for himself. There are many of that kind in this world of ours, who only look for the best for themselves and who don't give a darn if their closest neighbor dies from starvation even if they themselves have more than they need of the necessities of life.

These people also generally refuse to take part in any public services. They may attend a public meeting, but if they happen to be nominated for any public office they will decline and refuse to serve. Just think what would happen if we all did that! We would not have any government or public institutions, no township or community organizations.

During my life, I have tried to do my part as a citizen and to serve my community to the best of my little ability. I realize that I have failed miserably at times, but also I have had times where I succeeded better than I had expected. I am here going to take a brief inventory of the public offices I have held during the last 40 years.

My first experience, and I will say my first training in the art of public service, was when I joined the International Order of Good Templars, a temperance organization in Hibbing, in the spring of 1906. The lodge was small and there were only a few to choose from when officers had to be elected quarterly. During my active membership in the organization, I served almost continually as an officer in various capacities. It was training in many things. I learned how to keep records, how to conduct a meeting and how to express myself in public. These teachings have helped me a lot in life.

I was elected and served one year as District Chief Templar in the First District of Minnesota Grand Lodge. This district included Duluth and the Range towns.

After moving to Gheen, I applied for direct membership in the Grand Lodge and whenever I had the opportunity I attended some of their annual meetings in different parts of the state. At the Grand Lodge meeting held in Fertile in 1929 I was elected "Grand Superintendent of Legislative Work" for the Grand Lodge jurisdiction which included both Wisconsin and Minnesota. There were about 85 lodges working in that area and I had to be in touch with them all at least twice during the year. I did not have to visit them personally but received reports from them and had to write replies to reports and send information on the political situation in both states. There was a lot of correspondence to take care of but I enjoyed the work. I served two years as "G.S.L.W." As far as I know I am the only "effective card" member in the Grand Lodge who has served on the executive committee of the organization for two years.

1891-1916 Scandinavian Grand Lodge of Minnesota 25th annual session card.
John Ostlund collection

Grand Lodge Meeting in Fertile, Minnesota.
John Ostlund collection

My training and experience in public service came well to pass when I moved out to my farm in Gheen. Here a Farmers Club had been organized a couple years earlier and I joined it in 1915. None of the officers had any idea how to conduct a meeting and probably had never heard of Robert's Rules of Order. The members just talked about their problems just like in any informal gathering, without asking for the floor or in any way recognized the chairman. The chairman never presented a question for a vote and I felt that there was no head or tail to anything. Finally, I could not keep quiet and when I asked for the floor everybody listened as this was something new and unusual in this group. I tried to explain as plainly as possible the usual proceedings of a public meeting. I told them that a decision not voted upon was not legal according to law, that nothing could be accomplished when all talked at once, like they had been doing and that the chairman was there to keep order and conduct the meeting according to rules. I tried not to make them feel that I criticized them, but I suggested that we should join in making the meetings more orderly and more interesting.

1915 Farmer's Club picnic in Gheen, MN.

John Ostlund collection

The following meeting they had an election of officers. I was elected secretary and served as such for five years in succession. I have, during thirty years membership in the Willow Valley Farmer's Club, served as officer 23 years. I served 10 years as president, 10 years as secretary and 3 years as vice president.

One of my most responsible appointments in public service was when the Township was to be organized. I took the initiative to have a petition circulated among the setters in the township and for two days I walked from one place to the other in securing signatures to my petition. When a hearing was called at the Board of County Commissioners meeting in Duluth, I was elected by the settlers here to represent them at that meeting and fight for the dissolution of this township from Linden Grove and permission to organize as a separate organization. I was fortunate to have a good friend working at the Courthouse, P.J. Borgstrom, and he took me over to the Commissioners and introduced me to nearly all of them before the meeting started. I had a few minutes to talk with each of them and when the matter came up for consideration before the entire Board, my requests were granted. I returned home very happy over my successful mission. We called a meeting and organized the Willow Valley Township in February of 1916. I was elected the first Town Clerk and held that office for many years or until I resigned. I then served as Township Assessor for 2 years, was again elected Clerk for four years and resigned again. I served as Town Treasurer for 10 years and in 1948 I was coaxed to resign and accept the Clerk's office once again.

Now I will relate one of my most
miserable failures as a public servant.

During my first years as Secretary of the Farm Club, the members pooled their orders for feed and kerosene. In 1918 we resolved to organize a cooperative store where we could buy our necessities without paying the exorbitant profits charged by the lone storekeeper in Gheen. I was elected a member of the organization committee and sent out to sell shares in the new enterprise. For three days I traveled through the Greaney and Silverdale communities and returned with over $800.00. We had raised $250.00 within the club and now we went to work in earnest. We purchased an old school building which we moved onto a lot purchased earlier in Gheen. When we had our store building ready, most of our share capital was spent. With A.P. Olson, I was sent to Duluth and Superior to purchase stock on credit. In Duluth we went from one wholesale house to another, but very little was promised. We had been informed about a cooperative wholesale in Superior, the Central Cooperative Wholesale and we succeeded in securing the confidence of it's manager, John Nummivuori. He gave us a nominal supply of what he had in stock and then accompanied us to another large wholesale concern where he convinced the manager to trust us with a considerable supply of what was most called for in a small country store. Happy we returned home.

The first Farmer's Coop Trading Company General Store in Gheen, Minnesota 1922. It was formerly an old school building, located across the tracks, which was moved to a lot in the townsite at Gheen.

John Ostlund collection

We hired a good manager and opened the store. Everything went fine for a year. We increased the stock, sold more shares and the cooperative store received more than its share of the business in the community. I served as Secretary of the company and every month two of us directors checked the books, sales slips and invoices. I did not know much about the bookkeeping and none of the other directors knew anything. Considerable credit was given to customers, which was something I always protested, but my fellow directors claimed that no business could be conducted here without credit.

Our manager resigned and we hired a new man. He was not a cooperator, but was a good salesman. The business increased considerably but so did the accounts receivable. When we checked the books he kept most of the invoices and bills in his pocket and we never suspected that anything was wrong. When he proposed a loan of $1,000.00 in the bank we began getting suspicious. He got the money on a note signed by all directors, but we decided to hire an expert auditor to go over his books. He immediately resigned. The auditor found a lot of discrepancies in the books and accounts which we local checkers had never noticed. We were in debt to wholesale houses and timber producers of $12,000.00 and while our inventory of stock plus accounts receivable amounted to about the same figure, we were unable to raise the amount demanded by the wholesalers and had to sign our store over to Duluth Jobbers Credit Bureau.

I had been director and secretary since it was organized and nobody had been closer affiliated with the store and it's affairs than I had been. For several months afterwards I felt discouraged and disgusted with myself. I had accepted a job that I was not qualified to handle.

Farmer's Club picnic at Nett Lake, July 4th 1925.

John Ostlund collection

In 1926 I was appointed and served as Director of the County Club and Farm Bureau Association. Every month the Board of Directors, consisting of three businessmen, three women and three farmers, met at various places in the county. These meetings were interesting experiences for me. We generally met at a luncheon and held our business meeting afterwards. At almost every meeting we had some faculty members of the State University or other distinguished guests. The Extension Agents also met with us and submitted their monthly reports. While we were allowed mileage and other incidental expenses, I soon found out that these meetings cost me a lot more than I received and I did not have any money to waste in those years. I was glad when the year was up and I refused re-nomination.

AWARD BUREAU PICNIC PRIZES

County Farm Bureau Gives Out List of Winners at Side Lake.

Virginia, Minn., July 4.—(Special to The Herald.)—The complete official list of winners of events at the county farm bureau picnic at Side lake has been given out by County Agent August Neubauer as follows:

Diamond ball, won by Brown School Community club from Lakeland Community club by score of 6 to 4.

Baseball game won by Cook from Pelican Lake by score of 11 to 1.

Horseshoe, men's — First, Mike Terska and Alex Watt, Linden Grove Community club; second, W. B. Thurman, M. A. Nichols, Buhl Civic association.

Tug-of-war, Lynwood Farmers' club from All Stars.

Rolling contest — First, Bobbie Parsons, Willow Valley Farmers' club; second, Norman Larson, Brooklyn; third, Jack Parsons, Willow Valley Farmers' club.

Zig-zag contest — First, Walter Beasy, Hibbing; second, Howard Nicholson, Hibbing; third, James McHardy, Hibbing.

Wheelbarrow race—First, Gus Parsons and John Gorenc, Willow Valley Farmers' club; second, Iver Erickson, Nonte Jarvi, Brown School Community club; third, Mike Terska and Toiva Annala, Linden Grove Community club.

Girls' race, 25 yards—First, Helen McKinnon, Brown School Community club; second, Ella Setter, Linden Grove Community club; third, Lillie Terska, Linden Grove Community club.

Girls' race, 50 yards—First, Ellen Grekela, North Hibbing; second, Anna Mattassich, Hibbing; third, Ellen Setter, Linden Grove Community club.

Boys' race, 25 yards—First, Bernard Dulong, Brown School Community club; second, Jack Parsons, Willow Valley Farmers' club; third, Donald Brown, Brown School Community club.

Boys' race, 50 yards—First, David Summers, Brown School Community club; second, Bernard Dulong, Brown School Community club; third, Herbert Lundberg, Willow Valley Farmers' club.

Fat man's race—First, George Pauley, Hibbing; second, H. W. Reik, Cook; third, Frank Wardas, Pelican Lake Farmers' club.

Married woman's race, fifty yards —First, Mrs. Bert Smith, Lynwood Farmers' club; second, Mrs. J. P. Clune, Bear River Farmers' club; third, Mrs. J. A. Withers, Willow Valley Farmers' club.

Newspaper race for women—First, Chloris McHardy, Hibbing; second, Mrs. A. Marvin, Lynwood Farmers' club; third, Ella Setter, Linden Grove Community club.

Horseshoe contest for women— First, Florence Lang, Virginia, and Mrs. Carl Munyer, Brown school; second, Mrs. Bert Smith, Lynwood Farmers' club, and Mrs. A. Marvin, Lynwood Farmers' club.

1927 Newspaper clipping for the Farm Bureau Picnic.

John Ostlund collection

At one of the director's meetings of the County Club I had suggested holding a Farm Bureau picnic each summer at some centrally located lake. In 1927 this question was taken under consideration by the directors and I was notified that I had been suggested as chairman of the committee. I accepted and met the other four members of the committee for a meeting at the County agent's office in Virginia. They were August Neubauer from Virginia, L.F. Luthey (banker) from Cook, James Butchart (retired businessman) from Chisholm and Joe Bauers (farmer) from Wilpin.

The event took place at Side Lake, north of Chisholm, and was officially attended by 11 Farmer's Clubs and 6 Commercial Clubs. The crowd was conservatively estimated at 500 persons and was considered an outstanding success as it was the first of its kind in St. Louis County. I received a sizable check as a remuneration for my expenses and time spent, from the secretary of the County Club.

During the years of 1927 - 28, I served as County Chairman of the Federated Farmers Clubs, an organization comprising about thirty farm and community organizations throughout St. Louis County. This association planned to take over the rural extension work in the county, rightfully claiming that County agents who are working for the extension of agriculture, also should be governed by strictly rural government, and not as here-to-fore, supervised by commercial clubs and other civic organizations.

Besides the F.F.C. was serving as a central organization for the rural clubs and assisted in promoting better cooperation between the sons of the soil throughout the county. The executive committee met with delegates from the various member clubs twice a year, in Duluth or on the Range. As Chairman, I had my traveling expenses paid to these meetings, but my time was donated.

When the Farmer-Labor political party was strong in Minnesota, party cubs were organized in almost every hamlet and town in the state. In our township the majority of the voters were in favor of the new liberal party and we decided to form a local club.

Martin Gorence was the originator of the idea but he came to me first for my opinion. We decided to call a meeting at the hall and about fifty people met up. The Willow Valley Farmer Labor Club was organized with twenty members but before the end of the year the membership had increased to 52. It was organized Jun 9, 1936.

I was elected and served as treasurer the first year. Then I served as secretary for the next two years and then the club dwindled and died. The last meeting we had only four members present.

However, during these three years I was elected to and took part in three County Conventions, one District Convention and one State Convention. I was also elected and served as District Chairman in the northern rural district, comprising about a dozen clubs north of the Mesabi Range. We generally met once a month at the Linden Grove County Garage with three delegates from each local club.

The most noteworthy experience that I had during these years in the Farmer Labor movement was when I was sent to the State Convention in January 1939. There were about 1,000 delegates present from all parts of the state and it was the most tumultuous convention that I ever attended.

However, I learned something about politics that was both disgusting and interesting.

In 1938 a revolution took place in Hibbing when a large group of farmers met and took over the St. Louis County Fair Association. During the last several years, the County Fair had been used as a racket by a group of unscrupulous gamblers. The racket was exposed when a number of large bills were presented to the Board of County Commissioners.

When the farmer delegation took over, the northern half of the County was divided into eleven districts, each district eligible to one delegate who would sit as director on the Fair Board. I was selected from the district comprising Gheen, Greaney, Orr and north to the Canadian border. The Fair Board meets generally two or three times a year and a Board member is receiving $4.00 for the day spent plus mileage of 5 cents. I have been re-elected for three 3 year terms to date.

In 1916 the Willow Valley Telephone Company was organized in our community. During the last 34 years I have been a member of the Board of Directors. The first years the offices were alternated and I served as President, Vice President or Secretary for different terms. Since 1932 I have served continually as Secretary. For many years no compensation was paid to the Secretary and a lot of my time was devoted to collection of dues and office work for which I did not even receive thanks, but often sneering remarks. When I complained at the annual meeting I was given a slight compensation, but nobody else would accept the office. A couple of times I flatly resigned, but was coaxed to continue. After 16 years as Secretary I finally told the members that I would not consider re-election under any circumstances and I consider myself retired from that responsibility.

When our first cooperative enterprise hit the rocks I resolved to not devote anymore efforts in that line. However, only four years elapsed until efforts were again made to organize a cooperative store in Gheen. This time it would be organized as a branch of the Orr Coop Company.

At the first meeting, held at the Farmers club hall, we had only three residents of the community who met with organizer George Jacobson and Orr manager Frank Biltonen. It did not look very promising, but we subscribed for two shares each and Jacobson decided to make a house to house canvas through Gheen and Greaney. Two weeks later another meeting was held, this time well attended, and the Gheen branch of Orr Cooperative Trading Company was realized.

We rented the ground floor of Albert Larson's hotel for the store. I refused to serve on the first Board of Directors as I thought that part of the blame for our first store's crash might still hang on me and discourage possible mistrusting members. However, I boosted for the new enterprise whenever I had a chance and soon I found myself on the Board of Directors again.

In 1932 we resolved to move our store out to the highway, one mile west of town. We purchased 20 acres of land, a building committee was appointed and every Board meeting was devoted to plans for expansion. It was June 1934 before we finally had our new store building completed and ready to move in. I was on a committee of three to arrange for a grand opening. Over 450 people attended and it was considered the largest gathering of humanity at one time in this area. We made a net profit of more than $100 from our Grand Opening.

Since then everything concerning the store has run smoothly. I have been a member of the Board of Directors almost constantly and now for several years also representing the Gheen Board on the main Board of Directors in Orr. In 1948 I served as Secretary of the Orr Board of Directors.

110
The Final Chapter of a Life Well Lived

Fun with a dozen grandchildren in 1957.

John Ostlund collection

John and Olga in 1958.

John Ostlund collection

John and Olga with youngest son, Kenneth - 1957.
John Ostlund collection

Olga and John at the farm - 1959.

John Ostlund collection

John and Olga's 46th Wedding Anniversary - 1959.

John Ostlund collection

Thanksgiving dinner at Kenneth and Barbara's 1960. This is likely the last photo taken of John Ostlund as he passed away two weeks later, on December 7, 1960.

22   Duluth News-Tribune, Friday, Dec. 9, 1960.

REGIONAL DEATHS

John Ostlund, 77, pioneer Gheen farmer, died Wednesday in Eitel Hospital, Minneapolis. He previously lived in Worthington, Hibbing and Chisholm. Survivors are his wife, Olga; three sons, Alvin, Crane Lake; Victor, La Crosse, Wis., and Kenneth, Minneapolis; two daughters, Mrs. Don Latendresse, Indianapolis, and Mrs. George Woods, Cook; a sister, Mrs. Mae Hedberg, Sunnyside, Wash.; 14 grandchildren, and four nieces, including Mrs. Walter Stockey, Virginia. Funeral services will be at 2 p.m. Saturday in Trinity Lutheran Church, Cook. Arrangements are by the Cron-Nelson-Harris Funeral Home, Virginia.

Death announcement of John Ostlund December 9, 1960.

*"I have now reached the age of the proverbial
'three score and ten'...During the years, or days, I have left
I am going to take it easy. I have nothing to worry about
anymore...I am happy and contented and like to live as
long as my health holds out. When I die, I hope that I do
not need to suffer too much and be a burden to my folks.
I hope death comes quick and I am ready for it..."*
John Ostlund 1953.

The Lord is my shepherd. I shall not want.

He maketh me to lie down in green pastures: He leadeth me beside the still waters.

He restoreth my soul: He leadeth me in the paths of righteousness for his name's sake.

Yea, though I walk through the valley of the shadow of death, I will fear no evil: for Thou art with me; Thy rod and Thy staff they comfort me. Thou preparest a table before me in the presence of mine enemies: Thou anointest my head with oil, my cup runneth over.

Surely goodness and mercy shall follow me all the days of my life: and I will dwell in the house of the Lord for ever.

THE 23rd PSALM

FUNERAL SERVICES
— for —
Mr. John Ostlund
Gheen, Minnesota

BORN
October 9, 1883 at Trangsviken, Jamtland,
Sweden

DIED
December 7, 1960 at Eitel Hospital, Minneapolis

AGE
77 Years, 1 Month, 28 Days

Services Held At
TRINITY LUTHERAN CHURCH
Cook, Minnesota
Saturday, December 10, 1960 at 2:00 p. m.

CLERGYMAN
Rev. James R. Peterson, Cook, Minnesota

INTERMENT
Family Plot, Willow Valley Cemetery

Arrangements By
CRON-NELSON-HARRIS-LEDING
FUNERAL HOMES
Virginia, Minn.   Cook, Minn.   Eveleth, Minn.
Tel. SH-1-9593   Tel. NO-6-3380   Tel. SH-1-6099

Funeral Remembrance card for John Ostlund.

Author and Cover Artist

Jenny Ostlund-Evens has been a self-employed memorial artist in central Minnesota since 1987. Most of her work consists of creating finely detailed pen and ink drawings for customized personal monuments and Veteran's Memorials. She also does freelance portraits and portrait collages in black pencil, colorful mural painting in children's rooms and churches/schools, designs nature-inspired essential oil diffusing jewelry, and creates original stained-glass mosaics. But she will probably be remembered most for her annual Christmas card art and has a large following of receivers who collect them.

She has always enjoyed writing, especially poems, and is excited to be finally delving into publishing and officially being an author. Publishing her grandfather's memoirs is her first book, but there are more in the works, so stay tuned.

In the not too distant future, Jenny plans to retire with her husband in northern Minnesota where she can spend more time writing/publishing, hiking and enjoying nature with her camera, fishing with her husband, and having the time in her studio to delve into the art ideas that are swimming around in her head just waiting to come out. She is currently working on setting up a business website for her creative endeavors, but until that is completed, she can be reached by email at:

JEvensArtist@gmail.com

CPSIA information can be obtained
at www.ICGtesting.com
Printed in the USA
BVHW032307160822
644778BV00008B/86